## Praise for *Every Landlord's Guide to Managing Property*

"Every Landlord's Guide to Managing Property: Best Practices From Move-In to Move-Out, *by Michael Boyer is a MUST HAVE for anyone who is currently a landlord or even thinking about becoming a landlord. The author, Michael Boyer, is obviously a seasoned professional and landlord who has taken the time to pass on his secrets to success so that you can avoid the many mistakes that (all too often) do-it-yourself landlords make.*

*It is well written and takes the mystery out of why some landlords are ultra successful and have great relationships with their tenants, while others have nothing but nightmare experiences that lead them to lose money, sell their rental property, and seek financial shelter in other (often less profitable) investments.*

*This book also provides detailed and practical advice on how to acquire and perfect technical skills involving property management (from property and tenant selection to when to do work yourself and when to call in a professional); people skills involving tenants (including how to attract and keep great tenants and how to work well with them once you have them); along with general management skills involving everything from short- and long-term planning to basic financial management. The advice and examples in this book will enhance the desirability of owning your existing rental property or help you select a new rental property, decrease the stress level and long term cost associated with being a landlord, and ultimately increase the success of your property investment business.*

*I cannot recommend this book more highly."*

—Gary Ransone, Esq.
    General Contractor, Real Estate Broker, Property Manager,
    and Author of *The Contractor's Legal Kit*

# This Book Comes With Lots of
# FREE Online Resources

Nolo's award-winning website has a page dedicated just to this book. Here you can:

**KEEP UP TO DATE.** When there are important changes to the information in this book, we'll post updates.

**GET DISCOUNTS ON NOLO PRODUCTS.** Get discounts on hundreds of books, forms, and software.

**READ BLOGS.** Get the latest info from Nolo authors' blogs.

**LISTEN TO PODCASTS.** Listen to authors discuss timely issues on topics that interest you.

**WATCH VIDEOS.** Get a quick introduction to a legal topic with our short videos.

**And that's not all.**
Nolo.com contains thousands of articles on everyday legal and business issues, plus a plain-English law dictionary, all written by Nolo experts and available for free. You'll also find more useful **books, software, online apps, downloadable forms,** plus a **lawyer directory.**

Get updates and more at
**www.nolo.com/back-of-book/PROP.html**

# Every Landlord's Guide to Managing Property

## Best Practices, From Move-In to Move-Out

**Michael Boyer**

NOLO
LAW for ALL

| FIRST EDITION | OCTOBER 2015 |
|---|---|
| Editors | MARCIA STEWART |
| | ILONA BRAY |
| Book Design | SUSAN PUTNEY |
| Proofreading | ROBERT WELLS |
| Index | ELLEN SHERRON |
| Printing | BANG PRINTING |

Boyer, Michael (Property manager)
  Every landlord's guide to managing property : best practices, from move-in to move-out / Michael Boyer. -- 1 Edition.
       pages cm
   ISBN 978-1-4133-2215-6 (pbk.) -- ISBN 978-1-4133-2216-3 (epub ebook)
   1.  Real estate management.  I. Title.
   HD1394.B69 2015
   333.5068--dc23
                              2015016510

This book covers only United States law, unless it specifically states otherwise.

### Please note

We believe accurate, plain-English legal information should help you solve many of your own legal problems. But this text is not a substitute for personalized advice from a knowledgeable lawyer. If you want the help of a trained professional—and we'll always point out situations in which we think that's a good idea—consult an attorney licensed to practice in your state.

## Acknowledgments

Special thanks to Marcia Stewart and Ilona Bray for stellar editing and helping make this book a readable reality.

This book is dedicated to small-time landlords everywhere, the men and women who roll up their sleeves to make a big-time difference through housing others.

## About the Author

Michael Boyer is a part-time landlord, college professor, and attorney. He has graduate degrees in management and law, plus over a decade of experience as a successful do-it-yourself landlord. He has been on both sides of the landlord-tenant equation, as a landlord and as a volunteer attorney representing low-income tenants. Boyer is the author of numerous articles and chapters, and has served on many boards, including several condominium association boards. This is his first book and it is a culmination of years of collecting notes, tips, and day-to-day observations about what practices really work for the small-time landlord (especially one with a day job).

# Table of Contents

## 5 The Art of Rental Maintenance ............................................................. 131

## 6 Working With Service Contractors ........................................................ 155

# Part-Time Residential Landlords: The Superheroes of Rental Housing

Whether you're simply exploring the idea of being a landlord or are already renting out property, you're in good company. Small-time landlords—real people like you—house much of the United States' tenant population, in single-family homes, condos, or multiplexes (such as a duplex, triplex, or fourplex).

### What Type of Property Do Most Renters Live In?

Residential properties (defined as one to four units), the staple of small-time landlords, provide much of the rental housing in the U.S. Recent Census data located 40 million renter-occupied housing units, of which well over half are small residential properties:

- single-family detached homes: 11.6 million
- single-family attached homes: 2.6 million
- two- to-four units (duplex, triplex, or fourplex, also known as quads): 7.7 million, and
- condominiums: 3.7 million.

**Source:** U.S. Census Bureau, General Housing Data—Renter-Occupied Units, 2013 American Housing Survey)

As one of these small-time residential landlords, I've learned a lot in my ten years of owning and managing residential rental property. I started out in this business when, rather than selling a condo that our family outgrew, I simply rented it out. I soon repeated the process so that I had four condo rentals, and then added a fourplex.

Like many residential rental property owners, I have a day job. Many times on my way to or from work, I do a quick change of clothes (and change of roles), from college professor to landlord. As a small operator without a staff, I am a hands-on property manager.

I've never changed clothes in a phone booth or leapt a tall building in a single bound, but with some exceptions (such as when I need to hire a contractor) I do everything myself—from choosing tenants to unclogging toilets. This book is about this endeavor, a guide specifically for the part-time landlord balancing a rental property with work and life. It is written for the mild mannered office worker by day, who may change into work clothes by night in order to clean and paint walls, just in time to show a rental unit that weekend. And while there are no diabolical villains (though I once inherited a tenant who was close) or trains heading off a cliff, this book is about managing regular people and keeping a residential property from going off the tracks—making it clean, safe, and well maintained.

## Filling a Gap in the Landlord Literature

While I read everything I can on real estate and residential rental properties, the primary guide I used in writing this book was my own experience as a part-time landlord. For example, the chapter on turnarounds (in which you get a unit ready for the next tenant) was from my years of notes on streamlining the process, and the tenant-selection and lease-signing practices described in this book are all largely my own practices, as well. That said, not every tip will work for every landlord or property, and I'm sure you will develop a few of your own tricks of the trade.

When I began, there was no detailed guide for what I would be doing. While there were some great books out there for professional landlords with apartment buildings and other major holdings, none really spoke directly to the part-time landlord with just a few residential rentals. And many books were short on details, just giving general landlording advice that, while sound, was quite vague: select great tenants, maintain your property, move tenants in, move them out, and so on. So the crucial granular detail of *how* to do all this was lacking. My goal in writing this book was to show exactly how I choose a rental property, create an ad, screen tenants, prep a unit, and even move out a tenant—everything I learned along the way.

Many books are also geared to larger operations. Some just tell property managers to have their staff or hired help handle all the details while they work the phone. But as a small-scale landlord, you won't have a staff, and you can afford to hire out only occasional jobs that you can't do better yourself. This book does cover hiring service contractors (Chapter 6) and using professional services

11). But for the day-to-day work, the person assigned to l the details will be the one in the mirror (you).

y-to-day work will contribute to your success and help you attract and retain good long-term tenants. I wrote this book to share the *how* and to cover the *details*. We will survey the skills, strategies, and general philosophy that can help the part-time landlord—from choosing the type of rental property that works for you (whether it's a single-family house, a condo, or a multiplex) to keeping every part of your rental units working smoothly; from communicating clearly and often with tenants to providing great service from move in through move out.

Each chapter covers a new area and is designed for part-time landlords—the people housing others in their spare time—the schoolteacher renting out a condo, the government worker with a duplex, or the semiretired person with several single-family homes. I feel these part-time landlords are modern superheroes of the U.S. rental housing market. They may not wear a cape or mask (speaking of detail, we'll even cover what a landlord can and should wear!), but they do amazing things—from refinishing dull cabinets to handling complex tax deductions. And the public benefits from their efforts to house others in their spare time.

## The Long-Term Landlord

Being a landlord is not about overnight success, but instead the ultimate long game. My approach is the exact opposite of the real estate shenanigans depicted on late-night, get rich-quick infomercials or reality television shows. Those may provide good entertainment or clever marketing. But slow and steady—mowing lawns, painting walls, shoveling snow, screening and communicating with tenants— week in and week out, year after year, wins the race for part-time landlords. The real gains will come over the very long term (think years, not months).

You've probably heard the phrase "buy and hold"—that is, to make money, a landlord should just purchase property, rent it out, and hold it a decade or two before selling at a profit. It is a common mantra in real estate investment. You've probably even seen it work, as real estate appreciates and rents rise over time.

But what's left out of the simple buy-and-hold equation, are the details of what you do in the meantime (the day-to-day property management) during the years that you try and hold onto the property. And the proverbial devil is in the details, because it's tough to engage in an activity for many years that you do not understand or find meaningful in some way. Fortunately, beyond financial gain, there are less talked about benefits of being a landlord (see my list of why I like being a landlord, below). And you'll find many of the other details in the best practices laid out within this book.

One of the top tips for holding a property long term is to select and retain long-term tenants. Most of a landlord's labor will be in this turnaround and rerenting process. But a tenant with a one-year lease may even renew a time or two, so your work (and money) can pay off in the following landlord's magic formula :

- you will have fewer costly turnovers and no or low vacancies
- over time, rents will rise but your mortgage will stay the same
- the value of your rental property will gradually appreciate, and
- tenants will pay down your mortgage with their rents,
  reducing your debt and increasing your equity in the property.

These four factors, combined with the power of financial leverage (most landlords put down 10%–20% of the purchase price but retain 100% of the upside appreciation), make a winning combination for long-term wealth building.

This sounds like a fail-proof proposition, but bear in mind that the appreciation in property markets can be sporadic (real estate moves in cycles). It may take decades for major profits to emerge. That's why landlords should focus on the long term, allowing appreciation to march slowly upwards—even if in fits and starts. Inflation will naturally drive up the rents in most markets, increasing your cash flow.

Another key advantage of owning residential rental properties is that they fit into many 30-year fixed-rate loan programs (ideal for a long-term approach) with more favorable terms than properties with five or more units. These larger apartment complexes typically require commercial financing, with higher down payments and interest rates as well as shorter repayment terms.

# How Skills You Currently Have (or Can Easily Acquire) Will Contribute to Your Success

Aside from the purchase price of the rental property, the biggest investment you will make in your rental business will be your time and skills spent improving your units and interacting with tenants. Part of the appeal of being a landlord is that you don't have to have any specialized skills: The endeavor best fits a generalist, or someone who can do many things fairly well. The things that landlords need to be proficient in fall roughly into three categories: technical skills involving the property, people skills involving the tenants, and general management skills, involving everything from planning to financial management. This book provides advice on how to become proficient in these areas and how doing so will enhance the desirability of your property and the success of your business.

Whatever your current skills level, you can continue to practice and develop them. In fact, every tenant will provide a new situation and a lesson or refresher course that never ends.

## Property Oversight and Maintenance Skills

A big draw of being a residential landlord is the average landlord's familiarity with the underlying property—or at least the type of property. Most people have lived in some type of residential property, and many have performed maintenance on a single-family house. So there is not a lot of mystery. Even residential multiplexes are generally quite similar to houses we live in, with all the same features. Condominiums are a unique form of ownership and are often part of larger buildings or properties. But since owners are generally prohibited from working outside or in common areas, you really need to know only how the inside works.

My general assumption is that you have the technical skills of an average homeowner. That should be enough to get most landlords through the maintenance and turnaround procedures in this book. There are a group of related skills any landlord can and should try to master because they are so central to the practice of landlording—cleaning, painting, and exterior maintenance—and I'll explain how to develop or improve these skills.

## Interpersonal (People) Skills

Almost all personalities can be good property managers with the right skills and some basic self-awareness when it comes to dealing with tenants and handling conflicts. Whether written, spoken, or even nonverbal, good communication is the glue that holds the landlord-tenant relationship together. How you respond and communicate with tenants can help make sure your rent checks come in on time and keep problems at a minimum. I'll give you many ideas in this book for establishing productive communications with tenants, such as verbal scripts, as well as strategies on things like establishing a high-trust environment and avoiding overemotional responses to typical tenant issues (from late rent to messy pets).

With well-screened tenants, you may not have to face many heated personal conflicts. But a good many minor issues can crop up with even the best tenants. I'll explain effective strategies for avoiding common conflicts in the first place, as well as how to handle those that do come up, by providing general scripted responses that have worked for me in various types of conflicts—whether a tenant's general dissatisfaction with the unit or an interpersonal issue with another tenant.

> **TIP**
> **My simple philosophy is to get good tenants and leave them alone.** That means I emphasize selecting the right people (those inclined to be long-term, respectful tenants). And then—other than routine maintenance or reminders—I leave them to live peacefully in the unit. Of course, if a tenant calls or contacts me about an issue, I respond right away. I aim to be a background presence in tenants' lives, helpful when needed, but not in the way.

## General Management Skills

Good managers, whether they're landlords or small business owners, share many traits. Here are some of the key skills that will contribute to your success.

**Delegating.** While this book has a strong do-it-yourself mentality, I don't recommend a "do everything yourself" approach. Knowing when and how to hand off tasks is important to running an efficient and profitable business—whether it's hiring a plumber for a tricky shower repair job or an accountant to do your taxes. Two of the chapters (6 and 11) include extensive coverage of how and when to delegate tasks, be it to blue collar or white-collar helpers. Sometimes you will be more like the maestro of the symphony than a one-man-band trying to play every instrument.

**Flexibility.** Rigidity can be a real liability for landlords. When you deal with people, you sometimes have to be able to absorb small imperfections for the sake of the larger task. For example, a little "wear and tear" is something you have to expect when you do the walkthrough that's a customary part of the tenant move-out procedure. No tenant is perfect, and there are tips (in Chapter 9) on handling your response patterns when tenants do make minor errors.

**Being firm but fair.** Try to treat all tenants as fairly as possible and also strike a balance between your interests and theirs. Whenever possible, split the difference or meet the tenant halfway. For example, I might let a tenant hang or put out potted plants, but only in areas where the moisture won't damage decks or building and the hanging plants can't fall on a car or passerby. Making such accommodations can show that you are open to compromise and tenants' needs but have to look out for your own interests, as well. Also, avoid being judgmental or imposing your values on tenants.

**Managing stress.** Choosing the right rental property and carefully selecting and managing your tenants can greatly reduce a landlord's stress. But added tension is an inevitable occupational hazard, because tenants can be unpredictable at times, and buildings seem to have a mind of their own; you can't control when a pipe will burst or another such problem will develop (midnight seems to be the most likely hour). Of course, you will always have total control over how you react or face such situations. Ideally, you can take a positive approach, using a tenant phone call as an opportunity to improve a unit or increase tenant satisfaction rather than viewing it as a stressful nuisance. Developing strategies for stress management, such as exercise, a good social network, and a spiritual practice can help.

### RESOURCE

**Cut down the stress.** *Why Zebras Don't Get Ulcers: The Acclaimed Guide To Stress, Stress-Related Diseases, and Coping,* by Robert Sapolsky (Holt Paperbacks), discusses the health links to stress as well as some major issues related to stress, especially related to control and predictability in our lives—key challenges for many landlords

**Staying organized.** You can never close a deal if you can't find your lease form. So a central theme in this book is putting simple systems in place to help you be effective, whether it involves organizing maintenance supplies or receipts and tax records. The secret for the part-time landlord is to integrate rental property systems with household systems (as it is a home-based business in many respects, as discussed later).

### TIP

**Be a list maker.** An amazingly simple (but crucial) organizational strategy for landlords is making lists. The average turnaround (when you spruce up a rental unit between tenants) may include dozens of small, separate tasks. You often need a product or tool for each one, plus a clear order to tackle the tasks. Getting your to-do list out of your mind and onto paper or your computer can help you stay sane and save gas (so you don't have to backtrack for forgotten items). Some sample checklists for common landlord duties—like turning units around and periodic maintenance—are included throughout the book.

**Setting priorities.** One critical skill for every landlord is prioritizing what to do and, in turn, what to leave undone. For example, when you budget for projects on your units, you'll need a sharp eye to separate budget wants (your ideals for the property) from budget needs, and to decide between urgent short-term projects and longer-range plans. Prioritizing tenant safety first, then property protection and preventive maintenance, will help keep you on course and prevent injuries and liabilities. Also, it is key to think about resource allocation not only in terms of money, but with regard to your scarce time.

**Financial skills.** This one may be the "x" factor some people lack, and it is key in landlording. Along with handling the people and the property, you have to handle the money. As an example, a successful contractor (with strengths in both carpentry and remodeling) and his spouse, who managed both people and property (as a property manager), were looking at buying one of my properties—and I thought we had a match made in heaven. They could be an ideal landlording team for my tenants (and I could exit stage left with a large check).

But there was one key ingredient lacking: They could not get the financing due to credit issues, so it was not to be. I realized it's doubtful that even those with great people and property skills can be successful landlords without strong financial management skills. They will have trouble buying the property and probably couldn't keep up with all the added bills if they struggled to handle their own personal finances.

## Why I Like Being a Landlord

Like any other landlord, financial rewards are a central motivation for me. No one's in this business to lose money. But I find if you do the job well and enjoy it, the money will follow: it is a byproduct of being a good landlord. Yet the positive factors about being a landlord go far beyond money. In fact if you are just *in it for the money*, it may not be sustainable long term. Here's what I like about owning and managing rental property—beyond the financial rewards:

**I'm my own boss.** The pride of ownership and sense of accomplishment in running my own rental business is a major reward. I like being CEO and 100% in control. The absence of oversight, staff meetings, time clocks, office politics, and bureaucracy is liberating. It can be a nice contrast to many day jobs in that respect.

**It's work I can do on the side (and keep my job!).** Like many rental property owners, I hold down a busy day job and do landlording work in my free time. Most part-time landlords will need a day job just to get financing for rental properties; you can't really start or expand your business without some source of steady income (largely because bankers dislike giving loans to the unemployed). So keep your day job (this is not a quit-work book). Even the best cash-flowing properties don't tend to generate enough income to live on right away (and they never offer benefits like health insurance). I like having the safety net of a day job, but also knowing that no matter what happens to it, I have the security of controlling my destiny with this side business. I offer tips for the best of both worlds— retaining the security of your job and engaging in the excitement of your own entrepreneurial pursuits.

**I make use of my existing skills and knowledge.** As discussed above, being a small-time landlord is an area that rewards people who can wear several hats. It involves many of the same chores I do at home: cleaning, maintenance, painting, repairs, gardening, and lawn care. (Thank your parents for all the on-the-job training those chores provided!) And whether you've practiced on your coworkers, employees, students, or family, you may already have the communication and conflict-management skills needed to work with tenants. Because I bought my own house, I was already familiar with mortgages, purchase contracts, and inspections before buying my first rental property. I'll target only residential properties, so the buying process is similar to the one any home buyer encounters. Finally, most of us may have been tenants at some time or other, so we have that perspective, too. Part of the allure of landlording is that the average adult homeowner probably already knows enough to be a part-time landlord.

**The business model is fairly simple.** You don't need a degree in finance to make money renting out residential property. You own a place, and people pay you money to live there (ideally paying you more than your expenses). Much of what you need to learn can be picked up on your own (and this book is a great way to start). Even endless family games of *Monopoly* have helped me understand property acquisition, rents, and different price levels in the rental market. As a landlord, just providing well-priced, desirable housing rentals will give you your choice of tenants in most rental markets. Everyone needs a place to live.

**Home based.** You don't need a shop, a storefront, or a warehouse in order to be a part time landlord. You can use your own home as a platform for delivering great rental service. Your garage or even an empty closet is your shop and storeroom, holding all your materials and tools. Your own kitchen table is the office. My favorite part: The commute is to your own file cabinet down the hall for a lease or to your garage to get standard white paint (you'll use the same color in all your units).

Best of all, the overhead will be low, with no franchise fees or extra office space to rent (of course, special rules apply if you are looking to deduct a home office, and some of the references in this book can help you there). An epiphany I had in writing this book was that small-time landlording is a real home-based business (not a gimmick but a real one). Even your business vehicle will be the one in front of your house right now (and a tax deduction). And if you follow the guidance in Chapter 2, your rental property will be conveniently located nearby, too.

**Landlording keeps me fit and healthy.** While not a substitute for a regular exercise program, one beneficial side effect of being a hands-on landlord is the added physical activity. This can be especially valuable if you have a day job, like mine, that is primarily sedentary. Landlords can expect to be pleasantly surprised by what the scales says after they've been working on their units. For example, completing a unit turnaround or doing an exterior paint job can increase activity for a couple of weeks and routinely melts a few pounds off me. The intense bursts of activity may be intermittent, depending on the season, vacancy rate, and building needs, but very real. More importantly, being a landlord has given me a strong incentive to stay fit year round in order to be prepared for a physical task or unit turnaround. All this bending and lifting saves me money on labor, improves my flexibility and balance, and burns off calories. (Of course, I'm careful not to overdo it, and I hand off hazardous tasks or those that are too physically challenging.)

## Landlording Can Burn Calories

There may be times when you can skip the gym and hit the rental property. Landlords can burn major calories doing these common tasks:

- sweeping: 240 calories per hour
- painting: 290 calories per hour
- mowing the lawn: 325 calories per hour
- shoveling snow: 415 calories per hour
- mopping the kitchen floor: 153 calories per hour
- vacuuming: 240 calories per hour, and
- intense bathtub scrubbing: 90 calories in 15 minutes.

**I'm always learning.** Owning rental property keeps my mind active as I learn new things about real estate, rental markets, taxes, the law, maintenance and repairs (from painting rental units to buying new appliances), managing people, and more. Learning can be fun, and it's hard to beat the feeling of solving a complex problem on my own and improving my rental units and tenant experience in the process.

**Housing tenants is meaningful and fulfilling.** While being a landlord is a for-profit venture, it has clear social benefits. Many areas of the country face dire shortages of affordable rentals, and I firmly believe that small-time landlords like myself are an important part of the solution to housing America. I like the fact that I can impact society in small but meaningful ways, starting by simply having well-maintained, safe, and clean units and encouraging and fostering "green" practices (many are listed in this book). I add to the standard of living and quality of life for my tenants, often in basic ways, such as by allowing pets (on approval), providing secure bicycle parking, and fostering community by encouraging tenants to get to know one another. Unlike stock quotes I watch on a screen, my real estate investment has me interacting with a variety of real people. My role as their housing provider is a pursuit that is active and social.

**I'm contributing to my community.** Being a landlord is also a great avenue toward civic engagement, as I pick up trash outside my

## Landlording Can Accommodate Life Changes

Being a landlord can lend itself to a wide range of lifestyle decisions or changes. Also, changes in demographics, tax laws, and the real estate market can create motivations for starting or growing a rental property business. Here are a few examples:

- **Moving.** If you don't want to (or can't) sell a current house, renting it out often makes sense, especially if you might return eventually, or feel the market may improve such that selling later will reap higher profits.
- **Downsizing.** This trend often has empty nesters or mature individuals and couples moving from a larger single-family house to a smaller home or condo. Such a move reduces costs and maintenance, and in some markets and situations, it may make economic sense to rent out the larger home.
- **Retirement.** This major life change may see people moving seasonally to a more temperate location. Snowbirds might rent out their main home or while they are away. Retirees may also be looking to live abroad, work intermittently, or stay with family for long periods of time. All of these could make renting your home an option.
- **College.** Buying a rental for the kids or grandkids while they are in college can be a good strategy. Or, if you're going to college or pursuing education, you might want to buy a place with that goal and later rent it out.
- **Second home.** Whether it is an inheritance, a place to return to, or an eventual place to move to or enjoy seasonally, people often keep a second home for work or play, and this can probably be rented in the interim.
- **Part-time work or extra income.** Industrious types looking for extra income or part-time work might choose a residential rental property over a second job.
- **New business venture.** It can be hard to beat the allure and excitement of the new business venture. And few businesses are as simple to start and understand. Buy a unit and rent it. Of course, the details of executing this simple plan can be critical, and this book offers a good framework for success.

rentals, paint a front porch, plant flowers, or perform some other service for appreciative tenants and neighbors. These tasks may seem small, but lots of people are looking to find volunteer work in their communities because it helps them make a tangible difference. You can also be active beyond your property boundaries in neighborhood associations and local affairs related to utilities, zoning, and urban planning. You will have an added stake in the outcome and can be active in local governmental affairs—whether it's attending local planning and zoning commission meetings or following city council discussions of services relevant to your rental property.

# What You Won't Find in This Book

The focus of this book is on management practices for the small-scale, part-time landlord. While it covers some financial and legal issues broadly, it does not go into extensive detail regarding real estate investment or landlord-tenant law in your state. Here are some resources for more information on topics this book doesn't cover.

## Large-Scale Property Management Tips or Practices

While many topics and tips in this book can work whether you have one or 100 units, it's geared specifically for the part-time landlord with a few residential (one- to four-unit) rental properties. Indeed, many of the same policies (be it openness to pets or more thorough communication with tenants) may not work if you had a large-scale operation. Also, you won't find advice on common apartment topics like swimming pools, managing the front office, hiring on-site apartment managers, or how to get tens of millions in commercial financing. This is about you, in your own vehicle, loading up to work on your own property. So we cover everything from painting your rental units to tackling the depreciation on your taxes. That said, I think many five-, ten-, 20-, or even 50-unit apartment owners can benefit from the ideas in this book. And more resources on larger-scale professional property management can be found at the Institute of Real Estate Management (IREM, atwww.irem.org).

## General Real Estate Investment Strategies

You'll find useful advice in this book on making sure a particular property pencils out in terms of positive cash flow and meets your needs as to location, type of property, and other factors. I recommend taking a long-term approach to owning rental property, but I do not go into all the possible strategies for making real estate investment decisions. For that, you'll want to check out books such as the classic *Buy and Hold,* by Dr. David Schumacher (Schumacher Enterprises), *How to Get Started in Real Estate Investing,* by Robert Irwin (McGraw Hill), or *Investing in Fixer-Uppers,* by Jay P. DeCima ( McGraw-Hill).

## Flipping

Television shows and investment seminars often promote flipping, a real estate investment strategy where someone buys property that is distressed or underpriced, makes improvements, and then tries to sell at closer to market value, for a quick profit. There is nothing wrong with this strategy for people who specialize in this activity. But flipping is not covered in this book, because it typically doesn't involve long-term landlording or renting out property, even for a short term.

## Renting Your Home Through Short-Term Vacation Rental Sites

Various online services act as a clearinghouse for short-term (typically less than 30 days) vacation rentals. These types of rentals involve different legal and practical issues concerning taxes, insurance coverage, liability for guest injuries, neighbor complaints, and municipal restrictions. And if your rental property is a condo or co-op, these may prohibit any and all short-term rentals. This emerging area of the residential rental world is not covered in this book, and the legal framework and management practices are still being developed.

## Other Helpful Nolo Books and Resources for Landlords

For many readers, this book will provide all the information needed to manage your rental property. But if you want specific legal forms or detailed legal information for your state, check out other Nolo resources.

Start with what's available for free in the Landlords center on Nolo.com (www.nolo.com/legal-encyclopedia/landlords). There, you will find charts with your state laws, including state security deposit limits, required landlord disclosures, rent rules, tenant privacy, small claims court rules, repair responsibilities, termination rules, and much more. You'll also find lots of useful articles on topics such as evictions.

Nolo publishes a comprehensive library of books (hard copy and electronic versions) for landlords and rental property owners, including:

- *Every Landlord's Legal Guide,* by Marcia Stewart, Ralph Warner and Janet Portman. Provides detailed state-by-state legal information on rent and security deposit rules, required disclosures, notice to terminate for nonpayment of rent, and more. Also dozens of legal forms you need from a lease at move-in to a security deposit itemization at move-out, as well as a property manager agreement (should you decide to hand off the day-to-day management duties).
- *Every Landlord's Tax Deduction Guide,* by Stephen Fishman. Includes all the information you need to take advantage of tax deductions and write-offs available to landlords, such as depreciation, legal services, and insurance, as well as instructions for completing Schedule E.
- *First-Time Landlord: Your Guide to Renting Out a Single-Family Home,* by Janet Portman, Ilona Bray, and Marcia Stewart. Covers the basics that first-time or "accidental" landlords need to rent and manage a single-family home or condo, including renting out a room in a house when owners are still living in it.

If your property is in California, see the two volumes of *The California Landlord's Law Book (Rights and Responsibilities* and *Evictions).*

Nolo also has many single-copy interactive online forms, such as state-specific leases and rental agreements.

For Nolo's full library, see the Landlord-Tenant and Leases & Rental Agreements sections of the Nolo store on www.nolo.com, or call Nolo at 800-728-3555. Also check your local bookstore or public library.

## Your State's Landlord-Tenant Laws

It's impossible to write about managing rental property without touching on key laws (primarily state) that affect your actions and policies—whether it be fair housing, limits on security deposits, landlord access to property, or nonpayment of rent notices. This is a management guide, not a legal resource, so I provide an overview of the key laws that affect the various aspects of property management, but leave the specifics to other Nolo titles, particularly *Every Landlord's Legal Guide*, and Nolo's extensive collection of free articles at www.nolo.com. See "Other Helpful Nolo Books and Resources for Landlords," above, for details.

---

### Get Updates and More on This Book's Companion Page on Nolo.com

When there are important changes to the information in this book, we'll post updates online, on a dedicated page:

**www.nolo.com/back-of-book/PROP.html**

You'll find other useful information on that page, too, such as Nolo's blog, covering various real estate issues.

---

# What's Your Competitive Edge?

Whether you are beginning, continuing, or expanding your rental property business, your chances of success and longevity as a landlord can be greatly improved by crafting a strategy that will give your units an edge over the competition. And make no mistake, there will be competition. Potential renters compare units based on price, location, condition, size, amenities, terms, and a host of other factors.

You need a focus, plan, and strategy to make sure people choose your rental unit over others. This may not take a highly complicated plan. In fact, crafting a competitive advantage can be surprisingly simple for the small-time landlord. First, get to know your market—the competition as well as the customers. Then, devise ways that your rentals, and your approach to property management, can stand out to potential tenants.

A major allure to being a small-time landlord is that you can compete, and even offer a superior product and better service than a large billion-dollar property firm, simply by putting in extra effort and doing small but meaningful things. There are two primary ways to beat the competition.

**First, be different**. Offer something other rentals on the market don't; you can differentiate, for example, by allowing a different lease term (like six months), allowing pets, or even offering better management and communication; all three are covered throughout the book. Also, choosing attractive features in the rental properties you own (like a yard or garage) can help differentiate, as can a more convenient location (all covered in Chapter 2 on selecting properties).

**Second, be cheaper.** Offer a comparable unit for less than the others on the market, which you may be able to do with low overhead and by reducing turnover.

The key is to employ one (or both) strategies; otherwise, you are offering the same thing at the same price as your competitors (and don't have an advantage). Don't leave it to chance: have a strategy to offer the price and unique terms or features, so the best renters call you first.

# Get to Know Your Market and Where Your Rental Fits Within It

You can never know enough about your rental market. After a few years of owning and managing rental property, you should be very knowledgeable about the price points, terms, needs, demographics, and demands for rental housing in your area. Read Craigslist and other rental ads constantly. View the photos. Drive by the competition. Look for subtle clues beyond price and size. For example, what is included in the rents charged? Do the units have their own washers and dryers? Do they provide adequate parking spaces? Do they allow pets? Are the terms flexible?

Doing your homework can help you craft your own pricing and marketing strategy. The good news is that everyone needs a place to live, and in many markets around the country, the demand for quality, affordable rentals outstrips supply. (Of course, different areas have different vacancy rates.) After educating yourself about your local rental market, think about your price (or rental amount), property type, and how you will promote it to grow your business according to your own needs and goals—for example:

- If your target market is college students in a college town, you'll be adding different amenities than if you're trying to attract families with children in a suburban community.
- Your strategies will differ if you own rentals in a super-competitive market with a high vacancy rate versus a community with a low vacancy rate and large tenant population.
- If you rent out a duplex in an area where income levels are low and unemployment high, you'll want to take a completely different approach than you would if renting a high-end condo in an affluent community.

# Differentiate Your Units From the Competition

A key part of your success will be a differentiation strategy. Think about practical and meaningful ways you can make your rental units—even when similar to competitors—more appealing to your target renters. This means you won't simply offer the exact same product at the same price as your competitors. (If you want to try that approach, you really will be relying on luck—hoping tenants happen to call and sign with you first.) This does not necessarily mean you have to add expensive amenities or commit to providing extra services.

Here are some simple ways to set your rentals apart from the competition, the details of which I'll discuss in subsequent chapters of this book.

## Pets on Approval

Almost half of all Americans have a dog and around a third have a cat, yet many rentals flat-out prohibit pets. With these facts in mind, Chapter 8 takes a detailed look at a "pets on approval" policy that will open up your rentals to sensible, responsible pet owners with well-behaved pets. This policy can minimize the risk of pet problems (noise, smells, damage) while maximizing your chances of getting great tenants. Your rental will automatically out-compete other units where landlords have a strict no-pets-allowed policy. Better yet, many tenants will base their decision to rent on this factor alone.

## Top-Notch, Personal Service

Small-time landlords can offer big-time service. Right away, you will likely know the tenant's name, needs, and preferences. Instead of "tenant in unit 179," your tenant will be "Jake" or "Jane." You can demonstrate this from the get-go by having the unit ready in pristine condition and arriving early and staying late to show the place to prospective tenants. You will study the applicants into the wee hours to try and find the best fit. Your response time to communications and requests should also be outstanding.

Other landlords and property managers may have dozens, even hundreds, of units to manage. They will do the job well enough to earn a fee and stay employed. Such a manager is not really incentivized to do more. If you're managing just a handful of properties, you should be able to easily best them on the service level.

You'll notice that some prospective tenants will be surprised to see the owner there, on site showing the place, rather than a proxy. They're used to dealing with hired managers who have neither the same incentive nor the power to be flexible. They can sense right away that you are *the* source for authoritative answers on a range of questions about the property, potential terms of the lease, or other factors related to the tenancy.

## Tenant-Friendly Features

Ideally, you have or will choose units with features considered desirable in your area. Adding costly amenities like a major kitchen remodel seldom pencils out for rentals, but there are low-cost items that can put your unit in front. Sometimes a fence for pets and kids, for example, may be a huge selling point, and not that costly. Secure bike parking and storage for items like kayaks and recreational gear can be big draws and are fairly simple to construct. Think about features that will sell with your target tenant without adding too much additional cost. Keep your potential tenants in mind if and when you buy a rental unit (see Chapter 2 for more information on property purchase decisions).

## Effective Management

When tenants rent a place, they are also getting a person who will work with them and manage the tenancy. Make sure tenants know that you, personally, will be there for them with competent help when they need it. Whether it is making a needed repair or resolving a problem with another tenant, your diligence and skills can set your unit apart from those offered by other landlords.

## Strong Communication

From the beginning, you can offer better rental application or lease forms and paperwork; a streamlined move-in process; clear (written) rules and policies, and exact answers for tenants when they need them.

I provide samples of useful forms and suggestions for helpful communication throughout this book, devoting all of Chapter 9 to the subject.

## Empowered Tenants

Many large apartment complexes have extremely restrictive policies governing tenant behavior, as are necessary for large-scale operations. Small landlords don't need to use the same cookie-cutter approach. You could, for example, consider allowing tenants some leeway in caring for and customizing their rental, such as by painting the living room or planting a garden. You could allow simple but meaningful activities such as holiday decorations in the window or on the porch and car washing (you provide the hose). Little freedoms like these generally don't cost much, are low risk, and often help tenants settle in for the long term.

## Flexible Rental Terms

Tenants may face a brick wall of rigid lease terms, costly deposit requirements, and other restrictions in some rental markets. If the norm is the one-year lease, think about whether you can do six-month renewable leases. Satisfied tenants will simply renew again and again. Take a customer- or tenant-focused approach and see what matters to them. The same flexibility may work with your terms regarding pets, parking, storage, occupants, and so on. Where your competitors say "No," you can say "Yes," or at least "Maybe" or "Under these conditions" to reasonable requests.

> ### TIP
> **Flexibility may be limited if your rental is in a condo or planned unit development.** Many condo associations have strict rules and policies governing lease terms and use of your property. So you may not have the same flexibility to offer a shorter lease or allow an extra pet or vehicle. Check the policies, bylaws, and declarations (often called covenants, conditions, and restrictions, or CC&Rs) of your condominium or community association.

## Offer Lower-Priced Units by Focusing on Keeping Long-Term Tenants

Long-term tenants are not only less hassle and more sustainable than ones who come and go, but they can help you reduce costs, thus allowing you to lower your rents—and ultimately reap higher profits.

Suppose you have a three-year tenant paying a slightly below-market rate of $1,000 a month. You'll make a grand total of $36,000 in rental revenue and have no vacancy for an entire three years. You won't need to paint, clean the carpets, or do anything but maybe an annual inspection and make any requested repairs.

Compare that to a $1,050 a month tenant in the same unit, in which you turn the unit over at the end of year two and three, and have a one-month vacancy at each turnover. You'll make only $35,700. Plus, you'll have to clean, renew, and show the unit, taking up your time (which is not free) as well as money. If you value your time and consider the costs of materials and supplies, you could easily spend another $1,000 on each turnaround. That leaves you at $33,700, or $2,300 less than you would have made keeping the same tenant with lower rents over the same time period.

One can begin to see the difference between success and failure, between sustainability and burnout for the small-time landlord. The moral of this story is twofold.

**First, there is very real economic value to long-term tenants.** A lease from a long-term tenant is an asset, a stream of uninterrupted cash that takes minimal labor and no extra capital other than your standard fixed expenses. (If you don't think constant monthly cash flow is important, consider trying to make two or three mortgage payments on your rental properties—not to mention your own home—without any rents coming in.) The long-term tenant just requires a renewal lease dropped in the mail. After that, you'll enjoy "mailbox money"—in which tenants pay you on time, month after month, year after year without causing problems. Your only effort is in getting the mail and cashing your rent checks.

**Second, keeping rents slightly below market will help turn good tenants into long-term tenants.** Why would your tenants want to go elsewhere, if they'll face higher rents in return for fewer amenities and less personal service? The result for you will be fewer costly turnovers and no or low vacancies.

> **TIP**
> **Create a tickler system for renewals.** Put a tickler or note on your calendar for when leases end. Contact the tenants about renewing. And if they are interested, send them the lease (with SASE) to sign and mail with the next month's rent. Be sure and let tenants know of any changes. Typically, the same lease will work, but update any new pet, vehicle, or tenant info.

## Make Strategic Decisions About Your Own Approach to Renting Property

There's no one single type of landlord, even among the small-time landlords. So let's take a moment to consider some of the major differences—or up-front decisions— affecting how you'll run your business.

First, think about your own SWOT (Strengths, Weaknesses, Opportunities, and Threats). This is strategy lingo for analyzing your abilities (such as your own maintenance skills) in light of the opportunities and threats around you (such as the type of properties, current prices, and available tenants in your market). Looking at your strengths and weaknesses in light of your market will help you make the early strategic decisions that follow.

## Type, Number, Location, and Condition of Rental Properties You Will Own

The scale and type of your rental operation should reflect your own abilities and resources. For example, if you are a full-time professional without a lot of free time or property maintenance skills, you should probably choose a property that requires minimal time and skills spent on management—a small condo, perhaps. If it's occupied by a trouble-free tenant; you may just collect rent checks and drop off an annual holiday card in winter. If something is problematic outside the condo unit, such as a broken step, it will be the condo association's responsibility to fix it. You may act primarily as an information conduit, taking the information from the tenant to the association or their property manager. On the other hand, if you grew up maintaining houses and have a flexible job, maybe doing shift work or with summers off, you might be a strategic fit with an older triplex in a working-class area. More work would be required, but you'd have the time and skills to handle them (think biweekly exterior maintenance such as mowing grass and removing snow, larger projects like painting, more potential vacancies, more toilets that could get plugged, and more potential tenant complaints or issues).

Look for a strategic fit between you (and your capacity as a landlord) and the property for success. Otherwise, your career as a landlord could be both short and stressful (and your day job even impacted negatively). Property choice is very important and is the primary focus of Chapter 2, which explains how to pick your properties to match your personal and business goals, including your desired lifestyle and work-life balance.

## How Much Work You Do Yourself

Along with your strengths and weaknesses, you can also assess how much work you can delegate (a key management skill). A major theme in this book is that when it comes to key tasks, such as choosing and managing tenants and handling basic maintenance, most people can become effective do-it-yourself landlords. However, this does not mean you should try and become a "do-everything-yourself" landlord. Hiring others to do some work is often more effective and practical. Indeed, effectively delegating tasks is one of the landlord's top skills. This book contains two chapters on effectively hiring others to do jobs (Chapter 6 on trades and other service contractors and Chapter 11 on hiring white collar professionals, such as lawyers).

If you plan to use a lot of help, you may even want to put the cart before the horse, and have good helpers lined up *before* you buy the property. That way, you can have a real estate professional or attorney help in the property transaction, a contractor give an impression of (or bid on work to be done) on the property, and have lawn or maintenance people lined up to start work when you close.

## How Long You Want to Own the Rental Property

The soundest strategy for most small-time landlords will be holding the rental properties for a long time period, such as a decade or more. If you have any doubts about this approach, study what property in your area sold for ten, 20, 30, or 40 years ago. With the exception of some economically depressed areas of the U.S., most locations have seen strong (even shocking) price appreciation over this span of years.

As your property price and rents go up, your debt on the property will go down. You can ride out multiple real estate and economic cycles by buying and holding. Owning a rental property for a number of years also produces tax benefits. You can defer capital gains taxes by not selling, letting that gain grow until selling works best for you or you retire and drop into a lower tax bracket.

CAUTION

**Beware of anyone touting real estate as a tax shelter or haven.** Such tax benefits may have been available in the past. But U.S. tax law contains very specific rules about deductions, and the amount you deduct may depend on your activity level. Tax breaks can be an added benefit of being a landlord, but should not be the driving force behind your decision to become one. *Every Landlord's Tax Deduction Guide,* by Stephen Fishman (Nolo), covers the tax deductions and tax considerations for small-time landlords, as well as the tax consequences of starting and growing a rental business and of using the rental personally for part of the year. Chapters 11 and 12 also cover taxes, record keeping, and hiring an accountant.

Don't forget that your skills and experience as a landlord will also increase over time, making your operation more efficient and easier to run. And you may even favor legendary investor Warren Buffett's ideal holding period for his investments: *forever.*

A short-term time frame (less than a year or so) doesn't make sense for most landlords, largely because of the transaction costs in both buying and selling. When selling a property, you will likely have substantial closing costs, contractor bills, and transaction fees (notably real estate commissions), which will likely devour much of your gains. Also, selling an asset like a rental property owned for less than a year will quite possibly move you into a higher capital gains tax bracket.

A short-term strategy also cuts off your opportunity for price appreciation and could leave you selling in a down market. And there are numerous costs involved in prepping a property for sale. Even if you recently turned around the unit, tenants can inflict a lot of wear and tear on a rental in just a year or so, requiring new paint, carpet and probably new appliances, fixtures, and more to reach pristine sale condition.

A short-term strategy works best for real estate investors who "flip" property—that is, buy a neglected rental property, do some modest cosmetic repairs, and then sell it. But this is a specialized type of real estate transaction beyond the scope of this book. And, of course, if you are an "accidental" landlord, perhaps because you inherited your parents' home and want to rent it out for a short while before selling it, a short-term approach may work just fine.

> **TIP**
>
> **Being a landlord should never be a life sentence.** Everyone's interests, financial goals, health, and energy change over time. The negatives of managing rental property may, one day, take a mental toll on you that outweighs the financial and other benefits. Perhaps you'll want to retire from the day-to-day oversight of your rentals after a few years and hand the management off to someone else. Or maybe you will simply sell the unit (or even finance it yourself, if it is paid for). Be thinking of an exit strategy even as you purchase a property, because one day you will need it.

## What's Next?

Having looked at your big-picture strategy, one of the most important decisions you will make as a new landlord is your selection of a rental property, our next topic (in Chapter 2). A poorly chosen property in a bad neighborhood that needs major repairs is a management nightmare. But a solid property in the right location can almost rent itself, reduce maintenance costs, and appreciate nicely on its own. One is a path to long term success; the other leads to short term failure.

# Selecting Rental Properties

n order to make the property-management model that I describe in this book work for you—with its focus on responsiveness to tenants and hands-on maintenance—it helps to have the right property in the first place. This chapter explains the key factors that go into choosing a rental property, including the location and property type (single-family house, multiplex, condo, or in-law apartment), as well as how to do a rental market analysis, estimate the cash flow for a hypothetical rental, and inspect a rental property.

Many of the insights are from my own real estate transactions and my belief that if you start with the right rental property, your operation is far more likely to be successful—in terms of profitability, ease of management, and attracting the best tenant pool. Conversely, if you choose the wrong rental property (in a bad location, with negative cash flow, or one with serious construction defects), you may be the best landlord on the planet and still fail.

Whether you are buying your first or your tenth rental property, read on and choose wisely.

## Location, Location, Location

One of the most important parts of choosing a rental is location. It's one aspect of the property you can never change. There are two main areas to explore regarding location—the fit for you as a manager of the property and the fit for the potential tenants who will live there.

### TIP

**Owning rental property out of the area.** This book is geared toward landlords who own rental property fairly close to where they live or work. For most people, owning out-of-town rental property—that is, more than an hour or two drive away—is not feasible. The expense and stress of being far away can take a toll on even the best landlord. Perhaps the only exception is if you use a good local property manager to oversee rental operations, a topic covered in Chapter 11.

> ## Make Sure the Rental Location Fits Your Safety and Comfort Level
>
> Remember, you will have to go to your rental units at all hours and usually alone. When choosing a rental property, look out for signs of neighborhood decay, such as graffiti, broken windows, or unusual street activity. Check online or with local police for data on crime in the area (and police responses). Many smaller towns print a police report in the newspaper. You can quickly identify geographic patterns to the criminal activity. Avoid rentals in high-crime areas or neighborhoods you find unsafe. Good tenants will probably do the same, so being safe also makes economic sense.

## A Location That Isn't Far Out of Your Way

As a diligent, hands-on landlord, you may have to visit your rental units often. You may go there daily when you are turning around a unit, or just drive by monthly, when things are going smoothly. There will also be countless trips to do chores each time it snows, when the grass grows, or when a tenant calls with a broken appliance or other repair problem.

So, whatever you do, make sure it is fairly easy to get to your rental property. Otherwise, the drive alone could quickly become a burden. Worse yet, your maintenance and oversight of the property could suffer, resulting in neglected repairs, delays in handling tenant complaints, and problematic tenant behaviors that could go unchecked (like unauthorized occupants or excessive clutter around the building).

Be on the lookout for desirable rental properties that match these criteria:

- **Along your daily commute.** This is ideal because you are in an easy position to stop by before or after work. Proximity will save fuel and time, and make the trip easier and more routine.
- **Near another rental.** If you already have a rental in one area and you like the neighborhood, it makes sense to add another

in the same location. You can mow both lawns or shovel both porches in one trip.

- **Close to home.** Of course, nothing beats having a rental down the street (or even on your property, such as an in-law apartment) in terms of convenience and ease of oversight. However, you are also very convenient to a renter who might want to stop by and see you, in which case you'll want to choose your renters carefully. (See "When the Tenants Are Your Neighbors," below, for more on this issue.)

## A Location That Fits the Needs of Your Most Likely Tenants

Along with finding potential locations that you can easily manage, think about the tenants and what's convenient for them—in terms of work, shopping, school, and recreation. Let the tenant's view guide your property selection, by looking for these characteristics.

**Proximity and access to work or school.** How close is the rental to major employers, such as factories, hospitals, government office buildings, military bases, or corporate headquarters? What about local colleges and universities? Is there easy freeway access? Nearby public transportation?

**Walkability.** See www.walkscore.com to find out how a property rates in terms of how easily pedestrians can get to work, parks, shopping, and other locations. A good walk score can be a real plus, and opens up your rental to people who may not have vehicles or want to use them daily.

**No hassle factors.** Be on the lookout for location-related issues that could inconvenience or deter renters, such as heavy traffic flow in the area (especially during rush hours), lack of adequate parking, and steep hills (especially problematic in areas with icy winter conditions).

**Privacy.** While you want a property that is accessible, one fronting a major roadway or overly exposed to passing cars, traffic noise, or neighbors' windows or views may be undesirable.

**School district.** Rentals within the boundaries of the best schools are often in the greatest demand. And families tend to look for long-term rentals.

**Other invisible regional dividing lines.** Certain neighborhoods have cachet. Even if you can't tell the difference from the place across the street, the trendy crowds may desire the added gravitas of a certain address.

**Other negative factors.** Look out for obnoxious noises, be it from factories, public areas, railroads, or highways, which make a property unattractive to renters.

# What Type of Rental Property Is Best for You?

Once you have identified your preferred location, think about the type of residential property you will focus on. You'll likely have several choices, each with unique pros and cons.

## Good News About Financing Small Rental Properties

Residential home financing is geared for the average homeowner, with loan programs designed to encourage home ownership. If you stick with one- to four-unit properties, you can benefit from residential financing through lower down payments and interest rates, a standard 30-year fixed rate loan, and common loan programs backed by government agencies. In contrast, commercial financing applies to properties with five or more rental units. With commercial financing, buyers are considered more sophisticated and face higher down payments and interest rates as well as shorter repayment terms. It will still be investor (non-owner-occupied) financing unless you live at the property (such as occupying half of a duplex), but these rates and terms are still quite favorable compared to commercial financing (the only option for five units or more).

No matter which property type you choose, I'm assuming that, at this stage in your career as a landlord, it won't be a major multiplex. One-to-four unit properties are not only easier to handle, but are defined as "residential" by housing agencies and, most importantly, for the associated financing programs (see "Good News About Financing Small Rental Properties," above). The next few sections cover the types of residential properties most recommended for small- and part-time landlords: single-family houses, multiplexes, condos, and in-law apartments.

# Single-Family House

Single-family homes (detached or attached) are staples of the U.S. housing market.

## Pluses of Single-Family Homes

Depending on their location and other factors, single-family homes in good condition are often the easiest forms of real estate to finance, sell, and rent. Their appreciation rates are also among the highest of any types of residential properties. Most people are familiar with the basic maintenance and features of single-family homes, as well. And in almost all geographic areas, there will be more single-family houses on the market than any other types of properties, giving you an ample selection.

## Minuses of Single-Family Homes

Some of the very features that make homes appealing to homeowners can make them problematic for landlords. Remember, you will be renting and maintaining the property—not living there. Here are aspects of single-family homes that can be challenging.

**Big yards.** Homeowners may like these (as will tenants with dogs or children), but there is more to mow and maintain for the landlord.

**Pools, hot tubs, saunas, fireplaces, or sunrooms.** These flashy features may attract some buyers, but can be costly for landlords to maintain, and even be risky liabilities.

**Specialized areas.** Wet bars, exercise rooms, media rooms, or just extra open areas are generally wasted space for landlords. They seldom increase rents. Worse yet, they could invite mischief or misuse. I once looked in one of my rental units and saw that the tenant (a well-paid professional, not a full-time biker) had wheeled her Harley Davidson motorcycle right inside the apartment, storing it in the large open area near the laundry and kitchen for the winter.

**High-end anything.** The mantra is "mid-grade" for the landlord. Higher-end appliances, finishes, or flooring tend to cost more to fix and replace.

**Numerous mature trees near the house.** This bucolic scene for an owner is a hassle for the landlord, who will be constantly cleaning gutters and clearing leaves, twigs, and other debris. There is also the risk of trees falling in a storm.

**Procedure-laden systems, such as septic tanks, irrigation piping, or alarm or sound systems.** Understanding and properly using these can be a challenge for the most diligent homeowner. The average renter may not be able to handle them.

**Large parking areas (if in a snowy climate).** Ample parking is great, but too much area is more to shovel and more to replace when the time comes.

**Steep drives.** These are maintenance risks, hard to clear for snow, and can even be risks for cars without good parking brakes.

**High-maintenance flooring.** Be it white carpet or an exotic wood floor, you don't want to be fussing over it. Look for durable floors that can handle wear and tear and hide stains, or you may need to replace flooring in a year or two.

**Almost any feature that is customized, fragile, or complicated, such as a delicate hanging lighting fixture.** These may not last through the first tenant's move-in and move-out.

> **TIP**
>
> **The best single-family home rental may be the one you already own.** Renting out your own home may pencil out better than selling it, if for example, you bought your house in the past at a relatively low price. Plus, you likely have kept it well maintained, so that it is rent-ready. You already

know your home's idiosyncrasies and how to handle the maintenance. An inheritance or gift may also present a situation where you rent a home you already own rather than one you are purchasing. For detailed advice, see *First-Time Landlord: Your Guide to Renting Out a Single-Family Home*, by Janet Portman, Ilona Bray, and Marcia Stewart (Nolo).

# Duplex, Triplex, and Fourplex

In most rental markets, some residential housing contains multiple units (or may be converted into multiple units). I'm not talking about apartment buildings here, but smaller rental properties, such as duplexes, triplexes, and fourplexes (a four-unit building with distinct units). Note: Fourplexes are referred to as "quads" in some areas, although this term may also be used to describe a large commercial apartment housing with four units per building or an apartment complex built around an open area.

## Multiplex Benefits

Owning and renting out property with two to four rental units has several benefits.

### A Multiplex Offers Economies of Scale

One weakness of the single-family home is the lack of economy of scale for landlords. Everything you do is designed around a single rental unit with separate tasks or repairs or individual expenses. The most alluring part of the multiplex is that you enjoy the opposite phenomenon.

Compare, for example, owning two single-family houses with a duplex that combines two rental units under one roof. With two single-family homes, you have two roofs to replace, two sets of gutters to clean, two yards to mow, two driveways to shovel, two houses to paint, two different trips to check on the units, two tax bills, two insurance bills, and—most crucially—two mortgages. Everything doubles.

With a duplex, you have one roof, one mortgage, one yard, one driveway, and so on. While the roof or driveway may be larger, you cut the overhead significantly. And you still get two rental checks. You can also visit both units in one trip. So a duplex often beats two single-family homes on a cash-flow basis and is more efficient to manage. The same holds for a triplex or fourplex—but to an even greater extent.

### Multiplexes Are Built for Landlords

Multiplexes are often built with landlords and tenants in mind. They typically contain individually metered electric service, simple layouts, and uniform fixtures and components, and all the same types of doors, windows, cabinets, and colors. This uniformity simplifies management when replacing items or maintaining the units.

### A Multiplex May Include a Home for You

If you like one of the units, you can target a one-to-four-unit property as an owner-occupied home and take advantage of the best residential financing available. There is no reason you can't live there, too. It can simplify management greatly. Should you move a few years later, you'll still have the same favorable financing and even more positive cash flow.

## Multiplex Drawbacks

There can be drawbacks to multiplexes, primarily when it comes to marketing and sales:

- Properties with two to four rental units may not be as common in some markets, so they can be harder to find.
- Selling can be more challenging, because few people think of a multiplex as a dream home. You may find the pool of buyers largely limited to other real estate investors or small-time landlords.
- Multiplexes may not appreciate in value as rapidly as single-family homes.

- Because of zoning regulations, multiple-unit properties may not be built in standard subdivisions or areas of single-family housing.
- Multiplexes are often in mixed-use areas or ones where greater density zoning is allowed, so you would often not find a multiplex in a new single-family subdivision or more desirable residential neighborhood.

## Adding or Decreasing the Number of Units in a Multiplex

If you own or acquire a four-unit building that has an extra common area for laundry or storage, resist the temptation to turn the extra space into an efficiency unit to derive more rent. This could drastically impact the sale price of the property and your ability to refinance. And it may even compromise your underlying mortgage terms, because you are making a residential property (defined as four or fewer units) commercial (which would typically mean less desirable mortgage terms or a pricier insurance policy).

The desire to be viewed as "residential" has prompted owners of five- or six-unit buildings to turn them into legal four-unit complexes, so as to access the larger pool of buyers and more favorable residential financing that can bring a faster sale and higher price. If you attempt to make a five-unit building into a legitimate fourplex, consult a contractor and obtain proper building permits to meet codes.

RESOURCE

**Learn more about the buying and selling of multiplexes and especially the financial advantages.** *Investing in Duplexes, Triplexes, and Quads: The Fastest and Safest Way to Real Estate Wealth*, by Larry Loftis (Kaplan), covers multiplex investing and makes a strong case for the financial benefits of buying and holding residential multiplex properties.

# Condominium

The conventional wisdom is that condominiums may not pencil out well as rentals, primarily because of the condominium association dues, management fees, and agency costs. However, many small landlords make condos work as rentals (nearly four million rental units are condos, according to recent Census data). To successfully rent out a condo, you must do your homework before buying, and understand the very unique traits of condos and the way they operate.

The story behind renting condos is more complex and nuanced than for other types of property. Renting a condo tends to mean less building maintenance for a landlord, but you'll be dealing with a more people-intensive and bureaucratic enterprise. You'll have to contend with a board of directors of the condo association and possibly even a property or site manager. Plus, you'll own the common areas in tandem with all the other owners.

But if you can live within these parameters, condos can be relatively worry-free rentals and marketable when you sell. Their monthly dues can eat away at cash flow, but in a well-run association, you should be getting a variety of services in return. These often include exterior maintenance, insurance, utilities, trash collection, and even some management of complaints, policies, and budget. A major factor in your success, however, will be finding the right condo and a strong association.

> **TIP**
>
> **Doing any work on common property outside your unit is forbidden in most condo associations.** That makes a condo a good fit for owners unable to do or uninterested in exterior maintenance. But if you want more control over work outside your unit, think twice about buying a condo. Either that, or learn to suppress your landlord instincts to paint a deck or tighten a loose handrail. You can always report problems or suggest maintenance projects to the onsite manager or association board.

## Review the Declarations, Bylaws, and Policies of the Association

It's crucial you check into the letter and spirit of the rules and regulations of an association (including the covenants, conditions, and restrictions, or CC&Rs) before buying a condo you plan to rent out. It's especially important that you find out the condominium association's stance towards renters.

Any listing agent should be able to tell you whether renting is allowed. The answer may simply be "no."

The more nuanced situation is when renting is allowed or conditional. Then you also have to look at the written and unwritten rules regarding renters, for example any extra fees, notice to the board about tenants, or limits on the term or type of lease. Also be sure to check any condo rules that may restrict your intended pool of tenants—for example, by prohibiting pets or limiting the types or size of pets a tenant may have. Condominium associations vary across the U.S., and a full discussion of condominium law is beyond the scope of this book.

## Research Owner-Occupant Levels

If renting is allowed, first find out what percentage of condo units within that community are currently owner-occupied. Some state and federal loan programs require a set limit. For example, the Federal Housing Administration (FHA) requires over 50% of units in the association be owner occupied. The condo association may also mandate owner-occupant percentages in its rules. Renting may be allowed conditionally or more openly, depending on how many of the other owners are already renting.

An ideal ratio from your perspective is around 60%–70% owner-occupants and 30%–40% rentals. This way, renting is accepted and widely practiced, but not overwhelming and a potential cause of community friction. Owners who rent their units will also have some clout in the voting and administration of the association. If you see a predominance of rentals, this could also be a red flag that could impact the marketability of the unit when you sell, due to a lack of financing.

> **CAUTION**
>
> **Renting may be allowed, but considered taboo.** Even if renting is technically allowed, some condo associations may have more restrictive policies or special rules for renters. This could be a clue about the condo association's openness to renters. If you see opposition to renters in the minutes of association meetings, complaints about renters, or proposed rules restricting rentals, consider steering clear of the association. Instead, look for a condo association with rules and norms that allow renters to live harmoniously with owner-occupants.

## Look Into the Condo Association's Financial Reserves

The primary benefit of investing in a condominium is that you don't have to do external maintenance and upkeep. A well-run association handles and manages the exterior of the complex and common areas. An additional benefit is that owners can pool resources and all chip in for larger repairs. You will get to split the costs for the roof or parking lot with a hundred other fellow owners, for example. Ideally, some or all of this money can come from reserves designated for larger capital projects. However, an association without monetary reserves is more likely to impose special assessments for larger repairs and projects, meaning you have to kick in more money more often for major repairs. Along with monthly dues, special assessments are a major culprit in preventing condos from producing positive cash flow for landlords.

## Check Condo Association Politics

Condominium boards and associations are like miniature democracies. Consider that a 100-unit complex may house several hundred people, roughly the size of a small village. All of the housing and living issues are handled by an elected group of directors. The politics can run from logical and lukewarm to angry and contested.

---

### Strategy for Condo Landlord Success: Be a Known Contributor and Get on Board!

Part of the ethos of condominium associations is owner involvement. Residents often attend meetings, volunteer their time on the board, and serve on committees to help operate the organization. So it is predictable that owner-occupants may look askance at landlords who don't live at the complex and who rent the unit out to nonowners.

The best way to counter this potential perception is to become a contributing member and known commodity in the association. Here's how:

**Consider living in the condo you plan to rent, either prior to renting a condo out, or perhaps seasonally or during an extended remodel.** If you can live in a unit, even for a short time, it may help alleviate the absentee-owner perception. You will get to know people and be seen as fully aligned with the owners long after you rent out your unit.

**Attend as many condo association meetings as you can.** Contribute in positive, constructive ways.

**Volunteer for any committees or get on the management board.** If you are a newer landlord, you will get the added benefit of learning more about property management. You will also get an inside view of how your association views rentals and learn all its policies and procedures.

Following these strategies should help you avoid being viewed as an uncaring, absentee landlord who is disconnected from the community's affairs and issues. I have served on three condo boards and benefitted in all these ways and more. I was able to see how a large complex handled annual maintenance, neighbor disputes, abandoned cars (not easy), and hiring contractors to completely rebuild units destroyed from a fire. Serving on condo boards gave me the confidence to buy more rentals. Having helped operate 40-, 50-, and 75-unit complexes, I felt I could handle at least a few units on my own.

Check the minutes of condo association meetings and bulletin boards, and ask residents about the tenor of the association's politics. You may find everything from cooperation to active lawsuits among members. As a landlord, you can't afford to be caught up in infighting. I once saw two neighbors in a condominium association so at odds with each other that one found his tires slashed.

## Accessory Apartment (or In-Law)

Sometimes referred to as mother-in-law (or simply in-law) apartments, accessory apartments are often built in the back, side, or basement of the main house in urban areas, and are a good way to start in the landlording business. If you buy a home with an accessory apartment, the rental income can help cover the monthly mortgage. Plus, the unit is nearby for easy management and maintenance. Of course, the proximity can also be a downside if you have a tenant who is loud, has friends or family visiting all the time, or complains a lot and wants immediate action. (See "When the Tenants Are Your Neighbors," below, for avoiding these kinds of problems.)

And if you are looking for a single-family rental house for yourself, be on the lookout for spaces, such as a finished basement, that could be turned into a small accessory apartment. They are increasingly common in densely populated areas, and can make the property a more viable rental. A potential single-family rental home may not produce positive cash flow alone, but one with an accessory apartment can be profitable. Often, a house can later be sold with the apartment as-is or rejoined to add square footage to the main house.

If you have (or are considering adding) an accessory apartment to your personal residence, pay close attention to the following issues.

**Tax considerations around depreciation and business and personal use.** For details on the issue, see IRS Publication 527, *Residential Rental Property*, and *Every Landlord's Tax Deduction Guide*, by Stephen Fishman (Nolo).

**Zoning and neighbor issues.** Make absolutely sure any accessory apartment is properly zoned, approved, and constructed with permits. In-law apartments can be contentious issues with neighbors, so also be sure the character of the neighborhood is not negatively impacted. Having ample parking, storage, and access for the tenant is critical to making the accessory apartment strategy a success.

---

### When the Tenants Are Your Neighbors

If you are considering an accessory apartment or a multiplex where you occupy a unit, it's a good idea to add specific rules and policies as part of your lease (covered in Chapter 8) that create boundaries (such as limited use of the yard or garage), quiet times, and complaint procedures (no banging on your door except in case of emergency) to protect your privacy (and sanity).

---

# The Rental Market and Your Target Tenant

Whatever property type you choose, your goal is to fill it with quality long-term tenants. As you select a rental unit, think about local vacancy rates, the larger demographics of the area, and economic growth, and how all of these can impact the type of tenant you will attract. Make sure the unit you choose is well positioned to attract a wide pool of potential renters.

This chapter will get you started, but a good real estate agent can be a great help in choosing rental properties and understanding a local rental market.

## Vacancy Rates—the Pulse of Your Rental Market

Of all the rental market data, the vacancy rate is probably most telling for landlords evaluating potential profits. It is like the blood pressure or temperature of a person, signaling in one rough metric the overall health—specifically the supply and demand picture—of your local rental market. Even a strong economy won't help you much if two existing units exist for every local renter.

The vacancy rate gives you a concrete number to consider when buying rental property and estimating your monthly cash flow (described below). For example, if there is a 10% vacancy rate in your area, expect to have a unit vacant just over a month (36 days) per year per unit (365 days x .10=36.5 days). If you rent a unit for $1,000 per month, your actual revenue will probably be, on average, a little less than $11,000 per year. On the other hand, in the unlikely event that your rental is never empty (a zero vacancy rate), your annual revenue for a $1,000 per month apartment would be $12,000.

Recent vacancy rates in the U.S. have trended between 5% on the low end and 10% on the high end. Some economically depressed areas have had double-digit vacancy rates, while thriving areas have very low, single-digit rates. Numbers also vary with recessions and expansions in the economy.

An average vacancy rate of 7.5% or less should provide a safe environment for an effective landlord to succeed in (see the Resource, below, for finding the vacancy rate for a particular area). Of course, if you find an area with a vacancy rate of 5% or less, that could be a sign of a tight rental market (more demand and less supply) and a real opportunity. A double-digit vacancy rate should give you pause about buying rental properties in that area.

If you own just a few units, you may be able to beat the average vacancy rate in your area. One-to-four unit properties generally have lower (about 1% lower) vacancy rates in historic Census data than larger apartment complexes. This makes sense, as a very large complex will almost always have some units vacant. Smaller landlords manage fewer properties and should be able to fill them faster and retain tenants longer through better response times and service. Along with the better financing and easier management, lower vacancies can be an advantage to residential rentals.

## Population Demographics and Economic Growth

Demographics—the statistical information about a population—are key for landlords to understand. If you buy a rental property in a small, isolated community of 100 people with few jobs or other attractions, it will likely be empty much of the time. There just aren't enough potential renters. More often, landlords face more subtle concerns when they look to buy rental property, particularly about the balance of supply and demand in rental housing or the relative merits of two nearby communities. To be an informed landlord, get some idea about the figures and trends in the area.

In addition to vacancy rates, local data on population, job growth, migration patterns, commercial activity, and housing starts/construction permits are highly relevant for small landlords. They can signal a strong local economy—which can translate into a strong demand for rental housing.

Information about the income levels and employment prospects in your area are also important to consider when selecting rental property. A significant portion of the local population needs to be able to afford the rent you are charging. While regions vary, many renters across the U.S. face significant financial challenges (see Chapter 7 for some sobering statistics), so keep this in mind in selecting and marketing your rentals. You won't want to price out the majority of your market by setting rents and deposits too high.

Other economic data that can inform your decisions about acquiring or selling units or even increasing rents, include:

- **Cost of living.** Your tenants' dollars need to cover such items as food, entertainment, fuel, and insurance. If your area has high costs for medical care, transportation, or other services, these can be competing factors for your rental dollars.
- **Construction permits and housing stock.** These important data can tell you about existing housing numbers and types, as well as new permits for construction.

- **Median home prices.** It is important to watch housing prices for two reasons. One, you may buy a single-family rental house. Two, many of your potential tenants will be weighing the merits of renting versus buying. If much of the population cannot afford to buy in your area, this increases the rental market, and vice versa. Look for published comparisons of the average rental rate of a three-bedroom home versus the mortgage and average homeowner costs of a three-bedroom home.

**RESOURCE**

**Where to find local information on vacancy rates, population demographics, and economic growth.** To find key data on vacancy rates, check out your local housing authority, community development agency, chamber of commerce, or city planner's office. The U.S. Economic Development Administration (www.eda.gov/resources) also publishes a directory of state and local resources that compile demographic, economic, and housing data.

# Choosing the Right Property: Don't Leave It to Chance

I've seen real estate purchase decisions make (or break) real estate investors and average people. That charming 100-year old bungalow can quickly turn into a financial nightmare (and even a lead and asbestos hazard zone). Or the ugly duckling duplex may turn into a swan when you cut the weeds, remove the junk cars, and paint the place. Indeed, the actual purchase decision is one that can have impacts (positive or negative) for years to come. To increase your chances of success, be sure to thoroughly study both the financial aspects of the purchase and the property condition.

Once you have some idea of where you want to buy (the location), the type of residential property you are targeting (such as single-family home versus duplex), and have reviewed local vacancy rates and economic and demographic data to see if owning rental property makes sense in a particular community, your next step is to decide on an actual property. The good news is that the process is not esoteric or rocket science, particularly if you have previously purchased a home. Two key questions to ask when considering a particular property are:

- Does the property pencil out in terms of cash flow?
- Is the condition of the property such that it would make a suitable rental? For example, is it free of construction defects, not in need of major repairs, and have features that make it a good rental?

You'll definitely want to involve professionals in buying, financing, inspecting, and insuring any property you are buying (or considering buying). See the section on inspections, below, for advice on hiring a professional inspection, and Chapter 11 for details on working with real estate agents, insurance brokers, and other professionals.

RESOURCE

**Never owned a house or condo before?** Check out *Nolo's Essential Guide to Buying Your First Home,* by Ilona Bray, Alayna Schroeder, and Marcia Stewart. It provides extensive advice on all aspects of house-buying—from finding and financing a home to arranging professional inspections and closing the deal. Also, the Real Estate section of Nolo.com includes many useful articles on legal, financial, and practical issues relevant to anyone buying property.

# How to Make Sure the Rental Property Pencils Out

Regardless of the type of property you buy as a rental, make sure it pencils out in terms of positive cash flow—the amount of cash coming in each month (your monthly revenue or rent) minus monthly expenses. There should be money left for you after *all* the expenses, such as mortgage payments, utilities, taxes, legal and professional fees, and any condo dues or HOA fees, are accounted for (deducted from the monthly rent), as well as some allowances for vacancies, maintenance (such as building and lawn care), and repairs (when a pipe breaks or you need a new deck railing).

## Cash Flow Example (Single-Family House)

Whether a property can generate positive cash flow depends a great deal on the local rental market, real estate prices, mortgage interest rates, and taxes. Single-family houses, for example, may pencil out as rentals in some neighborhoods but not in others. Or in some major cities, rent will never cover the mortgage, but might in nearby suburbs or outlying areas.

I've included a sample monthly cash flow estimate here (in this case, for a hypothetical single-family home), so that you can see the basic elements that go into a property's cash flow. This (very simplified) example shows a loss of $238 per month.

Doing an analysis for a rental property with generous positive cash flow or one that was hopeless would be easy: Simply make an offer (on the money maker) or walk away (from the money pit). A closer case, such as the one in my example, may be more realistic. It also prompts you to consider how tailoring an offer or changing other aspects of the transaction can shift the balance and perhaps make the property viable as a rental.

Let's drive by an imaginary single-family home located on 101 Sample Street and run the numbers. The Sample Monthly Cash Flow Estimate below gives you a glimpse of the average monthly expenses I face as a part-time landlord. However, monthly expenses and costs vary by region and type of property, so input realistic numbers for your area and prospective rentals.

### Sample Monthly Cash Flow Estimate

**Address and features:** 101 Sample Street. Three-bedroom ranch home built in 1979. Average condition.

**Asking price:** $300,000

| | |
|---|---|
| **Monthly revenue (rent)** (1) | $2,000 |
| **Monthly expenses (detail follows)** | -2,238 |
| **Monthly cash flow** | - $238 |
| *Details on monthly expenses:* | |
| Mortgage (2) | $1,288 |
| Insurance (3) | 100 |
| Taxes (4) | 250 |
| HOA or condo dues (5) | 0 |
| Utilities (6) | 0 |
| Routine building/lawn maintenance (7) | 100 |
| Repairs and/or reserves for major repairs (8) | 200 |
| Vacancy rate (9) | 100 |
| Management costs (10) | 200 |
| *TOTAL EXPENSES* | $2,238 |
| *TOTAL REVENUE MINUS EXPENSES (CASH FLOW)* | ($238) |

### Notes on Sample Monthly Cash Flow Estimate:

(1) Stick with a conservative figure for rent, based on actual comparable units nearby. Probably the best sources of area rents are online classifieds and local property management firms with many rental listings. You may be able to increase rent (subject to any local rent regulations) with some cosmetic enhancements or by allowing pets. But overpricing your rental may limit your market. See Chapter 8 for advice on setting rent.

(2) Mortgage payment in the sample is based on 20% down payment, 30-year fixed-rate mortgage at 5%. Terms will vary depending on the economy, market, the particular property, your credit score, down-payment amount, and other factors. Do everything possible to reduce your mortgage payments by finding the best loan, interest rate, and terms—for example, this sample includes no PMI (private mortgage insurance ) based on the 20% down payment.

(3) Your monthly insurance bill will depend on your policy type and several other factors. Consider not only the cost but also the coverage you get, and review some of the landlord insurance topics mentioned in Chapter 11. I just estimated insurance at $1,200 per year ($100 per month), but it is going to also vary by area, your property type and condition, and even the company you use and any discounts available.

(4) Find your local property tax rate; 1%–2% of property value is about average. Check with your local tax authority for more information.

(5) This sample property is a single-family home, with no HOA fees. If you buy property with association or condo dues, be sure to list here.

(6) This scenario has the tenant paying all utilities, such as water and electric. This is not uncommon in a single-family home with a long-term tenant, although some landlords may pick up a water/sewer or trash bill. Just add in any utility costs you cover.

(7) In many cases, 5%–10% of rent is a reasonable estimate for monthly maintenance costs, such as snow removal in winter. But the figure will depend on the location, age, and condition of the property.

(8) In this category (repairs/reserves), I just put 10% of rent, and anything I don't use on repairs, I put into reserves. My repair costs are closer to 5% of rents (leaving 5% for reserves), as I do about everything myself, with the exception of major plumbing and electrical work or highly skilled carpentry. This figure may vary depending on whether you are handy or have to hire everything out, so adjust accordingly. Also, try and adjust your reserves (upwards or downwards) to cover the useful life of major items like your roof, driveway, or heating and cooling systems. For example, if your roof has ten years of useful life left, keep enough money in reserve to replace the roof in ten years. That would mean if it costs $10,000 to replace the roof, you'd want to try and save a $1,000 a year in reserves for ten years, or roughly $85 per month. Then you can cover the estimated cost of the new roof when the time comes. A professional property inspection (discussed below) will help you estimate your budget for repairs and reserves.

(9) The 101 Street house is in an area with a 5% vacancy rate. See the discussion of vacancy rates, above, for advice on determining this figure.

(10) Be sure to include your valuable management time (screening and choosing tenants, handling routine repairs, collecting rent and security deposits, responding to tenant issues, and more), in your calculation of cash flow. Including this amount is important because should you ever need to have the property professionally managed, it can still produce positive cash flow. The amount listed here is based on 10% of the rent, a common property management fee.

## Analyzing the 101 Sample Street (Single-Family House) Deal

After running the numbers, this property on Sample Street may not pencil out well, with a negative monthly cash flow of $238. However, it is a close enough proposition that a lower asking price, larger down payment, or slightly increased rents may make it more worthwhile. For example, try running the numbers on the 101 Sample Street home purchased at $275,000 or $250,000 (rather than the $300,000 in the example). The equation begins to change, producing positive cash flow. Remember, you are looking at the property as business proposition. Don't be afraid to let the seller know this is an investment, so it has to work out financially.

Also, think about other creative bargaining tools using your cash flow analysis. For example, a savvy landlord might offer $275,000 for 101 Sample Street and also ask for repairs and other work, like a new roof, if it is near the end of its useful life. Having the seller cover some pricey repairs could reduce the amount you need to set aside for monthly repairs and reserves; combined with a lower offering price ($275,000), the deal could work out for you. Perhaps you also know you can cut the vacancy rate and that you can increase rents with some cosmetic repairs and curb appeal. These factors can help you find rentals that produce positive cash flow from the outset, using both the numbers and your own skills and creativity.

TIP

**Take the long view.** A strategy that may not make money on a monthly basis but is close enough to help you hold on to the property for years could be worthwhile. Consider whether you can take a small loss or break even over several years to take a shot at potential appreciation. This is not short-term speculation but a planned long-term goal. Rents may also increase enough to cover costs in just a few years. Best of all, the appreciation may eclipse the small loss you took in the first years from negative cash flow.

### Should You Wait to Buy?

As with many investments, your timing when you buy is crucial. A single-family home may not produce cash flow in your area right now, but may ultimately be profitable as prices change over the months or years. For example, it was hard to find single-family homes that worked as rentals in the real estate boom of the early and mid-2000s. However, by the time of the real estate bust and financial crisis of 2008-2010, many single-family houses could be purchased across the U.S. for an amount so low that the fair rental value would cover the mortgage and then some. Today, many of these properties not only provide positive cash flow monthly, they have also appreciated handsomely.

If few houses pencil out as rentals in your area, it may not be an ideal time to buy. Economists often look at the comparison between the costs of renting versus buying to measure a fairly priced market. If few of the single-family homes in your market cover costs, maybe look at another type of property or other nearby areas, or wait for a buyer's market.

## Finding Out All You Can About a Prospective Property

Unless you inherited your rental property, you will have a choice in selecting it. Just as landlords want to screen out tenants with spotty credit, serious criminal records, and poor rental histories, it is crucial that you screen out money pits and homes with faulty construction or other serious problems. It can be even tougher to fix an intractable building problem than a tenant issue. The problem tenant could be evicted, but you can't evict a problem property.

The quality of home craftsmanship in any area can vary widely. Serious building defects make being an effective landlord almost impossible. Problems in a property can be caused by design or construction problems or just from age and a lack of maintenance.

Even new construction can have serious defects. This section and the one that follows provide advice on inspecting buildings of any age before you buy.

## First Impressions: Your Own Observations and Research

Visiting a prospective property and doing some online research will give you many clues about the fitness of a property as a rental, and what repairs or maintenance will be necessary in the short or long term. If any of your initial observations or findings give you pause, walk away. It's not worth spending money on a professional inspector, who will probably find even more problems with the property. Here are some key things to look for.

**Age.** Older buildings, especially if not maintained, can present more repair and replacement costs. Set some age parameters that fit your desired area. In newer suburbs, you might exclude houses more than ten to 20 years old. In the older city centers, properties past 50 years may be too old. Or maybe you will look only at older homes if they have recent permitted updates of all major systems and been brought up to code. Whether it is ten years old or 100 years—the key is your neighborhood, your resources, and the criteria that work for you.

**Area.** Just as there can be people problems in some areas (like crime or traffic), some areas also concentrate building problems, such as a low-lying or waterfront areas prone to flood damage, a certain soil type prone to subsidence, or steep slopes that make for problematic structural problems.

**Low-maintenance entryway.** Look for properties with paved parking and walkways, and concrete or wood decks at the entry. If you have to cross gravel, dirt, or grass, your flooring will age at an exponentially faster rate. Also look for good lighting, ample off-street parking, and easy-to-maintain landscaping.

**Solid structure.** You can often spot serious structural problems and nonconforming additions right away. Watch for sagging buildings, sunken roofs, and crumbling foundations, and similar problems that can't readily be fixed (or at least not at a reasonable price).

**Signs of pests.** Be on the lookout for the telltale signs of termites, carpenter ants, roaches, rodents, raccoons (a growing urban problem), and other pests, which all leave subtle but detectable clues inside and outside a building. A professional pest inspection (discussed below) can provide specific information on all the potential damaging insects and rodents in your area.

**Condition of windows.** Modern windows are important for safety, energy efficiency, and convenience. Perhaps the best signal windows transmit is the overall building's upkeep and renovation history. If the past owners have lived with drafty 1930s windows that barely open, you can bet many other components and systems are of a similar vintage. On the other hand, newer windows may signal a recent major upgrade and active maintenance program in the home—a particular benefit, given that window replacement runs in the thousands of dollars.

**Water and moisture.** If not properly drained away or vented out of the house, water and moisture can cause mold and rot. Both of these can compromise the structure of the building and even lead to habitability issues. So be on the lookout for excess standing water around the building, a downspout that drains poorly, or a backyard sloping into a building. Some problems, such as clogged gutters may be easy to fix, while others (flooding due to the topography of the property), not so.

**Builder.** Different builders, past and present, whether large or small, develop reputations for quality. While sometimes more difficult to discover, try to screen out homes built by builders associated with lower-quality work and construction defects.

**Material and condition.** Find out what type of common building problems exist in your area. Often, these may be traced to certain materials or a design that was poorly conceived. Also, set some standards about age of certain systems and screen out properties that don't fit this profile. For example, avoid homes over 50 years of age with multiple layers of shingles or flat roofs; screen out those without updated (with permits) electric, plumbing, and HVAC; and cross off those in a flood zone.

## Property Information Available Online

Check the property's paper or electronic history just as thoroughly as you inspect its physical aspects. Try your jurisdiction repository for public records, such as the county recorder, assessor, building permit center, or other office. Consider the following caution lights in a property's records.

**Turnstile owners.** If the ownership has changed every few years, find out why. Perhaps a property or neighborhood issue prevents it being a viable rental. Or it may simply be that owners are profiting from rapid price appreciation. It could be coincidence; perhaps the various owners simply wanted to cash out, retire, or buy another property. Sadly, divorce and death are two of the most common reasons people sell real estate. Search court records (located online in some states) and other online resources to see if you can learn the story. Some states have past sale prices available; others may not. Ask your real estate broker about prior sales as the price and terms may be in their multiple listing system.

**Nonpermitted work or additions.** Find out about the building permit history of the property, especially if you anticipate additions, structural work, electric upgrades, major plumbing work, or an overhaul of heating, air conditioning, or ventilation (HVAC). A surprising amount of work is done without permits, and this can place you in a precarious position as the new owner—unsure if the work met codes or poses any risks of property damage or personal injury. If you find any additions that were done without a permit, consider crossing the property off your list.

**Crime or meth labs.** Online searches may reveal a property's dark history. Some states are also starting databases of methamphetamine lab sites. These properties can require extensive remediation and should be avoided by small landlords. Other crime information can be found by running searches on prior owners, residents, or the address. Even if the property is intact, its reputation could deter good renters.

**Geographic and environmental issues.** Flood zones, wetlands, slide zones, earthquake fault lines, and environmental hazards can usually be discovered through a bit of research. These are typically listed on official maps and sellers are often required to disclose them. But do your homework. The flood or landslide may not follow the prospective boundary exactly, so better to be safe than sorry. Steer clear of property near hazardous zones.

RESOURCE

**Learn about inspections.** For advice on home inspections, check out *The Complete Guide to Home Inspection*, by Roger C. Robinson and Michael Litchfield (Taunton Press), and *Home Inspection Secrets of a Happy Homeowner: A Guide to Peace of Mind for the Home Buyer, Sellers, and the Agents Who Love Them*, by Wally Conway (Someday Publishing). Another useful title, *The Complete Book of Home Inspection*, by Norm Becker (McGraw-Hill Professional), covers the more technical aspects of home construction, standards (such as electrical, plumbing), and codes, and is especially useful in helping you to understand a professional inspector's report (described below). For a more entertaining look at the inspection process, check out the television program *Holmes Inspection*, a video series (available at http://makeitright.ca) about what home inspectors can miss and the tremendous efforts required to repair home defects. Finally, you'll find lots of useful information on the websites of professional associations for home inspectors, such as the American Society of Home Inspection Professionals (listed below).

## Getting Information From the Owners

The previous owner is often the best source of information about a property. He or she may be able to tell you about any problems, offer maintenance tips, or provide details on what work has been done and when. The amount of information you can get from an owner will vary. Some types of transactions entail very little information exchange. For example, if you're buying a distressed "as is" property, a bank-owned property, a foreclosure at auction, or an estate purchase with a deceased owner, expect little or no information to be passed on. Similarly, a short-term owner may have little insight on the building.

However, there are situations where you could get a good deal of information from an owner. If the property is a FSBO (For Sale by Owner), you may be able to sit down and map out the entire maintenance history of the property with the current owner and even walk through maintenance together. These scenarios where you get no information or lots of information are the ends of the spectrum. Probably the most common situation is when the seller makes the required residential property disclosures required by state law (discussed below). Here, you are getting the minimal required legal disclosures in a written format. In most cases, you will also want to arrange a professional inspection (also discussed below) on any property you are serious about buying.

> **TIP**
> **Ask the seller for all information you think important, especially if the property is currently being rented.** In addition to repair receipts, get tenant information, such as details on leases and security deposits. You can either make an informal request in the negotiation process, or do so formally (making your offer contingent on receiving certain information). Your real estate or legal professional should be able to help you insert such contingencies or terms into your offer. As always, the seller will be more motivated to answer questions before the closing. After that, you are relying on the kindness of strangers for information.

## Required Seller Disclosures: Getting the Inside Scoop on Your Property

Most states require sellers in a residential property transaction to make some form of written disclosure to buyers prior to the closing. Generally, the disclosures are to help buyers get more information about a property, consider the wisdom of the purchase, and decide whether they really want to go through with the transaction. State disclosure laws typically require sellers to provide information on all the major components of the house (roof, foundation, windows, doors, etc.) and on many other topics, such as repairs, floods, electric usage, and nuisances or noise. Legal disclosure requirements vary by state, and a property that is not owner occupied may be exempt. Ask your real estate professional for details on your state disclosure rules.

> CAUTION
>
> **Disclosures won't tell the whole story.** State disclosure rules typically mandate at most that the sellers of residential property (generally one to four units) disclose what they *know or should have known* about the property. The property could still have problems that the sellers did not know about—that's why a professional inspection is so important.

## Arranging a Professional Inspection

If a property looks promising after visiting one or more times, doing some background research, and reviewing seller disclosures, you'll want to arrange a professional inspection before finalizing a deal. A thorough inspection should cover the condition and useful life of major components, such as the roof, driveway, and furnace, and include suggestions for needed maintenance and repairs. It is unlikely you will get a perfect rental, but a professional inspection will help you ascertain the problems and any serious building defects before the purchase, and decide whether to walk away or try and make it a successful investment.

### Including an Inspection Contingency

Make sure your offer or contract to buy any property has a contingency or escape clause that allows you to back out of the sale should you not approve of (or be willing to negotiate around) the results of a professional inspection. Also, make sure your purchase contract gives you plenty of time to inspect the property and review the report.

Your real estate broker should be able to help you negotiate the repairs (or a reduction in price or credit in escrow with which to make those repairs) or even an exit, if need be, after the inspection report comes in.

> **TIP**
> **Never go to a real estate closing until all required and negotiated repairs have been made.** As soon as you sign and close, you lose your leverage and will have to chase after the seller to try and enforce any agreed-upon conditions. Simply tell the seller you will sign when all the repairs are complete. Don't budge.

## Choosing a Professional Inspector

A key in getting the right property is getting the right inspector. Consider screening and selecting candidates well ahead of time. Getting recommendations from others (like your real estate agent) is fine, but remember after closing, you are on the hook for any property shortcomings.

Do your own research and try to get the most qualified, rigorous inspector possible. Your goal is to get a report that lets you fully comprehend the risks involved with a particular property. What the inspector misses—perhaps a serious structural problem or even a combination of serious defects—can cost you more than the property is worth to repair.

A seller may give you a copy of an inspection report he or she arranged, which can be a great starting point. But always insist on your own inspection, done by an inspector of your choosing, and be adamant that you be present when it takes place.

Here's what to look for when hiring a professional inspector:

**State license.** Make sure your inspector meets the minimum requirements in your state. The American Society of Home Inspectors (ASHI) website (www.home inspector.org) provides links to state-by-state requirements for education, training, insurance, and licensing. Look for "State regulations" under the "Inspector Resources" tab on the ASHI home page below.

**Qualifications.** Look for additional certifications, experience, education, background, licenses, and more. Membership in a professional organization for home inspectors is a good sign. Three of the most established are:

- American Society of Home Inspectors (ASHI), www.homeinspector.org
- National Association of Home Inspectors (NAHI), www.nahi.org, and
- International Association of Certified Home Inspectors (InterNACHI), www.nachi.org.

Look for the highest level of certification possible and any desirable specialized certifications (such as mold or radon).

**Reputation and experience.** In many jurisdictions, an inspector's longevity can be an indicator of competency. Not only does this help you avoid fly-by-night operators, the added experience often means the inspector has seen many types of properties and building issues. Picking an inspector who has inspected similar properties in the area can be helpful, too.

**Background in building or trades.** An inspector with a background in building or the trades can be a bonus. While this won't give the inspector X-ray vision, one who has been on many job sites and seen the various stages of construction firsthand can better spot clues and small defects that signal larger problems.

---

### Limits of Home Inspections

Every home inspection report comes with explicit caveats and exceptions. While this is partially for liability purposes, it is also because inspectors can only inspect what they can see. They won't generally move furniture, personal items, or debris to get a better look at an area. Some areas may be inaccessible or unsafe to view. So consider taking extra steps, asking more questions, or simply walking away if you can't get a full picture of the risks associated with the condition of the property.

---

**Ability to create a good report.** Even the best home inspectors are only as good as their reports, so ask to see a sample inspection report before hiring. If the inspector can't translate his or her expertise into a high-quality, readable report, you won't fully benefit from the help. Find out what areas of the property are covered and not covered in an inspector's report, whether the reports are customized or boilerplate documents, and whether photos and descriptions of problems are included.

## Following Up With Specialized Inspections

Inspectors may recommend other specialists such as a pest/termite expert, structural engineer to inspect the foundation, roofing inspector, chimney inspector, energy auditor, an environmental firm (for mold, lead, or asbestos testing), or a licensed electrician or plumber. Get their reports in hand, and study and approve them (or have required work done), before closing the purchase.

# Making an Informed Decision When Choosing a Rental Property

Selecting a residential rental property involves looking closely at many factors, such as location and physical condition. But another key factor is you—the landlord. A large part of your decision to buy a particular property will depend on your own skills, interests, and comfort level. Here are some key points to keep in mind.

**Play to your strengths.** Your time and skills are key factors to consider. For many busy urban professionals, renting out a couple of nearby condos—where you need only deal with interior maintenance and the tenant issues—is more than enough of a time commitment. A semiretired seasonal worker might manage four single-family homes. Your skill set, resources, and background are also important. If you've never started a lawn mower or hammered a nail, you probably don't want to buy an aged duplex, but it might be ideal for someone with a do-it-yourself background.

**Pick what you know and specialize in.** If you can learn the ins and outs of buying and renting one type of property, and it works well, consider sticking with it. For example, if you research and buy a condo and rent it successfully, you will already know the condo market, the type of tenants, the merits of different associations, and the management skills and time required. Then you can simply repeat the process of buying and renting another condo, because you are ahead of the curve. The same is true for single-family homes or multiplexes. Find a type of property that fits you and works in your market. Also consider specializing in one geographic area.

**Listen to the market.** Make sure the type and specific unit you choose is well positioned to attract a wide pool of potential renters in your area.

**Focus on buying property that should produce positive cash flow from the outset, based on your cost estimates.** Track real estate listings and also rental rates in your area so you know when a good value comes on the market. Then trust your judgment and make a decision.

**Don't take on more maintenance and repair needs than you can handle.** A professional inspection report should help you decide whether to buy the property or walk away, and know what you're getting into in terms of repairs and maintenance. Pass on any properties with too much work for you to handle.

## What's Next?

Once you have selected your rental property and closed the deal, you begin the next phase—the hands-on work. You move from abstract research on the property to actually working on its components. Chapter 3 covers some of the common rental maintenance tasks, such as painting, caulking, and dealing with toilets. It also covers the skills, tools, and supplies you will use in caring for your residential rentals and discovering your inner handy person. ●

# Discovering Your Inner Handyperson: Tips and Tricks

There is some truth to the stereotype of the landlord with a paintbrush, plunger, and a toolbox. To achieve maximum efficiency as a landlord, you'll need to tackle a certain amount of repair and maintenance on your own. (You can hire a property manager, but it will reduce your overall profits.) Most do-it-yourself landlords should not need to call in outside help for routine cleaning and fix-ups (the focus of Chapters 4 and 5) or for cosmetic repairs, such as patching holes in or painting walls. Similarly, after some experience, you should be able to handle a closet door that has come unhinged, a sticky window crank, a cabinet drawer that has come off the rails, and other sticky widgets. You may even be able to install some forms of flooring: Some laminate or vinyl flooring, or even carpet squares, can be installed with a razor knife and measuring tape.

This chapter will help you identify and develop your handyperson skills. If you've already got plenty of practical repair experience, you can skip ahead to the next chapters, where I discuss what tasks to take care of at crucial times in the tenancy, including before the tenant moves in and while tenants are living there. Some of the unique tips (like my kitchen-cabinet-refinishing recipe) may even be of interest to long-time landlords looking for a low-cost way to rejuvenate a tired kitchen. And some of the practices (like painting and caulking) are so central to the role of the hands-on landlord, it's always helpful to learn more.

## Your Basic Skills, Toolkit, and Supplies

With residential rental properties, most routine rental unit maintenance and repair is the same as what the average homeowner handles. Indeed, using what you already know from your own home maintenance is a major benefit of the residential rental property strategy of this book. Let's take a closer look at the skills and abilities involved in common landlord repair and maintenance tasks, and what tools and supplies you'll need.

## Basic Property-Repair and Maintenance Skills

If you can handle the following tasks, you can probably handle 75% of your routine rental property repairs and maintenance:

- clean and paint a wall
- start and operate a lawnmower or weed whacker
- shovel snow or dirt
- sweep with a broom and pick up trash
- hammer a nail
- drill a hole or drive a screw into wood
- use a handsaw
- climb a stepladder
- use a caulk gun
- clean a house, and
- bend and lift 25 pounds.

Of these, simply knowing how to paint, caulk, and drive screws will get you through many of your maintenance chores. In fact, I call these my "big three" landlord skills. With proficiency in painting, caulking, and using a drill (cordless or corded) and the abilities above, you can maintain the interior and exterior of most rental properties and even turn around most units to prepare them for future tenants.

## Basic Tools of the Landlord Trade

You may not need to buy much equipment, if you're willing to borrow the ones you use to maintain your own home. Your own drill, hammer, and wrenches will work fine on most rental properties. You shouldn't need heavy machinery, a shop, or even large or expensive power tools. If a task or repair comes up that requires them, such as an excavation or major demolition, think about hiring a professional to do the job, as discussed in Chapter 6.

See the "Landlord Toolkit," below, for a list of the items I most commonly use for my duties as a part-time landlord.

## Landlord Toolkit

Here are the basic tools and equipment the do-it-yourself landlord needs:

- ☐ paintbrushes and rollers (with extension pole)
- ☐ caulk gun
- ☐ drill (primarily used to drive screws)
- ☐ hammer
- ☐ nail set (small metal extension that lets you sink finish nails without ruining wood)
- ☐ utility knife with replaceable razor blades
- ☐ tape measure
- ☐ pry bar
- ☐ saw (a power circular saw or a manual hand saw with sharp blade)
- ☐ putty knives (for patching walls and scraping paint)
- ☐ plunger
- ☐ pruner (both a small hand pruner and limb trimmer on telescoping pole for pruning trees and branches)
- ☐ pliers, especially needle nose variety
- ☐ wrenches, including Allen wrenches
- ☐ screw drivers
- ☐ staple gun
- ☐ home improvement books (see recommendations, below)
- ☐ weed whacker and/or lawn mower (depending upon lawn)
- ☐ shovels (including snow shovels in snowy areas)
- ☐ ladder, and
- ☐ brooms and dustpan.

## Basic Supplies

If you've ever wondered who buys cleaning solution by the gallons, landlords certainly are prime suspects. Warehouse stores allow you to buy in bulk. I always buy the larger containers, and refill my favorite spray bottles. See "Landlord Staples," below, for a rundown of what you'll likely need.

## Landlord Staples

You can save money and ensure you'll have everything you need by stocking up on landlord staples, such as:

- ☐ TSP (trisodium phosphate, a strong versatile cleaner for paint prep), or TSP substitute
- ☐ baking soda
- ☐ vinegar
- ☐ all-purpose cleaner
- ☐ Lysol disinfectant spray
- ☐ scrub sponges
- ☐ window and glass cleaner
- ☐ paints and stains
- ☐ disposable wet wipes
- ☐ disposable gloves
- ☐ energy-efficient light bulbs
- ☐ drain cleaner
- ☐ toilet seats
- ☐ bleach, and
- ☐ smoke detectors and carbon monoxide detectors.

And stock up on the following items when they go on sale:

- ☐ caulk (interior, exterior, kitchen/bath)
- ☐ primer
- ☐ silicone-based lubricant for window cranks, sliding doors, closet doors, locks
- ☐ tarps
- ☐ super glue
- ☐ painter's tape, and
- ☐ filters (for HVAC and vacuums).

You'll also want to stock up on (look for neutral colors that work in your units):

- ☐ shower curtains and shower curtain rings
- ☐ door and bath mats and area rugs, and
- ☐ curtains and curtain rods.

## Storing Tools and Supplies

Keep an inventory of basic tools and supplies you need for all common maintenance and rental turnarounds organized for easy access in your own home. This way you can easily load and transport supplies from your house to the rental. You can essentially "shop your garage," one of the most convenient stores (with the best hours and prices!). All your tools will also be stored at your home and loaded up for work at rental units.

You'll want easy access to the right materials and tools. A simple shelving system or rack in a closet, garage, or basement of your home can provide a base for your landlord cleaning and preparation supplies. Make sure all your materials are visible, labeled, and easy to access. When I started with my first two or three rentals (all condos), I ran my operations and stored everything I needed in a large closet outside a condo that I owned. Today, I have an entire section in my garage with metal shelving. But many of my basic practices remain the same.

Store your paints and stains with clear labels reminding you of the rental units and areas where you have used them (and be sure they are protected from freezing). A simple milk crate or box on its side will hold caulks. Keep your screws, nails, and fasteners in one place. Keep tools in separate boxes in another area. And you can use individual containers for extra items like doorstops, switch plates, drain stoppers, hardware for cabinets, doors, door locks, and knobs. All your cleaners should be in a visible place where you can inventory them by sight. Keep your lightbulbs and detectors from getting smashed by putting them up high and away from heavier items.

Sort like items with like items, but also think about themes, such as keeping all curtains (including shower curtains), curtain rods, and hardware together. And similar areas can complement each other. For example, consider putting paintbrushes, rollers, roller covers, trays, and painter's tapes in a painting section above or near the actual paints.

The key is to make it easy for you to quickly shop your own storage area or garage the night before the job so you can easily find the right color of paint or type of caulk you need the next day. You will save time running around to several stores with a long list and also will have bought items in bulk or at the lowest cost.

## When to Buy Duplicate Tools and Supplies

While I recommend keeping your tools and supplies in your own home, in some cases, it makes sense to buy duplicates to keep at the rental unit. A multiplex, for example, may have an exterior closet, shed, or area where you can store and secure some of the following items.

**Lawn mower and weed whacker.** Loading and unloading a bulky mower is often harder than mowing a small strip of grass (especially all alone). Not only are lawn mowers and weed whackers awkward to load in your vehicle, they can be very dirty and smell of oil and gas. Better to keep these tucked away at the rental (unless you have a truck). You can use a bike lock to attach a lawn mower and weed whacker under a deck or to a back porch. Be sure and put in fuel stabilizer if they are left a long time or over winter and protect them from elements with a tarp.

**Ladders.** I hauled around a large ladder when I had a pickup truck, but actually prefer having both a stepladder and large extension ladder at my fourplex. It can be tricky to haul ladders without the right straps. Some new models do collapse, but can be heavy. If there's not a garage or other storage area at the rental property, use large ladder hooks or a padlock to attach a ladder to a fence or posts in the backyard and cover with a green tarp, or store ladders out of the way on the side of the house.

**Shovels.** These can be dirty and even sharp—not something you want in your clean car (assuming they don't fit in the trunk). Shovels can damage seats in a sedan or fly out of the back of a truck. If you live in snowy climate, for example, it's best to label a few snow shovels with permanent marker and leave them at the rental property. Tenants may even use them to help remove snow. You may have to store shovels out of sight or behind a fence if you don't have a locked storage area, or if you have a theft problem in your area.

**Brooms.** These get dusty and, with long handles, are unwieldy to transport. Tenants will often use brooms to clear dirt or snow off their cars and the steps. So these are worth the minor investment to keep on site.

**Miscellaneous supplies.** Consider having these items at your rental unit: extra weed whacker line, paint (same color as exterior and interior), hammer and nails, basic household cleaner, rags, tarps, painters' tape, a black magic marker and some blank paper (to make emergency or quick notes for tenants), a water hose, trash bags, and other items you may use regularly or need in a pinch. When turning around a unit, you could also stash any items you might use to tidy up a unit before a showing. Of course, your on-site storage will depend on your specific property and needs, with multiplexes having more room and a greater need for maintenance supplies, and most condos likely having little or none.

## Washing Painted Walls

Whether you're preparing a unit for a new tenant or getting ready to repaint, giving the surfaces a good wash is a key skill. Take a clean, newish sponge mop and dip it into a bucket with diluted TSP (trisodium phosphate). Wring the mop out thoroughly, allowing you to just dampen the walls (there should be no water flowing down). Then before the wall dries, rinse the walls with another damp sponge mop and clean water.

Cleaning the walls is important even if you plan to paint a unit. Not only does cleaning dirt and oils help paint properly adhere, you may notice a drastic improvement in the walls and ceiling after the TSP treatment, alleviating the need for a complete repaint.

CAUTION

**Phosphates can be hard on the environment if dumped in the water system, so mix only the amount you will use.** TSP is a strong inexpensive cleaner. If mixed and diluted properly, you won't need to dump any out. But you can use a more environmentally sensitive cleaner; several are marketed as TSP substitutes.

# Refinishing Wooden Cabinets

Another important surface that will need regular attention in your rental unit is the exterior of any wooden cabinets. Here's how to make older wooden surfaces (not painted) shine like new. The same formula can even work on wooden windowsills, trim, and handrails.

**Clean and prep.** Use a simple dishwashing sponge with an abrasive side, and dip it in warm water and TSP or substitute (mixed as directed). Lightly scour all the visible surfaces on the face of the cabinets (not inside). Put paper towels or rags on the countertop and floor to catch drips. You may have to do this twice; kitchen cabinets absorb a large amount of oils and grime from cooking and use. Your goal is to both degrease and degloss (slightly dull) the cabinet surfaces, making them receptive to the new finish. Stain (or paint) won't stick if dirt or oils are present on a surface or if there is a remaining glossy surface.

**Rinse off TSP with a clean, damp sponge.** The cabinets may look slightly faded, and the abrasive sponge will have slightly scored the surface. This preps the surface for the stain and polyurethane combination you will apply after it dries.

**Let the cabinets dry (overnight, at least).** Make sure you have other tasks you can do in other areas of the rental. Ideally, prep the cabinets before you leave for the day.

**Apply a combination stain-polyurethane product.** Use a high-quality brush to paint this on thin. Look out for drips. Just use the closest color stain you can find—slightly lighter or darker is fine. This widely available two-in-one product cuts your work in half. Avoid getting any dust, hair, or loose paintbrush bristles into the polyurethane, because these will become permanent. Also, do not shake polyurethane, or air bubbles will appear in your finish; stir it gently before using. After the first coat has dried, again lightly rub the cabinet surface with a dry abrasive sponge to score it slightly. Wipe away the dust on the surface and in the area thoroughly with a clean damp cloth. Then add a second coat. When applying a coat of the stain and polyurethane product, make sure this is your very last task of the day. Brush it on and head home. That way, you won't stir up dust, accidently touch wet stain, or inhale the fumes while it dries.

**Admire the final results.** Your cabinet surface will be dry—plus durable and stunning—the next day when you arrive.

---

### What About Cleaning Painted Cabinets?

If the cabinets in your rental are not already painted, I do not recommend painting them, as this can be labor intensive (as I learned from a couple of small galley kitchens). The process for refinishing wood cabinets is easier. But if your rental already has painted cabinets (white, for example), or the cabinets are very old, dark, or scratched, and refinishing won't hide surface problems, you may want to repaint or paint them. There are some new products that make this process more bearable. Low- or no-VOC paints offer a durability and viscosity that's ideal for cabinets. The preparation process is similar to, but a bit more involved than the wood-cabinet-refinishing process described above. (You'll need to prime unpainted cabinets or when changing colors.) For a useful article and video on painting kitchen cabinets, see this piece on the *Better Homes and Gardens* website: www.bhg.com/kitchen/cabinets/makeovers/kitchen-cabinet-paint.

---

## Painting

Painting is probably the number one skill all landlords need. Dollar for dollar, you get the most surface protection and cosmetic improvement from paint. It can protect your property's exterior from water and sunlight. And inside your unit, you'll get more visual appeal from fresh paint than any other low-cost project. You can transform almost any room with a few gallons of paint, and protect and renew everything from the front porch to the back yard fence.

You could delegate some painting tasks, but painting is so central to the do-it-yourself landlord theme that it may not be feasible, especially for touch ups or small areas. The ideas below can help you through the process whether you are a novice or expert.

Because you will be painting (a great deal), think about using a store that specializes in paint. The staff will likely have helpful advice on choosing paint and supplies, and can keep your paint color codes on file. Their added expertise and the quality of their paint can make it worthwhile to become a loyal customer. But shop around for paintbrushes and supplies, because these are usually more expensive at paint specialty stores.

## Gather and Organize Your Painting Materials

Painting will be easiest if you pull together your basics (paintbrushes, tarps, and the like) in one place. See the "Painting Supply Kit," below, for a list of essential painting items.

---

### Painting Supply Kit

Here are the basic items to have on hand before starting painting:
- ☐ numerous high quality paintbrushes of various sizes
- ☐ extra rollers and roller covers of different types
- ☐ a light, sturdy extension pole that attaches to your paint roller (one about the shape and dimension of a broom handle is ideal for interiors and will increase your efficiency and reduce fatigue, because you'll use your whole body to paint, not just your wrist and arm), and even consider a telescoping extension pole for high and hard-to-reach places
- ☐ paint pans and pan liners
- ☐ paint can openers
- ☐ drop cloths or tarps
- ☐ painter's tape of various widths
- ☐ sand paper and paint scrapers
- ☐ painter caulk or quick-drying spackle
- ☐ low-odor paint thinner for cleanup of oil paints or ammonia for shellac-based products, and
- ☐ disposable wet wipes for easy clean up.

---

### What Are the Best Types of Paint Brushes and Rollers?

My advice: Buy top-quality brushes and rollers (and reuse them). There is a false economy in the large packs of cheap brushes, (although it's fine to keep a few sponge or disposable brushes on hand for touchups). For most landlords, several sizes of high-end synthetic (polyester or nylon) brushes will serve nicely. Simply clean them up when the job is done. You can use a good paint brush dozens of times instead of buying the new cheap ones every time. If you can't clean paintbrushes until later in the day, wrap them in an airtight plastic bag so they won't dry out.

You often can do better in small spaces like kitchens, bathrooms, and closets with a smaller roller. As you get more proficient, use wider rollers to cover more space in less time.

## Select the Right (and High-Quality) Paint

Painting is mostly labor—in fact, the cost of the paint is minor compared to the amount of labor you will put into repainting an entire rental unit. Always use the highest-quality, longest-lasting paint you can find. You will get better coverage, too, cutting your time and labor. Cheap paint is often more expensive in the end, as you have to apply more of it and repaint more often.

The ideal sheen for a rental unit is one that's washable yet doesn't show imperfections. Flat dry flat latex can't really be washed off, and a shiny enamel gloss may show imperfections. My experience is that the best finish is somewhere in between. A low-luster finish, usually called "pearl," "eggshell," or "satin," is ideal. It is washable and appropriate for most rooms. It will hold up to touching and traffic. Staff at a specialty paint store will help you select the best-quality paint.

## Simplify Your Colors

Just one word on colors: Simplify. If you haven't yet done so, pick one shade and sheen of white for all your interior painting, and stick with it in every unit. The paint should look clean, hide stains, and not be overwhelming. There are a dizzying number of whites, so find one that works. As you gradually repaint your units, you will have the same paint and finish throughout, making your selection and buying of paint a no-brainer. Doing touchups and matching paint will be simple.

You can get a slightly higher gloss for doors, trim, and bathrooms, making it even easier to clean, but it is not necessary. For exterior painting, the best color is often the current color of the building. Using the original paint color will be easier than changing colors, so try and get the color code when you buy a property (ask the seller or try and find an unused can with the description or codes on top).

### Consider a Ceiling Paint

Ceiling paints are specially formulated to dry a bit slower and for less splattering and mess. They often come in a light, flat ceiling white. If you have a textured (often called popcorn) ceiling, try and match the color so you can touch it up with a brush. If you have to roll it, cover the entire floor with a drop cloth and roll once lightly in one direction, so you don't pull off the texture.

## Prep for Painting

The TSP routine described above for cleaning walls is ideal for cleaning and prepping both interior and exterior surfaces for painting. With exterior painting, you can also spray on TSP with a garden sprayer or hose attachment (just be sure and rinse it before it dries on the surface). Also on the exterior of a rental in a wet climate where mildew is a problem, use a house cleaner designed for this or diluted bleach as well as TSP. Cover plants near the house with a tarp or plastic. After cleaning, additional prep work may include the following.

**Patching.** Use a fast-drying filler or paintable caulk to patch small holes.

**Sanding.** Sand any paint that is peeling and prime any bare exterior wood.

**Removing light switch and outlet covers.** Remove and organize the light switch and outlet cover plates by room in a clear plastic bag (with the screws). Leave them in that room or label them to avoid confusion.

**Carefully masking or taping off areas you aren't painting.** This includes heaters, baseboard trim, window trim, lights, and fixtures. Painter's tape is expensive, but will save time cleaning up drips in the long run. For exterior jobs, do not let your painter's tape get wet, or it may be difficult to remove.

**Using tarp to protect interiors and exteriors.** Cover interior floors with a drop cloth or tarp and don't track the paint inside the rental unit. When painting outside, use an old tarp to protect your sidewalks and shrubs. Make sure tenants move any vehicles away from your painting area.

**Matching the texture.** Inside your units, you may find walls have varying textures, from flat surfaces to a popcorn ceiling to everything in between. There are spray-on and brush-on textures you can use to match any texture if you have a damaged area. These should be good enough for a small patch in rentals.

## Start Painting

At last, you can actually paint! It often takes longer to get to this point than one expected (because most of your effort in a quality paint job is actually prep work). Here's what to do:

**Make sure you have the right conditions.** The ideal paint conditions are dry days between 50 and 85 degrees for most latex paints. The ideal relative humidity should be between 40% and 70%. Also, make sure you let exterior surfaces dry a day or two after a rain.

**Cut in corners**—that is, paint the corners, covering a few inches, then roll out the ceiling and then walls. Do this before the paint dries, so you will not see the edges.

**Use primer when needed**—for example, if changing colors, covering stains, or painting faded, stained, or bare wood or surfaces.

## Environmental Considerations When Painting

The following tips will help protect not only the environment, but your health, your tenant's health, and your pocketbook.

- Low- and no-VOC (volatile organic compounds) paints are among the best recent product innovations for landlords, professional painters, and anyone who paints often. This means that little or no toxic fumes or gases are released as the paint is applied and dries. The result is that landlords of today can breathe easier than those of the past. Be sure to use a low- or no-VOC paint on any occupied units to protect tenants, as well. For more on VOCs, see this article on the EPA website: www.epa. gov/iaq/voc.html.

- Use up one can or bucket of paint before opening another. You should get 300-400 square feet per gallon, depending on coverage, preparation, and the thickness of your coats.

- Reseal paint properly to preserve it. Use a hammer or rubber mallet to secure the paint can lid and keep air out. And don't allow paint to freeze. Paint may last for years if sealed and stored properly.

- Once a can or bucket is empty, let any residue dry out before disposing of it in the trash.

- Donate extra paint to local charities that do painting projects. Theater and art groups have taken dozens of gallons that were left behind by my tenants. The paint gets a useful second life in murals or stage backdrops.

- Properly dispose of unwanted paint. Unused paint of any kind is hazardous waste and should be dropped off at your local center for hazardous waste.

**Dodge direct sunlight.** When painting the exterior, avoid applying paints directly under the glaring sun. Instead, follow the arc of the sun. When the sun is beating down on the front of the building, paint in the back or on the sides of the building. Then follow this pattern around the house, painting on the shaded or semishaded side. It will be cooler (and safer) for you in the shade and the paint will have a chance to dry properly, as the sun makes its arc. Today, most paints dry in four hours or less and under most conditions.

**Keep perspective.** You are not doing a magazine spread or a home show for your rentals. So your best is going to be good enough and a dramatic improvement. The tenants will love the new walls.

## Clean Up After Painting

Cleanup is always the last thing a tired painter wants to do. But you can minimize your effort with the following tips.

**Seal it up.** Bring along clean, airtight garbage bags when you paint. Use them to cover and seal your paint tray, brushes, and roller all at once when you finish an area. Then you can move to another job on your list or take a break. When you come to another painting task that day, just unseal the garbage bag to start again. Use the bag for trash at the end of the job. This advice applies to latex paint; with oil-based paints, you'll need to clean up paint equipment immediately after painting, using a low-odor mineral spirits or paint thinner.

**Paint in your socks.** To prevent tracking paint, step on to your tarp or drop cloth in your socks and leave your shoes at the edge. Then change into different socks or just slide on your shoes to prevent tracking.

 RESOURCE

**Advice on painting.** For a wide variety of useful how-to articles, go to the www.familyhandyman.com and look up "Painting" under the "Skills" tab. For more technical information on paint chemistry (to help your paint purchase decisions and application), check out www.diyadvice.com/diy/painting/paint/chemistry.

## Using a Drill

Today, the best way to affix wood to a structure, repair railings, tighten handrails, repair loose deck boards, or straighten sagging closets is all much the same: Use a cordless or conventional drill. Actually, the use of the drill is not so much to drill holes, but to drive screws. Using a drill for this is easier and more efficient than hammering nails, plus, there is no banging to drive the neighbors or other tenants crazy.

If you have not run a power tool since high school wood shop, the cordless drills of today are light, quiet, reliable, and effective. An old-fashioned corded drill will, however, get the job done. Also, be sure you have a large supply of bits to use with different types of screw head types and, of course, different-sized drill bits in the event that you need to actually drill holes.

Once you can drive screws well, you open up the possibility of making dozens of minor repairs. Almost anything that is loose and made of wood can be reattached with a screw with your drill. You can quickly change locks, install curtain rods, and tighten loose cabinet doors. You can even hang shelves or cabinets. Chances are, if your tenant calls about anything wooden that is loose—inside or outside—you can tighten it with a drill and screw. This versatility makes using a drill one of my top three landlord skills.

> **RESOURCE**
> **Useful article on drilling.** You don't need to be absolutely perfect to get common repair jobs done with a drill, but the *Family Handyman* article, *How to Drive Screws Perfectly,* will help. See www.familyhandyman.com/carpentry/how-to-drive-screws-perfectly/view-all.

## Caulking

Caulking is also one of the landlord's top three most-used skills. It's crucial for the classic task of sealing the edges in kitchen and baths, but the skill goes well beyond these primary uses. Caulking is really important in order to weatherproof the exterior of your rental unit from the elements and also the interior from the human element (including water from a careless tenant). If you get proficient with a caulk gun, you'll be able to handle a wide range of tasks:

- apply construction adhesives to affix loose baseboards or thresholds
- protect, fill, seal, and/or weatherproof exterior cracks
- prepare to paint with a painter's caulk and caulk gun, and
- fill in small cracks and gaps in concrete and asphalt driveways and sidewalks, using special caulks.

With practice, you will become skilled at caulking. The basic process described here works for all types of interior and exterior caulks and surface, with some variations by type of application.

Remove any old caulk. I like to use a plastic, not metal, putty knife or a tool designed for removing caulk, and the abrasive side of dishwashing sponge for any residue.

Use a high-quality caulk designed for the application. I generally use a bright white, for aesthetics in kitchens and baths (silicone is a plus, and some caulks offer mold resistance). For exterior caulks, I use a higher-end paintable product designed for the longest time period available (they are often rated by years). The purchase decision for caulk is analogous to paint— the process is mostly labor, so get the best product you can find. Any midgrade caulk gun should work, but don't be afraid to switch if you are having trouble with yours.

Cut off the tip of the caulk container with a razor blade at a slight angle. Penetrate the caulk with a poker on the caulk gun or a long nail. Pull back the hooked ratchet and place the caulk in the caulk gun cradle. Squeeze the trigger and push the tip against the corners and areas where the counter meets the walls. As a small stream of caulk emerges from the tip, drag it smoothly across the edges and gaps of the surface in question. Take your damp index finger and run it across the top in a smooth, fluid motion. If you're not wearing disposable gloves, clean caulk off your finger with a wet wipe before it dries.

If your caulk job looks decent, resist the urge to try and improve or touch it. If the caulk job looks poor, simply use a wet wipe to clean it up and try that again before it dries.

Seal the tube when you are done, so that the rest of the caulk doesn't dry out. Take a corrosion-proof screw and twist it into the opening of the caulk. Then wrap it in blue painter's tape completely, sealing the tube. To reopen, unroll the tape and back out the screw.

RESOURCE

**For an extended discussion of caulk and caulking,** search for the Tim Snyder article *Laying Down a Perfect Bead* on the This Old House website at www.thisoldhouse.com.

## Dealing With Drains

Even a conscientious tenant will probably clog a sink drain at one time or another, and may call you rather than doing self-help. For most slow drains, a simple commercial drain cleaner, used as directed, will solve the problem. For more troublesome clogs, try a sink plunger or repeat the drain-cleaner process (as directed) for clogs or slow drains. If you still can't clear the drain, call a plumber.

TIP

**Green drain cleaner.** Sprinkle a cup of baking soda in your kitchen drain (don't pack it in as this could clog). A quick burst of hot water can help send the baking soda into the drain. Then add a quart of vinegar. Allow the bubbles and foams to work for a few minutes and then let the hot water run a few minutes. Repeat until the drain flows well. This has worked for me for years and even has a science-fair type visual effect (and you'll avoid using harsh chemicals).

## Toilet Troubleshooting

In the recent survey on American housing quoted in this book's introductory chapter, tenants cited toilet issues as a top problem in their rental units. However, the survey data showed that few of these problems lasted more than six hours, indicating that common clogs or minor toilet tank issues were a likely cause (not major sewage line failures).

The basic strategies discussed here will help you handle most common toilet repairs—usually problems in the toilet tank mechanism (causing a running toilet or weak flush). Simple clogs are even easier to handle. Often, you can actually walk tenants through the process of unclogging a toilet over the phone. (Better yet, give tenants a plunger when they move in and advice on avoiding toilet problems in the first place, as discussed in Chapter 8).

## Inside the Tank: Troubleshooting Common Toilet Tank Issues

For an easy visual lesson, simply lift the lid off the tank portion of your toilet. Look inside. Then flush it. You have just seen how the gravity flow toilet works. It is remarkably simple.

There are two common types of mechanisms working inside tanks today. The older version has a large float (it looks like an oblong black or clear floating ball). Seeing this mechanism in the tank could be an indicator that it is time to replace the entire flush and fill mechanism. You can get an overhaul kit to do this, as explained below. The second, more modern type of tank has a plastic floating arm that rides up and down what is called a ballcock mechanism.

Whichever type of mechanism is inside the toilet tank, you will experience three common problems related to the tank. Some quick fixes are discussed here (and more permanent solutions later in this section).

RESOURCE

**Basic toilet anatomy.** The gravity flow toilet commonly found in rentals is really just two main parts: (1) a bowl or base (the part that you sit on), and (2) the tank attached to the bowl or base (behind where you sit on the toilet). If you have any questions, check out the basic parts of a toilet at *Toilet Basics: Understanding the Basic Components* at www.doityourself.com/stry/typestoiletparts.

## Toilet Is "Running"

The signs of this problem are that you hear water repeatedly or constantly filling the tank and then it shuts off but refills again; you see ripples in the tank; or you have to jiggle the handle to make it stop running. There are a few common causes of a running toilet:

- The seal on the flush valve is not closing properly or is corroded. You could try cleaning the flapper or ball or adjusting it. This could prevent water from escaping into the tank.
- Water may be going through the overflow valve. If you lift the tank and see water overflowing into the hole on the inlet valve (overflowing), then your ballcock mechanism is not properly shutting off the water to the tank, or (with the older type of mechanism), the float arm with a ball is not working. They may need adjusting.

> **TIP**
>
> **The rental unit's water bill may signal you have a running toilet.** If your water bill spikes and you can't find any leaks or abnormal usage, tell tenants to listen for a running toilet. One that runs nonstop for a month or more can raise your water bill noticeably. Make sure tenants in single-family home are on the lookout for this signal of a running toilet.

## Toilet Is Not Flushing Fully or Is Weak

A second common problem related to the tank mechanism is a weak or partial flush. Here, you can try and adjust the flapper and chain on the handle (or flush ball if it has that mechanism). Flush the toilet with the top of the tank open and make adjustments to get the tank to drain more fully before the flap closes. Some new ones have a dial or parts you can adjust. You can also adjust the float level to allow more water in the tank. Also, check that the fill tube is not unhooked or aimed improperly.

## There's a Leak from the Base of the Toilet Tank

If your tank is leaking (not just sweating), this is likely from a washer or gasket around the bolts and mechanism holding the tank to the bowl or the seal around the inlet valve. This may happen when tenants add toilet bowl fresheners—chemical- or bleach-based—to the tank. These corrode the seals quickly, especially if water is not flushed frequently. So drain the tank and replace the seals. However, if you have already done the work of replacing the seals for a toilet tank, you may as well replace the entire mechanism in the tank, especially if it is older. This tank overhaul option is discussed below.

## Three Permanent Solutions to Toilet Problems

The problems discussed above often signal aged tank parts and an adjustment may just be a temporary solution. If your minor adjustment does not work or you want a more permanent solution to a toilet problem, you generally have three main choices: replace the precise part, replace the entire internal mechanism, or replace the entire toilet. What's best depends on the age and condition of the toilet, your skills and time, and whether the unit is occupied all day long or accessible (a problem if there is just one bathroom!). You do not want to try and make a toilet repair with a tenant urgently waiting on you.

### Replace a Toilet Part

This is the precision strategy, and may be the cheapest and quickest option if the problem is clear such as a corroded toilet flapper or a broken toilet handle. If the rest of the inside of the tank and the overall toilet look good, try to just replace a specific part.

However, if you have a ten-year-old toilet, remember that your fill and flush valve assembly has flushed thousands of times and it may be easier to replace the entire mechanism or toilet. With older toilets, consider the two options described below. Otherwise, once you replace one part or seal, another is just as likely to break and you will face a call back and have to troubleshoot and repair the same toilet again.

This precision strategy is also less advantageous when the problem is a combination of parts or not easy to pinpoint right away. Then you may as well overhaul the entire toilet tank mechanism to be sure you get the problem fixed.

RESOURCE

**Advice on replacing toilet tank parts.** For a useful article with photos, see *Replacing Toilet Tank Parts* by Brian Simkins at www. doityourself.com/stry/typestoiletparts.

## Overhaul the Toilet Tank Components

If the toilet base and tank are not cracked, damaged, or unsightly, your best bet may be using an all-in-one, universal style overhaul kit that replaces everything in the toilet tank. These kits include a fill and flush valve, handle, lever, and all the bolts, seals, and parts to renew the toilet tank components. They also have fairly simple instructions and you can even watch online videos. These kits are primarily made by two manufacturers and are presently $20 to $30 at big box hardware stores.

You'll face a bit of a learning curve with overhauling the toilet tank. Your first installation will be tricky and may take several hours. If possible, try it on an older toilet in a vacant unit first, or hire and watch a plumber or contractor do the work. Properly installed, these kits can make a toilet work trouble-free for many years.

## Buy a New Toilet

You might think it's the most expensive option, but buying a completely brand new toilet may actually cost less than the average repair call and visit from a plumber, including parts and labor, in some areas. For example, when a plumber diagnoses and replaces something on an old toilet, you still have an old toilet and may have spent the equivalent of buying a new one after you pay the parts and labor. You can buy a new toilet in a box ready to seat on a wax (or waxless) ring for less than three hundred dollars. You just unhook the old toilet and put the new one in place.

So it could be more economical in some cases to just replace an older toilet, especially if it is damaged or has other problems. It may also make sense if you are selling a unit and the cosmetic appeal of a new toilet could add value.

Replacing a toilet is also a good option for an occupied unit with one bathroom. It will just take a few minutes and the tenant will be delighted. As long as the toilet flange connecting the toiler to the floor is not damaged, installation is fairly simple. Make sure you have simple metallic braided cord supply lines to the toilet. These are easy to remove and seal without a problem.

If you have never replaced a toilet before, or the unit has a nonstandard or very old toilet, perhaps even attached to the wall (not the floor), or you encounter any other problems, call a plumber.

> **RESOURCE**
>
> **How to repair and replace toilets and other plumbing fixtures.** The *Ultimate Guide to Plumbing,* by Merle Henkenius (Creative Homeowner), has clear pictures and step-by-step information to help landlords handle or understand most residential plumbing repairs.

## Talking Tenants Through Minor Toilet (Clog) Problems

Nine out of ten clogs can be fixed with the simple use of a plunger, so make sure your tenants have a good plunger at hand, and directions on using it (included in your move-in materials). When a tenant contacts you about a clogged toilet, try this on the phone.

1. Calmly explain to the tenant how to turn off the water supply to the toilet. This will prevent or stop additional overflows.
2. If there is an overflow, ask the tenant to use old towels to clean and up and say you will provide reimbursement for new ones. This will prevent water damage to your unit.
3. Explain how to use the plunger you left in the unit. Have the tenant get good suction and push in and pull back (both ways), forcing water down the toilet. Sometimes the pull is as important as the push in plunging. The tenant should keep working the plunger until there is no water in the tank.

4. Tell the tenant to turn on the water supply and try to flush the toilet after the tank fills, but be ready to turn the water off again if necessary. The clog will likely be cleared.

5. If the toilet is still clogged, have the tenant repeat the plunging process. Sometimes you may have to plunge for five to ten minutes on a serious clog. Don't let the tenant give up too soon.

6. If the problem is still not fixed, tell the tenant to put a cup or two of liquid dish soap into the toilet and leave it overnight (if the unit has another bathroom), or an hour or so if not.

7. Have the tenant repeat the flushing, filling, and plunging process the next morning if the unit has second bathroom, or an hour later if not. The clog will likely be cleared.

8. If the toilet is still clogged, drive over to the rental unit with your best plunger. If you can't fix it, try a short toilet auger if you have one. Use as directed. Or call a plumber if you suspect a larger problem.

> **TIP**
> **Education is the best option.** You probably do not want to run right over every time a tenant has a clogged toilet. But if you do that more than a few times, make sure you have the tenant watch you fix the toilet and even have the tenant try the plunger. Tenants may have a clogged toilet in the middle of the night or while you are at work, so it will be important for them to be able to fix this type of problem themselves. Odds are, once the tenant can use a plunger, you will never hear about another clog during the tenancy.

## Dealing With Moisture and Mold

Moisture can be a big problem in rental units, in all but the most arid desert climates, and dampness or musty smells are often renters' top concerns. Yet it's often their behavior that leads to the moisture. Tenants will produce water vapor in the unit through boiling water, showering, bathing, cooking, and even breathing.

Moisture has become more of an issue than in decades past because new and upgraded rental units are often tightly insulated and sealed, but not always properly ventilated. This can trap moisture in the unit, leading to problems such as mold. If you see water condensing on the windows on a cold day, for example, your rental unit may have too much moisture. Also be on the alert for tenant complaints about any surface mold. Here are some tips on handling moisture problems.

## Ventilate

Make sure your bath and kitchen fans are working properly and venting warm moist air outside. To avoid buildup of dirt, turn off the power and clean any visible dirt or grease off the blades and spray some lubricant on the shaft of the fan. Also check that the exhaust outlet is free and not blocked. You can turn it on and go outside and see if the flapper opens when the fan is running. Upgrade your fans if they are working poorly or lack sufficient power.

Be sure the unit has adequate ventilation in the attic and crawlspace (if it has one). If you recently purchased the rental property, your inspection report should have identified any ventilation problems; if not, a roofing expert should be able to assess whether your roof is adequately ventilated. See Chapter 5 for more on issues involving crawlspaces.

## Check for Water Leaks

Always inspect to make sure you do not have a water leak in a wall or a flooded crawlspace, which can make units damper than usual. It is hard to maintain a proper humidity level with pooling water beneath a building or a slow leak inside a unit. These can create moisture problems in buildings.

## Check Dryer Ducts and Vents for Leaks

Clothes dryers can be a source of unwanted moisture in homes. Make sure the vent and outlet hose are attached, sealed, and venting properly outside.

## Educate Tenants

Make sure tenants are using bath and kitchen fans, and opening windows as necessary—for example, when boiling water or soups for long periods of time. Similarly, taking long, hot baths or showers without the bath fan on traps too much moisture in the unit. Exhaust fans are helpful only if they are turned on. Consider getting bath fans that go on automatically when the light goes on.

## Buy Dehumidifiers for Rental Units

If you follow these steps and still have some moisture building up in your units, consider buying a dehumidifier. These small appliances can help dramatically with moisture. It is worth a few hundred dollars to prevent mold and keep your tenant satisfied. The newer dehumidifiers are impressive. They will give you a humidity reading and come on and off when they hit a specified level. They also stop before they overflow. Be sure to show the tenant how the dehumidifier works and how to empty it.

CAUTION

**Get professional help with a mold problem.** Small amounts of surface mold (less than a few square feet) can be removed, but if you find large areas of mold or entire walls of mold, seek professional guidance. More on mold in residential homes can be found here (simply search the agency website for the relevant title):

- EPA's (Environmental Protection Agency) *Brief Guide to Mold, Moisture and Your Home*, at www.epa.gov
- CDC's (Centers for Disease Control and Prevention) *Facts about Mold and Dampness*, at www.cdc.gov
- U.S. Department of Energy's *Guide to Home Ventilation*, at http://energy.gov, and
- articles published on the Home Ventilation Institute website at www.hvi.org.

# Ways to Boost Your Repair and Maintenance IQ and Effectiveness

Even if you did not grow up doing basic home repairs or maintenance around the house (ideal preparation for being a landlord), you can still enhance your maintenance abilities with all kinds of online resources and books, as well as formal and self-study courses and volunteer opportunities. Experienced landlords can also take continuing education classes to learn more about construction and cutting-edge maintenance products and innovations. Here are some of the basic resources for improving your maintenance skills.

## Online Videos

Thousands of accurate and informative free clips can be found online (at YouTube and on most home improvement magazines' websites) to help landlords understand basic repair and maintenance tasks. As a soon as a tenant calls about a broken sliding door or leaking appliance, go online and look for a video demonstrating the problem, the repair, and the exact parts needed. Manufacturers' and retailers' websites also offer online assistance.

## Magazines and Websites

It is hard to beat some of the leading home improvement and maintenance magazines for readability. Today much of the content is also online, such as in the Home Improvement section of the *Better Homes & Gardens* website (www.bhg.com). One of the best, *The Family Handyman* (www.familyhandyman.com), has articles on everything from carpentry and plumbing, to appliance repair and landscaping. Also, check out www.doityourself.com for useful "How-Tos" on everything from exterior painting to home energy checkups, plus forums for advice on specific questions.

## Television Shows

Landlords are major beneficiaries of the genre of home-repair related television. There are now entire television networks on home improvement such as DIY Network (www.diynetwork.com) and HGTV (www.hgtv.com). Many shows demonstrate skills used in residential home repair and maintenance, especially painting, landscaping, and creating curb appeal.

## Courses

Whether short, one-hour courses for free at a big box store or your local hardware store, or a semester-long community college course, the skills of home maintenance and repair can be obtained in most communities through safe, structured programs. Some of these may even get into more advanced topics to help with repairs.

## Work or Volunteer Experience

Landlords with summers or weekends free might consider getting on-the-job training by taking a part-time position with a company or person doing property maintenance work. You could get paid and learn at the same time. You may even find volunteer opportunities in this vein where you could be helping out and learning. Habitat for Humanity (www.habitat.org/local) may have an active local affiliate, or even a skills learning program like Women Build (www.habitat.org/wb).

## Books

It's still wise—even in today's information age—to keep a couple of the old-fashioned home improvement books on hand. These are step-by-step and in depth, with useful photos and drawings. Bring your favorite book along to units when you work just in case you face an unanticipated problem. The following books cover a range of home improvement tasks with drawings, photos, and guidance (look for the latest edition):

- *Ultimate Guide: Home Repair & Improvement,* by Editors of Creative Homeowner (Creative Homeowner)
- *Home Improvement 1-2-3,* by The Home Depot (The Home Depot), and
- *Home Maintenance for Dummies,* by James Carey and Morris Carey (For Dummies). The authors also have a home maintenance website with tips, products, and more at http://onthehouse.com.

> **TIP**
>
> **Practice makes perfect.** Sometimes you just have to try and try again. If you have read up on a project or task, watched a video, and gathered all the necessary materials and tools, then nothing can teach quite like experience and trial and error. When you have a vacant unit and are confronted with a wide range of turnaround tasks, it is an ideal time to practice or even learn something new. You are the boss—no one can reprimand you for wasting time or not getting it right the first time. You will get quicker and more skilled every time you try a particular task. For example, if you want to perfect your caulking skills, find a place where any two materials come together, be it under a vanity or sink or in a garage or unfinished basement, rather than a high-visibility kitchen counter top. Practice there first. This same theme applies to other skills, too. If you have never painted, try starting in a closet where imperfections won't be noticed. The first linoleum I laid was actually in under-sink cabinets of kitchens and baths (which makes them waterproof and attractive), and let me practice in inconspicuous places.

## What's Next?

Once you have some of the skills in this chapter down pat, you are ready to apply them to one of the most important landlord tasks: preparing your rental units for tenants. This will help differentiate your units from the competition (by being cleaner and shinier), and also preserve and maintain your properties, helping lower your operating and repair costs. ●

# Preparing Your Rental Unit for Tenants

As a part-time landlord, by far the most labor-intensive part of your job will be the turnaround process—when you go over the entire unit after one tenant moves out and before another moves in, cleaning and repairing every area and component. The tips in this chapter are designed to make your turnarounds as thorough and efficient (in terms of time and money) as possible.

Early on, I rather dreaded having to go in and completely clean, paint, and prep units. Partly, this was because the units needed a great deal of work and I hadn't yet mastered the process. I also allowed too many seasonal renters and was turning around units too often. And I was, of course, worried about the vacancy that was part of the turnaround process.

Today, while I try to keep great tenants as long as possible, I actually look forward to "getting into" a vacant unit. With the tenants gone and all the furniture out, I have a brief window of time where I get full access to the unit. (Some nooks and crannies can be seen and worked on only when the unit is vacant.) It gives me a chance to assess all the small details, maintain or replace every moving part, and get the place ready for another long tenancy. Further, there are some tasks you simply can't do in an occupied unit because of interfering foot and pet traffic, the impact of fumes on tenants, or furniture clogging up the work area.

Rental units are assets you'll want to protect. Your thorough cleaning and preventive maintenance at turnaround time can add decades of life to the components of the unit, set it apart from the competition, and attract the best, long-term tenants.

## Understanding Fair Rental Condition for Your Market

Before you get your unit into shape for the next (or your first) renter, focus on what the final place should look like: Picture a clean, well-maintained unit that is on par with others for rent in your area in the same price range. Don't get caught up in any lofty notions of radical transformations or renovations you might have seen on television! Over-renovating can be a common and costly problem for landlords.

Understanding the average rental condition for your community or market is the first step toward knowing how to prepare a unit for rental. The concept of rental condition is also an important theme in this book and part of becoming an effective landlord. If your units lack features or are not as well maintained as those offered by the competition, then you can lose renters. Similarly, if you over-remodel your units, you can easily lose money. For example, a three-bedroom house will likely rent for around the same price whether you remodel the kitchen or not. Putting in special features or doing frequent remodels may bring a slightly higher rent, but the slight increase seldom covers the cost outlays. Plus, you may get fewer tenants to view your unit if it's priced higher than similar units in the same neighborhood. Of course, the features and condition of your rentals will depend on their price range, location, and property type. For example, luxury rentals commanding a high price will also need to have higher-end features and be in mint condition.

The vast majority of tenants will just need functional units in fair condition with everything (walls, floor coverings, bathroom fixtures, appliances, countertops, and the like) working, clean, and undamaged. View enough rentals in your area, online, or by visiting open houses, so that you get an intuitive feel for the fair rental condition of similar properties. If the other units have dated cabinets and floors and older laminate countertops, then yours (if clean and undamaged) can have the same features and compete just fine.

> **TIP**
>
> **The perfect is the enemy of the good.** Try to keep your rentals in good (not perfect) condition. You do not have an unlimited budget or full-time assistants. After you've been a landlord for a decade, you'll probably find that you can drive down most any street and spot hundreds of potential repairs (dated coolers, roofs near the end of their useful life, cracked driveways, aged windows, and some peeling paint). Most of these will not be done in the near future and the properties go right on housing people safely and, if they're rentals, producing cash flow.

# To Furnish or Not to Furnish

Most part-time landlords shouldn't rent their apartments furnished. While you could command a slightly higher rent and appeal to some people who may not have furniture (especially if your market includes students or seasonal workers), the negatives of furnishing an apartment or house usually far outweigh the positives, in that:

- providing furnishings (beds, bureaus, sofas, dining room tables, and the like) can be costly
- furnishings mean there are more items to maintain, clean, or repair
- many renters have their own furniture and don't want furnished units, so you lose them as customers (or you may have to empty the unit to attract them), and
- moving around furniture while you prepare a unit for new tenants can be labor intensive. Not only do you have to clean the furniture, you have to slide it around as you clean carpets and paint. It can wear you out.

My advice: Don't deliberately furnish a rental unit unless this is the norm for your rental market and expected by your target renter.

What if you buy a unit with some quality furniture already in it? Before getting rid of it, consider a compromise strategy that's worked for me. Leave some furniture in the unit—maybe a quality dining room table, sofa, and futon. Then rent the place "partially furnished." This technique can attract people with no furniture, just a few pieces, or even a houseful of furniture. People with little or no furniture will find it ideal, and those with furniture will seldom find a few items a deterrent. It also means you'll have just a few large items to shift when you clean or paint the unit. When things get dated or if you want to make the unit unfurnished, you can give the items to a departing tenant, call your local charity for pickup, or sell them cheap online.

> **TIP**
>
> **Inventory the condition of the rental unit and any furniture that you own when a new tenant moves in.** You should always prepare a move-in checklist at the start of a tenancy, describing the condition of the rental unit, including any furnishings. This is an invaluable tool when the tenant moves out and you need to assess the need for and costs of cleaning or damage repair (and security deposit deductions). Also, there won't be any question of which items are yours and which are the tenant's. (But as a backup, you'll probably want to find an unobtrusive place to write your name on each item.) For more on using move-in and move-out checklists, see Chapters 8 and 10.

# Preparing for New Tenants

Don't be tempted to rush into showing your property to prospective tenants. I've found that it rarely pays off to show them "construction zones" rather than finished units. Renters tend to lack imagination as to how a unit "could be," no matter how much you explain what you plan to do by way of cleaning, painting, or getting rid of odors. Besides, if you are distracted taking phone calls about the unit, or constantly cleaning up to make a path for the showings, you are courting disaster. Tenants will not be impressed and could touch wet paint or even trip over your cleaning and preparation materials. This chapter will help you make your rental unit completely ready for the renter before you show it.

## It Takes as Long as it Takes

You may have read or heard that a turnaround of a rental unit should only take a set time, be it two weeks or one month, but the truth is that is takes as long as it takes. While it's a good idea to set a time goal for your turnarounds, the time to get an individual unit ready will depend on how much work the unit requires and how much and often you can work on it. There will be times when a fastidious tenant will leave a unit so immaculate, you can check everything and start showing it in hours. Other times, you may walk into a unit that needs extensive work, and know you're looking at some long weeks ahead.

A part-time landlord may not even be able to work on the unit until the weekend. Then you may discover you need a new hot water heater or flooring in the bathroom. And it may take a week to get the contractors scheduled, or work through the steps to remove a pervasive smell. Many variables can impact the time it takes to complete a turnaround.

## Develop Your Own Make-Ready Rituals

The guidelines in this chapter have worked for me over ten years preparing units, but each landlord will have his or her own routines and strengths. Develop your own cleaning and preparation tricks. You will also learn more and more with each tenant turnover so each successive turnaround is easier and more efficient. Establish a process and order that works for you.

# Establishing a Cleaning and Repair Routine

An organized routine will help you make it through the detailed process of getting a unit ready to show and rent. Of course, the exact routine you follow and how much you will need to do will depend on the condition of the unit. You may buy a rental (or an outgoing tenant may leave one) that is dirty and needs extensive work. Or you may have had an ideal tenant who leaves the unit in excellent shape. This section describes a process that can work for most types of units and almost any situation.

At checkout, I will walk through the unit with the tenant and inspect it, using my move-out checklist (see Chapter 10 on moving out). While I am looking for damage, this is also a good time to survey the entire unit for your turnaround to-do list. After canvassing the entire rental unit and every surface, you will probably have a lengthy list of areas to patch, clean, paint, and polish. Try to keep one working list that you continually add to as you come across new tasks and needed repairs. I make notes on both major tasks, such as a new hot water heater, and minor ones, like loose doorknobs, that I need to tackle (or hire a contractor to handle). I keep this working list in a handy place in the unit and continue to add to or amend it in the coming days, checking off tasks as I complete them. See the "Cleaning and Repair Checklist for Rental Turnarounds," below for details.

TIP
**Cleaning the unit of a tenant who just moved out?** Also keep track of damaged items that you may be able to deduct from the tenant's security deposit, as explained in Chapter 10.

## Practice Safe Cleaning Techniques

Always use disposable gloves and wear eye protection (in case of splashes) in all the cleaning and painting routines recommended in this chapter. Even mild cleaners can cause skin and eye irritation. Use dust masks when sweeping, sanding, or when in contact with fiberglass insulation. When using paints, stains, and other chemical solutions, always use a respirator (a good one costs $20 to $40); it can save your health. And be sure to ventilate any areas you are painting or cleaning. Finally, don't forget to wear appropriate footwear (that means no flip flops).

RESOURCE
**Everything you want to know about cleaning.** One of the most prolific writers on professional cleaning is Don Aslett. His books, including *Clean in a Minute, Make Your House Do the Housework, Construction Clean Up,* and *The Cleaning Encyclopedia,* can be ideal reading for landlords, especially novice cleaners. Aslett has also written books focused on spot removal, wood floor care, clearing clutter, and professional cleaning. Some of his best tips center around techniques and tips to organize and systematize the cleaning process. For more information on Don Aslett's books and strategies, see Don Aslett's Cleaning Center at www.cleanreport.com.

## Cleaning and Repair Checklist for Rental Turnarounds

Here are the items, areas, and issues that you will likely need to clean, repair, or otherwise attend to when preparing a rental unit for new tenants:

- ☐ walls and ceilings
- ☐ floors and floor coverings
- ☐ air quality (odors)
- ☐ kitchen cabinets
- ☐ appliances
- ☐ kitchen sink and drain
- ☐ kitchen counters
- ☐ bathrooms
- ☐ light fixtures and outlets
- ☐ doors and windows
- ☐ closets
- ☐ smoke detectors, fire extinguishers, and carbon monoxide detectors
- ☐ other interior items
- ☐ front door and porch
- ☐ windows
- ☐ yard
- ☐ driveway, sidewalk, and parking areas, and
- ☐ bugs, pests, and rodents.

# Walls and Ceilings

Start by thoroughly wiping down the walls and ceilings, as described in Chapter 3. Then decide whether you'll need to repaint them. Sometimes you know right away it needs to be done—for example, after a long tenancy with lots of wear and tear or when you have recently bought a poorly maintained unit. Other times, it can be hard to tell at first. Give the walls and ceiling a good cleaning, let them dry and your shoulders rest, and then see which of the following three situations you're in.

**No painting necessary.** The walls may be fine after just the TSP treatment (described in Chapter 3). This is an ideal situation and not that uncommon with a recent paint job or good tenants. Using a high-quality, easy-to-clean paint can help increase the chances that a simple cleaning will make the walls ready for the next tenant.

**Paint touch-up required.** The most common scenario is where you see some isolated stains and faded spots on the walls. You can simply touch up paint on these areas, as the walls are already prepped with the TSP. Painting all your interiors the same color (as I recommend in Chapter 3) will make the touch-up process easy.

**Full paint job needed.** You're most likely to need to completely repaint a rental unit that you recently purchased, or one that hasn't been painted in a long time or has endured rough wear and tear. After the TSP cleaning, do any hole patching and caulking before painting. Or, if you have to cover a dark paint color or troublesome stains, try a primer first. Chapter 3 covers painting in depth, including how to choose paint supplies and do the actual painting.

## Floors and Floor Coverings

After cleaning (and painting) the walls, you want to move to the floors. Prospective tenants tend to look down first when they enter a unit, so your floors should be in good shape. What you do with floors can be very simple or more complicated depending on the age and type of flooring and how the previous occupants treated it. Here are the basic steps to tending to different types of flooring.

## Carpeting

Start by vacuuming all carpeted areas, including the edges where the floors meet the walls. This will prolong the life of the floor and give you a chance to scan the entire floor and lower wall areas of the unit. Next, use a home carpet cleaning machine to remove any stains or spots. Buy the best such machine you can afford. The features and technology are constantly improving. I find that using a really good vacuum and my home carpet cleaning machine can get my rental floors clean enough for most average turnarounds.

**RESOURCE**

**Read reviews of carpet cleaning machines.** Check out the websites of *Consumer Reports* (www.consumerreports.org) and *Good Housekeeping* (www.goodhousekeeping.com) for useful articles.

If your carpet is badly soiled and can be saved, consider hiring a professional carpet cleaner. You may also want to use one after a long tenancy. Select a carpet cleaning service using the guidance in Chapter 6.

If a carpet or rug is badly stained and can't be cleaned properly, or has bad odors you can't remove (say, from a pet), buy new carpeting. If a departing tenant is responsible for all or some of the damage (above ordinary wear and tear), deduct an appropriate amount from the tenant's security deposit, as described in Chapter 10.

## Wood, Laminate, and Other Flooring

Sweep and vacuum all noncarpeted areas, including wood floors, linoleum, tile, or laminate. Use an extension wand to vacuum along the corners and edges. Then use your favorite floor cleaner and mop on linoleum floors. Only use a slightly damp mop for laminate or wood flooring (or products designed for cleaning these surfaces).

Fix any scuffs and holes in the linoleum (common in kitchens where dropped pans and utensils may create small indentations or imperfections in the floor). You can often keep these small holes from becoming big ones using two items you should have on hand or can easily find: (1) appliance epoxy, especially if your floor is white, off white, or almond (you'll also use this epoxy on your range top or appliances, as discussed below)—just brush on and dab it in, and (2) a strong, clear fingernail polish or topcoat (or be daring and try to match the color with a polish).

## Tarp and Tape Galore: Do No Harm to the Unit

When prepping a unit, you will routinely have to paint, patch a hole, have an appliance delivered, or replace a hot water heater. You may even need to have a contractor replace a window or exterior door. The opportunities for mishaps are legion: spilled or dripped paint, gouges in the kitchen floor from moving a refrigerator, and dust or debris that will need to be picked up later.

You will save yourself hours in cleaning, stain removal, and heartache if you keep several new and used tarps on hand. I just buy the all-purpose polyethylene tarps ("blue tarp") with grommets. Keep various sizes and also several bungee cords on hand, and then: drape new tarps on the floor when an appliance or hot water heater is delivered (to prevent stains from the dolly and floor damage; use tarps as drop cloths in painting (old ones are great outside and new ones protect well inside); and lay tarps down over carpet and furnishings when a window is replaced or wall or ceiling work done.

Tarps have several potential lives. When they get dirty or covered with dry paint, use them outside to cover the sidewalk or shrubs in an exterior paint job or cleaning. When roofing, cover the lawn to catch nails and loose shingles. If it looks like rain, you can also cover equipment or materials in a flash. Finally, when you have sand, gravel, or other rock delivered, have them dumped onto an old tarp so it catches everything and can be easily rolled back up.

Another favorite item for landlords is blue painter's tape. With it, you can temporarily adhere clear plastic (like visqueen) onto walls and furnishings, so as to protect them from dust and debris. You can even construct an effective dust barrier, walling off a room or area with visqueen and blue tape. As long as it stays dry, you should be able to remove the tape without damaging surfaces. Also, use only blue tape to attach notices to the tenant's door. It will keep them looking nice and not damage the paint or finish.

Often, contractors tell me I need not have covered a room so thoroughly, but by the end of the job, my plastic is covered thick with dust and the tarp on the floor is littered with nails and discolored from traffic. We—the contractor and I—are both very glad in the end that I covered everything.

## Area Rugs and Mats

Dollar for dollar, a good mat is worth its weight in gold. A high-quality doormat will trap dirt, sand, and gravel before it gets into the unit and grinds into your flooring. Buy the best mats you can and put them outside the front door, as well as by any back door or garage entry. Put sturdy mats in the kitchen and bath to absorb any water that might drip and create problems.

Use large area rugs to protect laminate, vinyl, and tile floors (with the added bonus of reducing noise). Look for overstocks and closeouts at discount stores that complement your unit's size and existing colors. You can simply roll out a new rug at each tenancy and provide an instant wow factor. More than once, a tenant has called me about a disastrous spill or pet accident, only to find it was largely contained by an area rug or kitchen floor mat. I simply rolled the mat up, discarded it, and replaced it with a new one.

## Pet, Tobacco, and Other Odors

One of the lowest points for any landlord is walking into a unit and discovering a nasty stench. Many smell issues, especially related to pets, originate in the carpets, but walls can be a problem, too—and smells can be tough to conquer. I have battled quite a few odors and won most of the fights with the following procedure.

Start by closing doors to various rooms and see if you can pinpoint precise areas within rooms with odor problems. Use enzymes if you encounter pet odors and a proven odor neutralizer for other smells. Especially target the sites of cat litter boxes, spills, or tobacco use. Clean up any mystery gunk.

If you find that an odor is coming primarily from a closet, hall, or just one bedroom, consider replacing the floor covering in that area. Be sure to clean the subfloor with bleach and seal it with a strong primer before putting down new flooring.

## Smoking Out Tobacco Smells

The smell of tobacco is noxious to many people, and you want to make sure that's not a problem in your rental. You may have purchased rental property that previously allowed smoking. Moving forward, you can prohibit smoking in your rental units. But that doesn't mean you won't end up with a tobacco-smelling rental unit, especially if your tenant is a smoker or frequents bars or clubs that allow smoking. Also, in condos that allow smoking, you may find tobacco odors drifting in from other units or areas. I don't allow smoking inside my units but still encounter faint tobacco smells from time to time, and these tips are designed for that level of odor.

If you still detect carpet odors after following the cleaning process described above, try some of these steps (always wearing a dust mask or respirator when using chemicals).

**Ventilate.** Open the windows while you are working or put a fan in the doorway or windows.

**Spray.** Hold an aerosol disinfectant, such as Lysol, close to the carpet and cover the entire floor area. Use a respirator and do this prior to leaving the unit for the day. Repeat on your way out after the first few days you work at a rental unit. Focus on areas you think are the most malodorous. Allow some airing-out time before the next showing.

**Sprinkle.** Use baking soda (sodium bicarbonate) to dust all carpeted areas. Wear a dust mask or respirator and fling the baking soda outward with a small cup or ladle, thinly dusting the entire floor area. Then use a stiff broom to disburse and spread the powder into the carpet. Much of the baking soda will disappear into the fibers. Let it remain for a day or more then vacuum it up. Repeat if necessary.

If you have followed all these cleaning and odor fighting tips and the smell remains, then the carpet may not be worth saving.

But before you pull it up, try a sealer or odor-blocking primer on the walls. Often odors have seeped into walls and remain there even after you have cleared them out of the carpet. Several times I have been about to pull up the carpet in a unit when I found that using a shellac or oil-based sealer on the walls actually eliminated the smell (pet urine or tobacco), as it had permeated the walls and ceiling. Be sure to use a respirator and proper ventilation for oil-based primers and shellac sealers.

## Workflow Symphony

Getting a unit ready can require a hundred small tasks that interrelate. Take time to plan how you will approach them each day. Have a list of the order and process before you even leave the home. Here are a few tips.

**Put two or three easy tasks on the top of your list.** By walking right in and checking these off, you will be able to get into the workflow. For example, make your first task a useful one where you can't get stuck. Sometimes, I will just make "organize tools" and "clean out the vacuum filter" the first order of business, simply to knock off two items within a few minutes of walking into the unit. These types of tasks can also keep the workplace orderly and clean. If you think you may run into a tough task involving sticky parts or lots of elbow grease, put it last on the list, so that if you get stuck or it takes the rest of the day, you will have already done most of your tasks beforehand.

**Never watch paint dry.** Make sure you know dry times, and plan accordingly. Ideally, painting or staining is the last task on your way out the door; that way it can dry overnight. The same goes for cleaning surfaces for paint. Let them dry so they are ready to paint the next day. Always have an alternate item to move on to while paint or adhesive dries.

**Don't do it twice.** For example, clean the walls or counters before the floors, or else you just end up getting the floors dirty again with debris falling off the walls.

TIP
**Market your older carpet.** Landlords who allow pets can actually make outdated carpet a selling point (I often do). As long as it is clean and does not smell, older carpet can be a plus for tenants with pets. Let them know that the carpet is older and they should be careful, but not paranoid. Note on your move-in checklist that the carpet is worn, old, and near the end of its useful life. Some tenants are relieved to see older, darker carpet rather than brand new white or light carpet or expensive high-end flooring. They know the realities of pets and are more than happy to be free from the stress of worrying about their pet's paws. If you allow pets and have aged, dark carpet with some stains, think about keeping it if it is odor-free and clean.

## Kitchen and Appliances

Without a doubt, the most work for the landlord is usually in the kitchen, with its many features and moving parts. It's also one of the most important rooms to tenants, so you'll want to pay special attention to it.

During a showing or rental open house, tenants naturally gravitate to the kitchen. They open cabinets, fiddle with appliances, and feel the surfaces. More often than that not, the kitchen is also where I lay out all the forms and sign the paperwork with new tenants, and I don't want a stained floor or dirty countertop giving them second thoughts.

However, kitchens can also be among the most expensive parts of a house to remodel. So your better bet as a cost-conscious landlord is to use some simple techniques to renew and shine up your kitchen without spending a lot of money. This will also prevent a vacancy during a lengthy remodel. The tips below can help make your kitchen stand out from the competition.

## Cabinets

Clean cabinets inside and out. If faded or worn, refinish the surfaces of wood cabinets using the guidance in Chapter 3. Touch up any painted cabinets. Clean out all cabinets and drawers and lay down fresh lining paper. Tighten any cabinet knobs, handles, hinges, and interior doorknobs.

## Major Appliances

Landlords quickly learn some of the common problems, remedies, and life spans of most major appliances. You can also learn some tricks of the trade to spruce up the appliances in your unit, saving you money and time in the process.

### Testing Appliances

Tenants who are leaving do not always report appliance problems (perhaps for fear they may be implicated for misuse). So, inspect all the kitchen appliances when you clean. Look behind and under appliances for leaks and listen for problems when they are on and running. Also test them out by: running curtains or towels through the washer and dryer; turning on the dryer and going outside to check the air flow (it should feel like a blow dryer at the vent's exit); running the dishwasher empty, to rinse it out, and heating the oven after you have cleaned it and testing all the burners and surface elements. Set the oven temperature and put an oven thermometer inside to verify proper heat.

**RESOURCE**

**Check appliance user guides or manuals for troubleshooting and cleaning advice.** If you no longer have copies, you can usually find manuals on the manufacturer's website or at websites such as www.homeappliance.manualsonline.com or www.manualsonline.com. If a repair problem seems too complex, hire an appliance repair specialist.

## Repair or Replace?

The most important early decision to make regarding a questionable appliance is, should you try and repair it or just replace it? The answer depends on the age of the appliance, the type of problem, and the labor costs for appliance repair work in your area, as follows.

**Repair the appliance if:** the repair would be minor, like a broken handle, hose, seal, adjustment, or small part, and the appliance is relatively new (three years or less for most appliances). This is especially true if the repair cost is far less than the cost of a new appliance.

**Replace the appliance if:** the repair involves a major component, such as a motor, or would cost (with labor) one half or more of the cost of a new appliance. No sense throwing good money after bad by replacing parts on a used appliance that's reaching the end of its useful life.

To find out the age of your home's components, check your purchase receipts or tax records. Or, for appliances that came with the unit, try sites like these:

- Appliance411: www.appliance411.com/service/date-code.php, and
- ApplianceAid.com: www.applianceaid.com/how-old-is-my-appliance.php.

By simply entering the manufacturer, these sites will give you that company's code for the month and year of production (found in the serial number).

CAUTION

**Replace an old hot water heater before, not after it springs a leak.** As a general rule, you'll need to replace a hot water heater every seven to ten years. If your unit's hot water heater is in this age range, consider buying a new one. Replace the hot water heater immediately if it is causing problems, performing poorly, or is over ten years old. Previous owners often forget to list the age of the hot water heater in disclosures or simply do not know when it was installed. As with many appliances, you will practically need a code breaker to determine how the numbers in the serial code indicate the date of manufacture. For helpful information, check websites like the International Association of Certified Home Inspectors (www.nachi.org/water-heater-dating-chart.htm).

## Life Span of Common Appliances

Consider the relative life span of appliances when making the decision whether to repair or replace them.

| Appliance | Average Life | Appliance | Average Life |
|---|---|---|---|
| Exhaust Fan | 10 years | Microwave | 9 years |
| Compactors | 6 years | Ranges, Electric | 13 years |
| Dishwashers | 9 years | Ranges, Gas | 15 years |
| Disposal | 12 years | Range Hoods | 14 years |
| Dryers, Electric | 13 years | Refrigerators | 13 years |
| Dryers, Gas | 13 years | Washers | 10 years |
| Freezers | 11 years | | |

**Source:** *Appliance Magazine*, September 2005, Grainger

**TIP**

**Consider the environmental impact of your appliance decisions.** Of course, you want to try and keep appliances out of the landfill and avoid the carbon footprint of producing and shipping a new one when you can. This may sway you to repair an appliance with some useful life left in it. However, also consider that older appliances, even those from just a decade ago, are far less energy efficient than the ones on the market today. So it may be better in the long term to replace an older appliance with a new, energy-efficient model. This can also save the tenant money and use fewer resources in the long run.

## Ovens and Ranges

Here are some tips to make an aged oven work well and look good enough for another tenancy:

- Spray low-odor oven cleaner on the inside of the stove and on stains and burned-on debris on the door and lip. Let it sit overnight and wipe clean. (Always use gloves for this task.)
- Replace the stove drip pans or bowls (the exact pan will vary by stove model); it is often easier to replace these than to clean old blackened ones.
- Apply the proper color appliance chip/scratch repair to any scratches. This product comes in a nail polish container and is available in most common appliance colors. It is a durable epoxy with strong fumes, so use a respirator when applying.
- Take the metallic filter from the oven hood vent and place it in a bucket of leftover TSP solution (the same bucket and solution from the wall cleaning is ideal). Rinse it clean. Let the filter dry in the sun or in the sink. Then put it back in place.

## Refrigerators

Refrigerators are among a home's largest and most expensive appliances. The good news is, they usually don't need much maintenance. Beyond cleaning (especially the interior where bad food smells can linger for a long time), most new models are maintenance-free. The more common refrigerator problems include clogged drip lines, failing door gaskets, and fan or compressor malfunctions. Unfortunately, the labor and materials costs for many refrigerator repairs can make replacement a better decision. This is especially true when you suspect a potential failure that might one day ruin hundreds of dollars of the tenant's food and beverages. Failure to properly keep food cool can also be a safety risk. So it often pays to replace a refrigerator if there is a substantial problem.

Experience has taught me that more often than not, when a tenant complains about a refrigerator (loud, not cooling, condensation, and so forth), it means a replacement is in order. It is seldom worth the risk to try and move these heavy appliances around in order to work on them, due to the risk of injury. And most of my attempts at repair just delayed the inevitable purchase— and left me with a sore back.

TIP

**Buy right.** If you do purchase a new refrigerator, buy the most reliable, longest lasting basic model, without any extra features (like ice makers or water dispensers, which require extra lines and can cause problems). You can look for energy efficiency, a selling point for tenants if they pay the electric bill (and a selling point for you if you pay). Be sure to negotiate for delivery of the new refrigerator and make sure the vendor will take away your old one. Refrigerators can contain environmental hazards and must be properly disposed of.

## Dishwashers and Garbage Disposals

Other than cleaning, dishwashers and garbage disposals are often maintenance-free. However, tenants frequently drop bottle caps, plastic utensils, and other debris in garbage disposals. To remove items from a disposal, turn it off, then use needle-nose pliers to fish them out. With dishwashers, check your model to see if it has a screen or drain on the floor. Debris can build up here and need periodic cleaning.

## Sinks and Drains

Slow-flowing drains are an inconvenience for tenants and can create a disaster if someone leaves the water running, causing a small flood. So don't ever rent out a unit without clear, fast-flowing drains. Test for trouble, and use the guidance in Chapter 3 to fix drains.

Don't forget to check under the sink, where it probably looks like a maze of hoses and lines. Use a flashlight to check for leaks and signs of water. If you suspect moisture but are unsure, place newspaper under the sink and run the water, or even put in the stopper and let the kitchen sink fill up. Look again for drips and try to locate their source. Pause before detaching your drain lines or supply lines. That may be your first instinct, but these can be fussy. Sometimes a slight twist to tighten a piece will do the trick. If you think you need new undersink supply lines or drain lines, call a plumber.

In your onboarding process and walkthrough with new tenants (described in Chapter 8), show the tenant the undersink area and explain how these pipes can be delicate. Ask them to avoid banging and forcing bottles or bags into the undersink area. Also, ask tenants to keep an eye out for leaks.

## Kitchen Counters

It usually does not make economic sense to replace countertops unless they are badly damaged or coming apart. Instead, clean them and make the edges up against the wall look shiny and new with caulk (see the caulk tips in Chapter 3).

# Bathrooms

The bathroom procedures you'll want to implement are largely a repeat of others discussed earlier in this chapter. To make the space appealing to tenants, thoroughly clean walls, floors, and countertops; spruce up the cabinets (just like you'd do for kitchen cabinets) and vanity; clear slow drains in sinks, showers, and tubs; and caulk around vanities, sinks, and in showers and bathtubs. That just leaves the toilet. This feature found only in bathrooms is covered in depth in Chapter 3.

After cleaning and sprucing up, add a new shower curtain, floor mat, and toilet seat (leave the plastic on so the seat stays brand new), and you are well on your way to having the room ready for the next tenant. Also, tighten or replace all towel rods, replace burned-out lightbulbs, and make sure any bath fan is working and that the shower and/or bathtub, toilet, and sink are all operating properly. Buy a new flat bath stopper (or insert style), and leave it with the tub, in its package. Consider adding a new nonslip tub mat and extra hooks on the back of the bathroom door.

## Light Fixtures and Outlets

Check that all electrical outlets are working, clean the light fixtures, and check lightbulbs, including those in the stove and refrigerator. Check all exterior lights, including any motion detector lights.

## Doors and Windows

Clean all doors and windows. Spray sliding glass door rails with silicone lubricant. Repair or replace broken window screens or cracked or cloudy windows (that have lost their seal). Touch up any scraped or stained areas on windowsills or doors. Make sure all door and window locks are in good working order (more on this below). Clean the curtains or blinds and replace if damaged.

## Closets

Someday, someone will research the unique relationship tenants have with closet doors. For whatever reason, a smoothly operating closet door that works flawlessly when you rent the unit will be off the rails, stuck, or simply removed and tucked away in the closet corner when it come time for the move out.

Even a small unit can have four or five closets, counting bedrooms, pantries, hallway, entry, and utility closets, and you want to make sure all are in good shape before new tenants move in. Check the tracks, the rollers, and all the hardware on closet doors. Look for gaps, sagging, or friction. Because they are under constant use, closet components can often loosen or need adjustment. Add silicone-based lubricant to the rails and rollers. Tighten screws, and adjust the height or plumb if the door is dragging on the floor.

The closet rods that hold the clothes and hangers along with the shelves often get broken or overloaded, so buy extra brackets and support for your closet shelves. And you can buy adjustable metal closet rods, or use an unfinished wooden dowel rod (sold in long sections at a big box store, cut to size, and finished with a stain/ polyurethane product).

At the move-in process, mention closets and how they operate to the new tenant. Go over common reasons closet doors go off the rails (overcrowded, abuse), and show tenants how to get them back on the rails. Also, many tenants try to do creative things with closets (making them book or desk areas). Be sure and remind tenants that if they are taking off a closet door, you can help with this process, and to be sure to save all the hardware and label it.

---

### Creative Closet Solutions

If you have a closet door that looks broken, lost, or beyond repair, try this simple solution that has worked a dozen times for me:

- remove the broken closet doors and hardware
- find an attractive adjustable tension curtain rod or use a shower curtain rod (making sure that the rod spans the opening), and
- measure the height and length and find an attractive curtain with loops or grommets and attach it to the curtain rod—just make sure it slides easily.

You now have a "curtain" closet door. This is a trouble-free, low-cost way to create a closet door that's hard to break. It's attractive, covers the closet clutter, and the tenant can easily open and close it. The tenant can even pull the curtain to one side or take it down easily. You can run the curtain through the washer if it gets dusty, and ultimately hang a new curtain in its place, most likely when the unit turns over.

---

# Smoke Detectors, Fire Extinguishers, and Carbon Monoxide Detectors

Check your smoke detectors, fire extinguishers, and carbon monoxide detectors. Make sure you comply with all related safety requirements (check your local fire department for details). Pay particular attention to:

- smoke detectors—test their function and replace or add batteries

- fire extinguishers—if you don't yet have them, it's best to mount fire extinguishers on the kitchen wall or under a sink or accessible spot in a closet, and
- carbon monoxide detectors—even if your city or state doesn't require carbon monoxide detectors, consider putting them in the bedrooms of your units, especially rental units with garages, near parking areas, or with any fuel-burning heater or appliance.

# Perimeter and Outside

Most exterior maintenance will be covered in Chapter 5, but some items are important to handle when the unit is vacant.

## Front Door and Porch

The best time to paint and/or maintain the front door and porch is when the tenants (and their pets) have moved out. Otherwise, you risk one of them touching (or wagging a tail against) the newly painted door or walking on the freshly painted porch. And if you need to leave the door open to let the paint dry, it is really feasible to do so only when the unit is vacant (and while you are working there).

Sweep and possibly wash the porch area to make sure that it's clean and free of debris. Check that the doorbell works and that the steps or railings haven't come loose.

## Door Locks

Changing the locks is a routine you will get used to. It's best to do it when the unit is vacant, because otherwise you'll have to dodge traffic going in and out, and potential escaping pets. Locks come in a range of prices and styles. Because they are used every day and relate to safety, you're better off buying a higher-end model. In fact, I struggled replacing doorknobs, locks, and deadbolts until I happened on a higher-end brand that installs flawlessly in minutes every time. I noticed it was the only kind the local locksmith would use. So, find out the brand your local locksmith uses and give it a try, check out reviews online, or hire a professional locksmith. Make sure you comply with all state rules regarding security and locks.

## Windows

Clean both sides of the windows well, and spray silicone lubricant into the window cranks or sliders. You can use the same wood-refinishing process on the sills that you used for cabinet refinishing. But use rubbing alcohol to clean any surface mold or dark areas first.

## Yard

If you have a yard, trim back shrubs or trees around the house, mow the lawn, and clear all litter or debris. Add bark or gravel to paths and repair gates and fences. There are more tips for minimizing lawn and yard work in Chapter 5.

## Driveway, Sidewalks, and Parking Areas

There are some remarkably simple "add water and mix" products for small cracks or holes in your driveway or sidewalks. As with many projects in highly trafficked areas, the ideal time for these is when the tenants are gone.

 **RESOURCE**
**For useful products and advice (including videos) on concrete patching and repair**, see the Sakrete website at www.sakrete.com.

## Bugs, Pests, and Rodents

If you have a pest problem or suspect one, consider hiring an exterminator or firm specializing in the type of problem you face. Even if you don't have a pest problem, it's worth taking precautionary steps, by covering perimeters and nooks and crannies with pest deterrents. Some of these are harsh chemicals, however.

One of the best less-toxic deterrents for ants, cockroaches, and other pests is a Borax and sugar mix. Mix one part Borax to nine parts sugar. My method is to put a teaspoon of borax into a plastic bag and nine teaspoons of sugar. Shake. Sprinkle this under appliances or behind cabinets. The ants or roaches will take the mixture back to the colony, causing a collapse. The mix stays effective as long as it is dry.

> **TIP**
>
> **Most of my successful battles with pests have involved outthinking them—not winning a chemical battle.** Avoid potentially dangerous pesticides and traps by identifying the pest and what may be attracting it or causing it to come to your rentals in the first place. For example, there may be openings that are allowing rodents into the units. Trying to kill them after they've entered may not solve the underlying problem. Learn more about Integrated Pest Management (IPM) at this Cornell University website: www.nysipm.cornell.edu.

## Marshalling Your Materials and Supplies

Half the job in turning around a unit can be having everything you need to do the job in the right place at the right time. Nothing stops your momentum on Saturday morning like a missing item or running out of a needed product. Properly mobilizing your materials and tools efficiently can dramatically speed up your turnaround process and save you time and money.

A full-time landlord will likely have a van already stocked with needed items and perhaps a shop as well; but this is not feasible for a part-time landlord. Instead, you'll have your supplies and tools organized at home, following my advice in Chapter 3. Whenever you have a turnaround (or any time you need to do repairs or maintenance), you will load up your personal vehicle, and transport everything you'll need to the rental unit. The first few times may be hectic, but with a good system and process, it becomes easier and even relatively efficient. You can even do it in one trip.

## Organizing Supplies

Start a week out from a turnaround and begin making a list of the materials, cleaners, and tools you will need in the upcoming project. I like to post my list in my materials storage areas, then I add to it when I get new ideas for what I will need to complete the turnaround. The entire scope of every task and material needed in a turnaround will seldom hit you in one fell swoop. Rather, as you think about the process and the unit, you will incrementally recall its maintenance needs and problems, which may number in the hundreds.

Keeping organized maintenance records, as recommended in Chapter 5, will also help. You may think back to prior work in the unit, its needs, or get new maintenance ideas. And your "to-do list" for the turnaround will actually mesh with your materials and tools list, because certain tasks will require specific tools and supplies. I like to list the task (like paint the door) on one side of the paper and the materials needed on the other (brushes, paint, tape, etc.). As you get closer to the planned work date, start loading the actual items on your lists into your totes, bags, or boxes (discussed next).

## Carrying the Weight

How do you carry a hundred things of various sizes, and keep them relatively organized and ready to use when you get to the job? Someday, someone will probably market the landlord carryall kit. Until then, you need sturdy, low-cost, containers that allow a lot of volume but keep visibility. Ideally, your containers are not one more thing to buy, but rather something you already have or can appropriate or give a second life.

The best containers I've used are laundry baskets (often giving a second life to damaged ones); plastic totes; and very large, reusable synthetic shopping bags from the local warehouse store. You can segregate your items so that one tote or bag has painting equipment and another has cleaning products. Your storage containers may be dictated by what you have or what fits best in your car.

The best vehicle for almost any landlord, in my opinion, is the one you already have. It is the cheapest, and should work just fine unless perhaps you drive a motorcycle, two-seat convertible, or exotic sports car. The small-time landlord won't need a van, truck, or trailer. Any sedan or hatchback is ideal, and you can fit everything you need for the average turnaround into your trunk. Lay-down seats work great for larger objects like vacuums. Use delivery services from the vendor for lumber, appliances, and large quantities of landscaping material.

---

### What to Wear: Rags to Riches

You can save a fortune in paper towel expenses, help the environment, and protect your clothes with a simple process. When your daily or day job clothes get too frayed, stained, or old, they can become ideal landlord clothes. When your landlord work clothes get too damaged or torn for landlord duty, make them rags for your cleaning arsenal, saving paper towels. If the rags are just used for cleaning with household cleaner, you can even wash and reuse them. Keep the cycle going from work clothes to landlord clothes to rags.

---

## Setting Up Shop at the Rental Unit

Once you've toted all your supplies from your car into the vacant rental unit, pause and think about how you can situate them for easy access over the coming days of work. It's often best to keep cleaning supplies and other items in the bags, totes, or boxes. This serves to organize them and lets you move them easily. Think about a corner of the kitchen, a hallway closet, or any existing shelving for your main storage area. You will ordinarily want to store supplies off the carpet (vacuumed first) and away from the walls (cleaned right away). The top shelf of a closet can be a place where you can take some items out and arrange them. Then remaining totes, bags, or boxes fit into the closet.

Think about a system that lets you see all your materials and make sure you will not trip over the items or have to move them repeatedly.

This completes the process of getting the tools and supplies selected, transported, and organized in the unit in preparation for your turnaround process. However, keep a running list of additional supplies you may need, and bring these items from home or pick them up on the way to the unit.

## The Minor Remodel: Doing It on the Cheap

Your goal is to try and be a refinisher and cleaner rather than a remodeler. But occasionally, a unit will need enough improvements that you soon find you are practically remodeling it.

When you turn around a unit to prepare it for the new tenant, there will no doubt be certain items that need extra attention. Occasionally, you may face a unit that needs almost everything. This is particularly likely when you buy a new unit or have a very long tenancy with a lot of wear and tear.

A minor remodel without breaking the bank might include:
- removing old carpet or other damaged flooring
- repainting the entire unit
- refinishing the cabinets
- replacing flooring (use an easy to apply laminate flooring or hire a flooring contractor)
- replacing appliances
- replacing faucets and showerhead, and
- replacing toilets (or using the overhaul kit described in Chapter 3).

Try and leave your existing counters, doors, windows, interior trim, cabinets, vanities, and sinks. If you have one newer appliance, keep it and make the other new ones match it.

With a well-timed process, you can get through the minor remodel in less than a month and well under one year's gross rent, depending on the size of the unit, grade of flooring and appliances used, and use of outside contractors, such as plumbers.

### Don't Let Up

Even when you're all done prepping the unit and just driving over to show it to tenants, keep a bottle of spray cleaner, a small vacuum, and some wet wipes in a closet at the rental. Keep cleaning and dusting every time you stop by. Develop a plan for a pleasing but not overpowering smell, as well. Clean and shiny units attract better tenants. Remember, you are seeking to get an excellent tenant to sign a legal agreement to live a year of his or her life in your property. Don't let stray dust or some trash out front drive the person away.

Also, try to arrive at your units 15 to 30 minutes before showings begin. This way, you can sweep the front porch and pick up any stray trash, leaves, or debris. While you wait inside for showings, continue to clean even the small details of your unit with a pleasant scented all-purpose cleaner. More detail on planning and preparing for showings is in Chapter 7.

## Handing Off the Turnaround Work: Hiring Help

Every landlord should try and turn around a few units for the education and experience. But time, costs, skills, distance, or health may necessitate handing off part or all of the duties. How much or little of the process you delegate depends on your given circumstances.

If you are looking to hand off most of the duties surrounding unit preparation, look for a "make-ready" service that specializes in all the small tasks. There are often firms that do this in larger population centers, serving property managers and rental owners.

Or you could hand off some of the common turnaround tasks by using a painter, carpet cleaner, or housecleaning service.

Perhaps part of your turnaround process will involve hiring a handyman (or woman) to handle some minor tasks which you don't have the time or skills to do—whether it be getting a gate fixed, a hole patched, or a half dozen sticky widgets repaired. The labor and materials for these minor tasks may only be a few hundred dollars, which is not enough to attract a larger contractor or company.

All the same rules and best practices on hiring contractors in Chapter 6 still apply (and that chapter has more info on hiring a handyperson). Always screen your handyperson candidates closely, check their references and insurance, get written estimates, and make sure they have any required business license and no record of outstanding complaints.

## What's Next?

Preparing a unit for a new tenant can be a challenging and rewarding frenzy of activity. But even after your tenant is moved in, your work on the rental property continues in the form of regular and seasonal maintenance. This is our next topic in Chapter 5. Ongoing rental maintenance entails not only specific routines and tasks, but also developing some personal habits and practices to help keep up your building and retain your tenants. ●

# The Art of Rental Maintenance

Maintenance and repairs are about more than just tips and procedures for completing a task. Adopting certain patterns, practices, and habits will help you develop a maintenance mindset as a landlord. This can help you keep your tenants happy, your rentals in top shape, and you from getting burnt out (or sued). You won't be able to be a long-term landlord (our goal) if you're constantly rushing from one property crisis to another.

Whether you face saltwater corrosion at your Hawaii beach rental or deep snow removal in Minnesota, the guidance in this chapter should help you develop a systematic approach to the maintenance of your rental property.

## Maintenance—It's About Tenant Satisfaction, Too!

While you want to develop an active maintenance plan to preserve your building and retain its value, I find that maintaining a property is just as important to retaining tenants. If you have any doubt, let your roof fail (leak), and the first thing you'll see is an exodus of your former tenants (and their reliable rent checks). In fact, tenants will leave over far more minor concerns (one tenant once told me she was thinking of moving on at the end of her lease because of a clogged drain, which I quickly fixed with five dollars' worth of drain cleaner).

Remember, we invest in rental properties primarily for the rents they produce, and these rents come from satisfied, long-term tenants. And while most books focus on the preservation of the property as the motivating factor behind maintenance, I suggest thinking about the people, too. Often, when working on your rental property, you are also simultaneously cementing your relationship with tenants. I even find if I'm working on the unit near the end of the month, tenants like to hand me the rent check in person (even though I give them SASEs) and let me know they appreciate the work. It's a tangible example of our respective duties in the lease—mine to keep up the place and the tenant's to pay the rent.

But the task of providing ongoing maintenance is not always easy. There are countless moving parts in every rental—from major components (such as the roof and plumbing) to smaller parts (surfaces, knobs, rails, hinges, switches, and cranks). Ideally, every piece of the machinery contributes to your tenant's satisfaction—but the opposite effect can occur, if you allow these moving parts to fall into disrepair. Tenants' interest in a unit can deflate over something as small as a broken oven door handle, a worn out bedroom light switch, or a sagging cabinet door. Don't lose a great tenant because a $50 faucet leaks or the toilet won't flush properly.

Attending to the smaller details can also prevent larger problems. Without a 79-cent doorstop, a doorknob will eventually get slammed through a wall. And small leaks under sinks can cause mold, rot, and structural problems over time—all of which could make the unit uninhabitable or expensive to repair.

Neglecting maintenance not only decreases tenant satisfaction and leads to bigger repair bills, it can, in the worst case, result in legal problems (such as tenant rent withholding), and liability issues (if a tenant or guest suffers an injury because of an unsafe condition at your rental). Your challenge is to keep every part working safely and to the tenant's satisfaction for the entire tenancy.

## Learning What Level of Maintenance and Repairs the Law Requires

While the level of maintenance and care I recommend in this book should generally keep you well away from legal trouble, acquaint yourself with what your state's statutes, case law, local housing codes, and other regulations say about your responsibilities to keep rental premises livable. These include meeting minimum requirements for heat, hot water, plumbing, and other essential services, as well as a more general legal obligation to provide safe, fit, and habitable housing—for example, you need to avoid dangerous or unsafe conditions such as a slippery surfaces in winter, loose boards on walkways, and any uneven surfaces. You must comply with all state and local housing codes, and provide special care depending on your climate (I include a whole section on managing snow and ice below). Your duty of care extends to tenants as well as their guests and invitees.

If you fail to maintain minimum housing standards, you face the prospect of conflicts with tenants and legal liability. A disgruntled tenant might (depending on where your rental property is located):

- withhold rent
- make the repair and deduct the cost from the rent paid
- sue you to cover damages to personal property, medical bills, and so on, or
- move out before the lease term is up.

Not only must you meet your legal responsibilities to provide habitable housing, you must respect tenant privacy when doing so, More than half the states set specific rules for landlord's access to rental property to make repairs (24 hours' notice is common), and they sometimes limit the landlord's right to make periodic property inspections. At a bare minimum, landlords have to meet these standards and should do so. However, the larger goal is not just to keep out of legal trouble, but to keep up your property and retain great tenants over the long term with an even higher level of service than your competitors.

## Resources on Your Legal Responsibilities for Repairs and Maintenance

*Every Landlord's Legal Guide* by Marcia Stewart, Ralph Warner, and Janet Portman (Nolo), provides detailed advice on landlord responsibilities for repairs and maintenance, including environmental hazards; tenant options if you fail to meet these responsibilities; your liability for injuries and losses to tenants and others; and related issues, such as limits on how and when you may enter rental property to make repairs. This extensive book includes a detailed system for tracking and handling repairs and tenant complaints.

For dozens of free articles on the subject of repairs and maintenance, including state-by-state rules regarding tenant rights to withhold rent and make repairs or deduct the cost of the repairs from the rent, notice required for landlords to enter rental property, and related issues regarding your responsibility to provide habitable rental premises, see the Landlords section of www.nolo.com.

## Developing a Maintenance Mentality

An active and effective maintenance program begins with the one doing the maintenance or hiring people to do it—that is, you. You may wonder what level of expertise you might need. No doubt, your interests in maintenance and diligence are strong in some areas and weaker in others. Think about how you approach car ownership. Are you the type who performs every maintenance task right on schedule (even doing the work yourself), or someone who drives until the car breaks down? Most car owners probably are in the middle—trying to follow the recommended maintenance plan from the dealer and handing off most of the maintenance tasks. This analogy works for your rental property, too.

As a part-time landlord, your goal should be at least in the middle and preferably toward the more diligent end of this maintenance spectrum with your properties. This will involve doing the routine maintenance recommended in this chapter and handing off major projects to contractors (as described in Chapter 6), such as work involving HVAC, or heating, ventilation, and air conditioning. This will keep your property running smoothly.

 TIP

**Know which projects must be done and which ones can wait.** Knowing your property condition, available funding, and useful life of common home components is crucial. As you build equity in your rental properties, there may be available financing for some major projects (equity loans or lines of credit), but the building should, in theory, pay for its repairs through rents.

## Do-It-Yourself Maintenance Helps You Keep an Eye on the Property

Along with saving money, one side benefit to doing a number of maintenance tasks on your own, such as lawn mowing or painting, is that you will be spending time at the rental unit. This can help you better understand the property and the people living there.

When on site at your unit, you could spot and fix a small building problem, like a clogged downspout or gap around a window, before it becomes a big one. You will see which cars come and go, which units are quiet, which are noisy, and whether there are any problems, such as unauthorized pets (or occupants). You might spot a nuisance or safety issue, like clutter blocking back doors or barbecues propped against your building (a fire and smoke hazard). The maintenance routine is, in short, also a simple way to simultaneously do regular property inspections, make your presence felt, and catch little problems (be they tenant- or property-related) before they become big ones.

> ⓘ **CAUTION**
>
> **Don't be an overly intrusive landlord.** Taking care of needed maintenance and problems is well and good, but don't overdo it, such as by stopping by the rental at all hours, "just to check in." A rental unit is your tenants' home and you should respect their privacy. Also, many states have rules restricting landlord access to rental property (you'll find details in the resources mentioned above), so be sure you stay on the right side of the law.

## Enlist Your Tenant's Help in Identifying Repair and Maintenance Issues

A key to successful maintenance is to enlist tenants as your eyes and ears. Keep them aware of how they can help and their role in the process. Your lease and move-in letter to new tenants (discussed in Chapter 8), should request that tenants immediately report safety issues, such as a loose step or broken lock, or major problems such as leaking pipes. You should also encourage tenants to report things like evidence of mice, unusual noises in appliances, or clogged roof gutters. Because tenants live in the unit, they usually know better than anyone if something is wrong.

Early reporting of repair and maintenance problems can help prevent small issues from becoming big, expensive fixes. I recently had a tenant tell me she heard the sound of water below her unit. Sure enough, a pipe in the crawlspace had a small pinhole leak. It was caught quickly before the crawlspace filled up with water and overwhelmed the sump pump, which would have caused flooding and damage.

## Make It Easy for Tenants to Report Maintenance and Repair Problems

Most of your tenant contacts about repair and maintenance will probably be by phone, text, or email. Be sure to thank the tenant and follow up (as mentioned below). This informal channel is how I get most tenant maintenance or repair requests, and this is especially how you want to hear about a potential leak or dangerous problem—right away.

Be sure to keep a record of how and when you handled tenant repair and maintenance requests (as explained at the end of this chapter), including reasons for any delays in fixing something. This will help avoid problems such as a tenant withholding rent, claiming you failed to handle repairs in a timely manner (check your state law on when and how tenants may withhold rent or pay for a repair themselves and deduct the cost from the rent).

But you can also be effective at catching maintenance or safety concerns with an annual or semiannual form for tenants to fill out. This is not as much for emergencies or immediately needed repairs but for issues the tenant may have spotted—like the dryer not heating up well, carpet starting to come loose, the refrigerator running loudly, or signs of mice. Plus, it's a good place for any safety or security concerns the tenant might have.

I actually send a letter requesting any information about maintenance problems or repair needs with my holiday card to tenants (along with a small gift certificate). That way, it is routine and easy for me to remember each holiday season (and ideally, fun for them to receive, too).

You could develop your own method of getting regular input from tenants. For example, you could use the sample Semiannual Safety and Maintenance Update shown below as a model in preparing your own form for tenants.

## Should You Let Tenants Paint the Unit Themselves?

Eventually, you will have tenants who want to paint a rental unit—either before they move in or sometime during their tenancy. This poses many risks and few rewards for the landlord. The tenant could spill or drip paint on the floor, make a mess when cleaning up (it will stain the sink and bathtub), or even fall off a ladder. I do not let new tenants paint.

If the place really needs painting (walls are stained, full of nicks and holes), I suggest doing it yourself or hiring someone to paint before you show the rental (per my advice in Chapter 4).

I feel differently about my good, very long-term tenants. If they are strongly interested, I sometimes let them personalize their space in a minor way with paint, and maybe limit the initial painting to one small room or an accent wall. This is good tenant relations, helping them settle in and stay even longer. Ask about the tenant's level of painting experience; give adequate instructions; stress the problems related to drips and spills. I even buy tenants a drop cloth or tarp and painter's tape.

Try to limit the tenants' color choices to neutrals. Then make sure you get the paint codes, in case you need to touch it up later. If your tenant is really set on an unusual color choice (which is often the case), such as dark red, explain that you expect the tenant to repaint the unit to its original neutral color upon moving out, or to have the cost of repainting deducted from the security deposit. In my experience, however, asking tenants to do a perfect, clean paint job on the way out is unrealistic. They probably wouldn't have the incentive (even with a deposit at stake) or energy to do it well or even at all. Moving alone is an exhausting task.

If you do let tenants paint, set clear limits and expectations. Put all of your agreements regarding painting in writing—for example, what you've agreed upon regarding paint color and brand, and your expectations as to what color the paint will be when the tenant leaves, the condition of the walls, and other key issues.

## Be Responsive to Tenant Concerns

Keep open communications with your tenants and encourage them to let you know about any repair or maintenance issues or problems. Be open and responsive: "*I am glad you caught that. Thanks for letting me know.*" (Responding with annoyance or hostility tends to inhibit tenants' reporting problems.) Then follow up with a resolution. Reward the behavior and keep open communication.

Communication breakdowns can be costly. When tenants feel they can't get through to you, or do not feel like it's worth contacting you with issues, then a small unreported maintenance problem easily becomes a costlier fix.

# Establishing the Maintenance Habit

I highly recommend that every landlord develop a regular system for maintaining property. This won't happen on day one. But ideally, it can become a habit over time, something you can do without thinking too much about it.

> **RESOURCE**
>
> **Get in the habit.** The book *The Power of Habit: Why We Do What We Do in Life and Business*, by Charles Duhigg (Random House), discusses the tremendous power habits can have in business and personal management.

The key to developing and imprinting effective habits is to identify cues that signal you to engage in some routine, and then to have a reward of some sort at the end of the routine. The reward may be a treat for yourself, or it may simply be the sense of accomplishment at the end. You can build your own cues, routines, and rewards.

Living in Alaska as I do, I've learned that two inches of snow means it's time to start shoveling. I watch the local weather for this cue or just look out the window. The announcement or sight of two inches of snow or more is my cue to do my snow removal routine (shovel, sweep, spread ice melt). It can be exhilarating exercise and I

## Sample Semiannual Safety and Maintenance Update

### Semiannual Safety and Maintenance Update

Please complete the following checklist and note any safety or maintenance problems in your unit or on the premises.

Please describe the specific problems and the rooms or areas involved. Here are some examples of the types of things we want to know about: garage roof leaks, excessive mildew in rear bedroom closet, fuses blow out frequently, door lock sticks, water comes out too hot in shower, exhaust fan above stove doesn't work, smoke alarm malfunctions, peeling paint, and mice in basement. Please point out any potential safety and security problems in the neighborhood and anything you consider a serious nuisance.

Please indicate the approximate date when you first noticed the problem and list any other recommendations or suggestions for improvement.

Please return this form with this month's rent check. Thank you.

—The Management

Name: _____Mary Griffin_____

Address: _____392 Main St., #402____Houston, Texas_____

Please indicate (and explain below) problems with:

☐ Floors and floor coverings _____

☐ Walls and ceilings _____

☐ Windows, screens, and doors _____

☐ Window coverings (drapes, miniblinds, etc.) _____

☐ Electrical system and light fixtures _____

☑ Plumbing (sinks, bathtub, shower, or toilet) _Water pressure low in shower_

☐ Heating or air conditioning system _____

☑ Major appliances (stove, oven, dishwasher, refrigerator) _Exhaust fan broken_

☑ Basement or attic _Front door lock sticks_____

☐ Locks or security system _____

☐ Smoke detector _____

☐ Fireplace _____

☐ Cupboards, cabinets, and closets_____

**Source:** *Every Landlord's Legal Guide,* by Marcia Stewart, Ralph Warner and Janet Portman (Nolo). Copyright Nolo 2014

## Sample Semiannual Safety and Maintenance Update, continued

☐ Furnishings (table, bed, mirrors, chairs) _____

☐ Laundry facilities_____

☐ Elevator _____

☐ Stairs and handrails_____

☐ Hallway, lobby, and common areas _____

☐ Garage _____

☐ Patio, terrace, or deck _____

☑ Lawn, fences, and ground   _Shrubs near back stairway need pruning_

☐ Pool and recreational facilities_____

☐ Roof, exterior walls, and other structural elements _____

☐ Driveway and sidewalks _____

☐ Neighborhood _____

☑ Nuisances _Tenant in #501 often plays stereo too loud_____

☐ Other _____

Specifics of problems:  _____

_____

_____

Other comments: _____

_____

_____

Tenant _Mary Griffin_____   Date _February 1, 20xx___

• • • • • • • • • • • • • • • • • • • • • • • • • • • • • • • • • • • • •

### FOR MANAGEMENT USE

Action/Response:  _Fixed kitchen exhaust fan and sticking front door lock on_

_February 15, and adjusted water pressure in shower. Pruned shrubs on February 21._

_Spoke with tenant in #501 about keeping stereo low on February 2._

Landlord/Manager _Terri Zimet_____   Date _February 22, 20xx___

**Source:** *Every Landlord's Legal Guide,* by Marcia Stewart, Ralph Warner and Janet Portman (Nolo).
Copyright Nolo 2014

get to see walkways clear of snow—a reward that has worked for me. It's a sense of accomplishment, at least until the next snowfall.

Cues for maintenance habits are important, because most landlords will not randomly get up one day and decide off the top of their heads, "I need to clean out gutters." And even if they did, the randomness would make them less effective at the task. Rather, some regular, periodic habits or routines will allow you to handle major maintenance tasks when the work is necessary. Some of the easiest cues are the changing seasons, weather conditions, or other hints that I'll discuss further along in this chapter.

**TIP**

**Sync home maintenance with rental property maintenance.** I do this with my home and my fourplex. For example, when my own lawn is ready to mow, I know it's time to mow the fourplex. I can even finish one and do the next the same day (wearing the same work clothes). I get only one set of clothes dirty and have to take one shower after both. The same goes for gutters, tree trimming, and snow removal. If your rental is nearby, the weather is likely very similar, so you may have around the same snowfall, growth of grass and trees, leaves in fall, and more.

## Common Maintenance Cues: A Seasonal Routine

In much of the country, the natural changing of the seasons provides good cues for routine property maintenance. This works best where there are distinct seasons or weather changes, such as on the East Coast or in the Midwest.

For example, my cue to clean out the gutters in the fall is watching the falling leaves. As soon as all the leaves are gone, I know I can go up one time to clean out gutters (no sense going up repeatedly). By now, I've developed a routine with water hoses and a ladder. Of course, as I clean out the leaves from the gutters, I can see the tree branches that have grown too close to the building and cut them. While I'm there with a ladder, I brush and vacuum out the dryer vents from the outside as part of my fall maintenance ritual.

Seasonal or periodic maintenance will vary by climate, but the key is in having routines. Even if you have a steady year-round climate, you can do maintenance around certain holidays, or mark tasks for certain months on a calendar. For example, even if the weather has not changed, you could set spring-cleaning at your rental (for cleaning the yard or outside of windows) for the first day of spring. Or you could make your annual Inspection early in the new year, like every January.

## Winter Maintenance

Winter poses one of the most challenging times for landlords in much of the country. Cold climates with significant snow, ice, or wind and other storms can create hazards and test your property-maintenance skills and abilities. Just getting your own driveway and steps cleared of snow or debris may be more than enough of a challenge. As a landlord, you'll have one or more additional properties to maintain. Here are key tips for surviving winter challenges. This section focuses on areas of the country with heavy snowfall. If you live in a milder climate, you may have different challenges in winter, such as heavy rains.

### Clarify Snow-Removal Duties

Before you start shoveling snow, be sure and clarify your duties (versus the tenant's), which may depend on:

- your state and local laws—these may require property owners to clear the adjacent sidewalks of snow and ice (check your state landlord-tenant laws, or seek legal advice to clarify your responsibilities)
- your lease or rental agreement, and (especially)
- the type of housing unit you are renting out.

**Snow removal for single-family homes.** If renting out a single-family home with a private drive and walk where the tenant has exclusive control, the snow removal could be the tenant's responsibility if you agree to this in your lease. Check your state laws and conform your lease and policies accordingly. If the tenant is willing and able to remove snow in winter, this actually makes sense. The tenants are living right there and can best monitor snowfall and remove snow or hire someone to do it. Continue to monitor whether your tenants are removing snow reasonably. If they aren't, you may want to hire the task out and recoup the cost through increased rents at the next lease renewal.

**Snow removal for multiunit properties.** Clearing the shared driveways, parking areas, and walks of multiunit properties is generally the duty of the landlord. That means you either need to find a way to remove snow yourself or hire someone to do so. Depending on how much space you have and whether there's someplace to throw the snow, you have several options. If you have a small area the size of one or two driveways, a standard snow shovel could work, or a sleigh-type shovel, which allows you to push snow with your whole body. There are ergonomic and wider blade versions on the market.

For larger areas with a yard or vacant area to throw snow on, you may want to invest in a snow blower, particularly if heavy snowfalls can be expected where you live. Long or winding driveways and large parking areas should be cleared by a plow truck, probably one you hire. The best lead for finding plow services tends to be neighboring properties, as the contractor will already be on site when it snows and can easily do another unit without making a separate trip.

Use the guidelines for hiring a contractor in Chapter 6 to select a snow-removal firm. Pay close attention to insurance if a truck will be used (in case it hits a tenant's car, for example). And find out if the contractor will do the sidewalks and steps in addition to the driveway.

**Snow removal for condominiums.** Condos are probably the easiest for landlords in winter, because the condo association should handle snow removal. It's likely paid for out of your dues. The association may only do common areas like parking lots and walkways, however, so an individual deck or porch may need to be brushed off with a broom or snow shovel. Arm your tenant with these items.

## Make Winter Property Inspection a Routine

With any luck, you were (as mentioned in Chapter 2) able to buy rental units near your home or even on your commute to work. This way, you can stop by daily, to shovel snow or spread ice melt; or even twice daily, if the weather has been particularly severe. If it's cold enough to freeze, you never know where ice may form. What was once a puddle can become a slip and-fall hazard to tenants and others.

## Empower and Educate Tenants About Winter Maintenance

Few tenants are interested in large-scale snow removal, but most don't mind scooping ice melt from a bucket and slinging it on slick spots to provide instant traction. Keep brooms and shovels available for tenant use, too, and make sure every unit has its own bucket and scoop. Take some empty five-gallon buckets with lids (a great way to recycle old paint buckets) and write the address or unit number on it with permanent marker. Fill these with ice melt. Check their level when you make the rounds.

**RESOURCE**

**Consider the best ice-melt product for your property and weather conditions.** Ideally, you can pick an effective one that will do the least harm to plants, pets, and concrete. *Consumer Reports* has an entry on "Best rock salts and ice melts reviews: Top products for your driveway, walkways, and steps" which you can find at www.consumerreports.org.

Send tenants a brief winter safety note around the time of the first freeze or snowfall, which outlines your snow removal policy, explains where the ice melt is located, and recommends any special safety precautions. Let tenants know in advance when they need to move their cars for snow removal. This is also good time to touch base regarding any humidity and ventilation issues (discussed in Chapter 4) that may be more problematic in winter.

## Light It Up in Winter

Lighting is especially important in winter, because it's often not just ice, but slick spots you don't see, that can cause injuries on those short, dark days. To brighten sidewalks, walkways, and parking areas, attach low-cost rope lighting to stair rails, or install battery-powered motion lights to hit any dark corners. Both are easy to install. While these are ideal for the dark days of winter, I leave them up almost year-round.

## Take Special Care With Steps and Stairs

Use metal, grated steps for porches and second-story rentals. Snow and ice will fall right through, and these steps have great traction. Or if you have wooden steps, you can use roof shingles cut to size and attached with roofing nails to provide a long-lasting surface with great traction.

## Do a Simple Insulation Check

If you haven't inspected your attic insulation recently, stand on the street on a snowy day and check your roof. If you see melted snow and icicles, while neighboring roofs have several inches of snow on them, you're losing heat and lack adequate insulation. Odds are, you need to upgrade the insulation or at least replace it where missing. Inspect it or have a professional make a recommendation. Try to note which areas the snow is melted from, then target these for added insulation.

## Don't Forget to Clear Snow Around the Dumpster and Mailboxes

My trash company will not pick up the dumpster if it's in a snow bank and not shoveled out well. So keep yours clear of snow and make sure tenants or contractors do not bury it. The same advice applies to other trash or recycling containers. Mailboxes should also be cleared out and made safe for daily access by tenants and mail delivery persons.

TIP

**Sprinkle ice melt around the base of the dumpster or garbage cans the night before trash day.** This can make it easier to roll the dumpster out and more likely to get it picked up. You can do the same thing for the mailbox area around delivery time.

## Landlord Negligence and Winter

As mentioned earlier in this chapter, landlords have a general duty of reasonable care toward all people on their property. To avoid "negligence," you must act as a reasonable landlord would under the circumstances, and not create foreseeable risks of harm to others. You can't be careless or neglect your duties. This can present a unique situation in winter where, in much of the country, snow and ice will blanket rental properties and make weather-related injuries such as slip-and-falls all too likely. To protect yourself:

- have a snow removal plan and routine in place
- remove snow and ice in a reasonable time frame
- conduct regular property inspections
- stay aware of any special winter-related hazards
- avoid unreasonable risks
- provide adequate lights, rails, and ice melt on site, and
- establish an easy way for tenants to communicate risks and problems.

Curious whether you are a reasonable landlord? Look at neighboring driveways and sidewalks after a heavy snowfall. I try to be the best or one of the best on a block with a few dozen multiplexes. Having the clearest driveway all winter doesn't immunize you to a slip-and-fall case, but it makes it less likely. Remember, you don't have to be superhuman or even perfect to be a good wintertime landlord—just act as a reasonable landlord under the circumstances would, and don't act carelessly.

Of course, the goal is not to only to avoid lawsuits, but to keep tenants safe and happy, in winter and in every season.

## Take Special Precautions Yourself in Winter

Winter safety is key for the landlord. You can't help anyone else if you're stuck in a ditch or in a wreck, or if you hurt yourself removing snow. Follow these guidelines to get you through the winter in one piece.

**Wait until it's safe to leave your own home.** If your street is impassable, you probably won't make it to the rental unit. Set tenant expectations, letting them know you will be there as soon as you can safely arrive.

**Be a weather tracker.** Weather service guidance and reports have gotten more and more accurate. You can often tell when a storm will start and end. I like to wait, when possible, until just after the snowfall has ceased, so that I can clear the snow only once. In a large storm, you may have to also shovel midway through. But don't make extra trips.

**Consider delegating.** Snow removal can be physically exhausting, and you also have to drive, as well as work, in cold and icy conditions. Perhaps someone else can do the job better, at a reasonable price. The risks can increase with your number of units and your age and physical condition, so it may depend on your circumstances.

## Spring Maintenance

Spring is a relief for many landlords, as the immediate risks and unpleasant surprises are fewer. Nevertheless, parts of your property may have been neglected or inaccessible over the winter months, and summer will be arriving all too soon. Now is a good time to do the following:

- Sweep your parking lots and driveways to remove winter debris and reattach garden hoses.
- Clean windows and any glass doors.
- Clean your air conditioner condenser unit (if any). You can find a useful article on this fairly simple do-it-yourself task by searching the *Family Handyman* website (www. familyhandyman.com). Have your unit professionally serviced by a licensed contractor.
- Begin scraping, sanding, and prepping any areas you plan to paint in the spring. Schedule any exterior summer paint

projects or contract them out to professionals. Let tenants know when you've set the dates and times. Research the best paints and products for your application.

- Spray for pests, if you need to do so. Consider other barriers to prevent pests from entering your units, remove attractants, or implement natural pest management techniques.
- Lightly fertilize plants and grasses. Consider an organic, slow release fertilizer like compost.
- Put out any hanging flower baskets (an easy way to brighten up any building). Just wait until there is no frost danger in your area. Also, secure any second-story baskets so they will not fall (and hit cars or people).

## Greener Lawn Care for Landlords

A small yard or strip of grass does not need to be a burden (unless you're in California or another area with a major drought). Consider some of these tips to help make yard work more manageable.

**Leave the clippings!** For areas you mow, grass clippings can provide one-third of nitrogen (the nutrient that makes grass lush and green) and improve the soil and help it retain water. You will also save a bundle on trash bags and fertilizer—plus you can skip the nastiest part of the job: bagging and hauling grass. For more information see *Leave those grass clippings lie* by Ruth Davis, which you can search for at the Colorado State University website at www.colostate.edu.

**Let it grow.** Higher grass is healthier grass. It shields the sun from the roots and shades out weeds. Your lawn need not look like a putting green. Very short grass is actually more vulnerable to damage from heat and insects. I tell my tenants I try and keep it below their ankles—about two to three inches. Best of all, it means less work for the landlord and less water. The ideal height may vary depending on your climate and type of grass.

**Read more on the subject.** Search for the article "What is the ideal height to cut the grass?" by Julie A. Martens on the diynetwork website at www.diynetwork.com.

## Summer Maintenance

Summertime can be a good time for property maintenance. Even if your property is wellmaintained, now is a good time to think about improvements and beautification.

**Add curb appeal for under $100 with potted or hanging flowers.** You can reuse the pots every year. Ask tenants if they'd like to adopt a plant in front of their door or on their back deck. Tell them how much and often to water it.

**Do exterior painting.** Start by walking around the exterior of the house or rental unit—slowly. Find areas where the paint has cracked or where you see any gaps. Caulk and prime them. Then paint, to prevent rot. Do exterior painting. Summer is an ideal time in most of the U.S. for paint projects, following my guidance in Chapter 4.

**Prepare to be a part-time project manager.** Summer is construction season in much of the U.S. (other than in extremely hot areas, where you may be more apt to shift these tasks to spring or fall). Everything is easier when you don't have to battle heavy rain or snow. Schedule your major exterior construction and be available to facilitate the process. For more information on the landlord's role in major construction projects—new windows, roof repairs, decks, or paint jobs—see Chapter 6.

## Fall Maintenance

Fall is the prelude to winter and great time to do some routine tasks. It is the last chance in many parts of the country to touch up paint and protect exterior surfaces before winter. Consider some of these fall maintenance items.

**Service heating systems.** Hire a professional contractor to do this before winter.

**Beat the frost.** Cover exterior faucets and drains or store hoses before the freeze.

**Store and clean lawn equipment.** After the last time you cut the lawn, clean equipment well, spray with WD-40, and add a fuel treatment to mowers or weed eaters.

## Drought-Resistant Landscapes for Arid Climates

Especially if you own rental property in California or another area with a drought, explore the concept of xeriscaping—a landscaping technique that conserves water, fossil fuels, and labor, and can be very attractive. You can replace all or some grass areas with a drought-resistant landscape of plants requiring little water.

In combination with cover (bark, mulch, pavers), you could reduce or even eliminate the need to water, mow, and fertilize a yard. This could be a huge saving for you and the planet. In the past, tenants may have expected a lush green lawn, but many now realize the resources necessary to maintain the lawn could be better spent elsewhere (plus you may not have a choice, if tough local rationing rules restrict your water use).

Xeriscaping does not require much herbicide, pesticide, or fertilizer (because the plants naturally grow in the arid conditions). Lawns are becoming such a burdensome use of water in some arid areas that municipalities are paying property owners for every foot of lawn they will convert to a less thirsty landscape.

Some areas, however, may not have caught on yet, and you could run afoul of homeowner's association covenants, conditions, and restrictions related to lawn maintenance. Check your state and local guidelines—California, for example, restricts homeowners' associations from prohibiting low water usage plants. Search your state and local websites for useful articles on xeriscaping, drought-tolerant plants, and water conservation. For example, state agricultural extension agents often have advice for your area. And municipal water authorities and districts in arid areas like Southern California (see the Los Angeles County Waterworks District) or Nevada (see the Southern Nevada Water Authority) have abundant xeriscaping information on their websites.

**Clean out gutters.** Use a rounded potting scoop or wear rubber gloves and use your hands to scoop out heavy leaf debris and sticks. Then spray out your gutters with a water hose. Make sure gutters are flowing freely at the downspouts.

**Cut back tree limbs.** Late fall or very early spring is ideal for trimming back trees. An ideal time is when you are already out cleaning gutters with a ladder. Trimming limbs away from your building will deter critters from leaping onto the roof, prevent limbs from falling on the roof, and keep branches from brushing against the building. For more information, try your local agricultural extension agent or the U.S. Forest Service website (www.fs.fed.us) and search "tree trimming for homeowners."

**Leave the leaves.** Rather than raking or bagging leaves, try either mowing them to break leaves down into excellent fertilizer, or collecting them in a mesh area or corner of the lawn. They will break down into a rich soil within a year or two.

**Check insulation and gaps around windows and doors.** Make sure your insulation is in top-notch condition. Enlist the tenant to help you find drafts or cold spots. Turn off the lights and look for light shining in from gaps around doors, or feel for drafts. Consider door sweeps to seal gaps under doors.

---

### Crawling in the Crawl Space

If your building has a crawlspace, fall is an ideal time to peek inside, look around, and check the following.

**Pipe insulation.** Make sure all the pipes are wrapped to protect them from freezing.

**Presence of an adequate vapor barrier, such as heavy plastic or visqueen, on the ground.** This will prevent moisture from bare soil from rising and entering the building.

**No water within sight or sound of leaks.** The crawl space should be dry. If you see any water, try to determine its source and repair the leak.

**Functioning sump pump.** If your property has one, make sure it is high quality and working well.

**No gaps in any insulation under your building.**

**No signs of rodents, termites, or other pests.**

**Adequate ventilation and no signs of mold.**

**Prep for snow removal.** Get out your equipment. Have snow blowers serviced. Add clear polyurethane finish to wood handled shovels and rust proof coating on any metal shovel parts.

**Consider sending tenants a safety and maintenance update, such as the one shown above, before inclement weather comes.** Take care of any problems before winter. If you have a duplex or fourplex, you may be able to have a contractor come and do work in multiple units at the same time, with careful planning.

**Consider an energy audit.** If you have never done one, a professional energy audit of your rental property will help you determine the overall efficiency and identify air leakages, and even give you ideas about low-cost improvements.

## Making a Maintenance Record and Keeping It Up

Once you have made a repair, or spent time and money on maintenance, it's a good idea to record what you have done. The money spent is required for your tax records (discussed in Chapter 12), but your time, labor, and the type of repair can also help you plan ahead. You'll be able to see when a repair or maintenance was last done and how much time and money you are spending on a unit.

Probably, the easiest system for record keeping for the part-time landlord is to replicate the way you record your own personal events and expenditures. For example, I keep one file for personal tax-related expenditures and one for rental business-related expenditures. Put all your rental property receipts, invoices, and records in this business-related file (and note the unit, address, date, and repair if it is not evident from the receipt).

Then consider some type of calendar where you can record activities on rentals and the date, time, location, and brief description of your tasks. You can simply note the activity and time on the date—for example:

*October 20, 2016, cleaned gutters of Unit A on Baker Street, three hours*

If you communicated with your tenant about the repair or your notices of entry, you could also put copies of those in the file on that rental unit (which should have the current lease, rental application, checklists, and so on).

As you get more rental units, or time passes, you may find it hard to remember what repairs you did to which units and when you did them. Knowing you already replaced a part or made a type of repair could help you make future maintenance decisions about that unit or similar problems in other units.

## What's Next

As you maintain your property, you do not have to be alone. There are times when a complicated task, be it a furnace repair or an exceptionally large job, like a new driveway, are just beyond your skill or energy level. Our next topic is how to get help on your property. Chapter 6 covers hiring the service contractors that can be a part of your team when you need them. ●

# Working With Service Contractors

ontractors will be important members of every part-time landlord's team. They're the skilled players on your bench, ready to jump into the game when needed—whether you're handling an unexpected plumbing emergency for a current tenant, updating the kitchen of a rental house between tenancies, or looking to hand off a painting job because you're under time pressure to get a rental unit ready to show. Hiring contractors with professional expertise in these areas will improve your effectiveness and boost your tenants' satisfaction (not to mention reduce your stress level).

This chapter provides an overview of key issues involving contractors, including:

- when you should call in contractors instead of doing the work yourself
- how to choose and screen contractors
- when to use a fixed-price versus a cost-plus payment agreement
- what to put in your written agreement with a contractor
- legal issues to watch for when hiring contractors, and
- how to establish the best and most effective working relationship and avoid many of the pitfalls that occur when juggling tenants, contractors, and your life.

Clearly, the best approach to some of these matters will depend on several factors, including the particular type, number, and location of your rental properties, your own skills in repairs and construction trades, and your time and interest in doing the needed work yourself. This chapter assumes that you have the understanding of an average homeowner—that is, you can handle the tasks in Chapters 3 through 5, perhaps with a little training. If you are far more skilled, you may largely do without outside contractors unless they'll save you time or aggravation. If you are far less skilled than the average homeowner (you're not comfortable installing shelves or painting the bathroom), or you don't want to spend your time preparing rentals between tenants, you'll be especially interested in the advice in this chapter.

The chapter also assumes that you aren't interested in taking on the role of general contractor, overseeing various subcontractors. This role tends to be too big for the average part-time landlord. You're better off hiring a general contractor if you face new construction of an entire building, major rebuilding from a loss (fire, flood, or earthquake), or a complete remodel of numerous units.

## Who's a Contractor?

I use the term "contractor" or "independent contractor" throughout this book to refer to both licensed specialized tradespeople, such as an electrician, as well as less-skilled workers, such as a non-licensed handyman (or woman). A contractor may be a one-person operation, such as a landscaper or electrician, or a firm of several people. A licensed general contractor is a specific type of contractor, who might do a large construction project for you and hire subcontractors, such as painters.

But not all contractors wear overalls and carry tools. This chapter focuses on hiring service contractors to help maintain, repair, or remodel your rental property. Contracting with white-collar professionals, such as lawyers, accountants, property managers, or real estate agents, is covered in Chapter 11.

The main thing to remember is that contractors are not your employees. This is an important distinction for both tax and liability reasons, as you'll learn later in this chapter.

## When It Makes Sense to Hire Contractors

There's no mathematical formula to use in deciding whether to call a contractor to make repairs or improvements on your rental property, but at least you can know all the factors to put into the equation. Remember, just because you hire a contractor does not mean you won't be a part of the project. You'll have more than enough to do in properly selecting a contractor, communicating with the tenants, scheduling the job, and making everything flow smoothly.

Let's take a closer look at some situations when it's wise to consider bringing in outside help, namely projects involving work:

- requiring specialized skills or major repairs

- needing immediate attention in order to comply with habitability codes
- requiring specialized or expensive tools
- requiring a specialized license or permit
- that is time-sensitive
- requiring heavy lifting
- that would compromise your health
- that's more dangerous than you should take on
- in a unit that is part of a condo or homeowners' association
- that can be done more efficiently or faster by a contractor
- that's done in preparation for selling your rental property, or
- that just seems better suited for a contractor to do.

> **CAUTION**
>
> **You are still legally on the hook for your property's condition and safety even if you hire someone else.** Property maintenance is generally a nondelegable duty. By handing off a major repair job, you are still intimately involved (or should be). Later sections in this chapter discuss your role in the selection of a contractor—and the importance of doing it wisely.

## Repairs Are Major or Require Specialized Skills

Always view major issues—ones that could harm the integrity of the unit or the safety of its occupants—like a flashing yellow caution light. These almost always merit a call to a professional (even if only for an opinion). Often the level of expertise and precision required in such situations can quickly exceed the skills of an average landlord.

Here are a few examples of typical repairs that are beyond the scope of most landlords:

- plumbing problems, such as replacing pipe or sewer lines, beyond the classic clogged toilet or toilet repair
- electrical work, beyond adding a new outlet or light fixture
- heating and cooling system repairs
- exterior issues compromising weatherproofing, like major roof, window, or siding deficiencies

- completely reflooring, such as installing wall-to-wall carpet
- building code and safety concerns that involve ingress/egress issues (new doors or window used for fire exit), ground fault circuit interrupter (GFCI) power outlets, or building entire runs of steps to required dimensions, and
- major remodels, reroofing, or adding large areas of concrete (such as in a driveway).

## The Work Is Required Under Your State's Warranty of Habitability

Every lease (whether written or not) requires the unit to be livable or "habitable." Many habitability rules are common sense, requiring that rental units have water, heat, electricity, no vermin, and otherwise meet building codes and standards. Chapter 5 discusses your legal obligation to provide habitable rental premises and the consequences (such as tenant rent withholding) if you fail to do so. It also explains where to find information on your state and local housing codes, which vary.

Particularly if a tenant has given you notice of any condition that may impact the habitability of the unit, it would be highly advisable to use a professional in order to obtain: (1) an immediate, qualified response, (2) professionally insured service, and (3) documentation of your response (in the form of the contractor's invoice). Chapters 5 and 12 provide more advice on the importance of record keeping, and Chapter 9 has tips on maintaining good communications with tenants through all kinds of situations.

## Specialized Tools or Expensive Equipment Are Needed

Sometimes, the cost of buying a tool or renting a piece of equipment may make the job less economical, even if you have the skill and time, so hiring a contractor would be more efficient. For example:

- While you may pay a reasonable fee to rent a sander to refinish wood floors or a chainsaw to remove a small tree, renting a larger piece of equipment, like a skid steer or excavator, may make the project too costly. You probably want to use a contractor who owns this equipment already.

- If the pipes in your recently purchased rental unit are made of the newer PEX (polyethylene) material, rather than copper, they may require specialized tools that only a plumber with expertise has.
- If your rental house has a major vermin infestation and a few mousetraps won't do the job, you need a professional exterminator.

> **TIP**
>
> **Budget realistically for any equipment rental.** When penciling out whether renting a piece of equipment will save money as compared with hiring a contractor, be sure to add in costs for fuel, oil, associated materials, and taxes and fees. Also add in the time you'll spend picking up and dropping off the equipment, and learning how to use it properly. Gaining proficiency with equipment can require extra hours or even days. You may need the equipment much longer if your project schedule gets delayed or you face a steep learning curve with the new equipment.

## The Work Requires a Licensed Contractor Working Under a Valid Permit

Major electric upgrades, structural repairs, new additions, plumbing, and grading often require special licenses and/or permits from a municipal or local government. The same applies to work on sidewalks adjoining a public right of way, retaining walls or fences over a certain height, decks, carports, or a load-bearing wall. Check your local or municipal guidelines for details and procedures. Your contractor should have a valid state license, and plenty of experience in obtaining permit approval. Going without these won't save you money in the long term. Proper permits, licenses, and inspections will be vital in obtaining insurance for your rental, avoiding liability, and even properly marketing the property for sale in the future.

**RESOURCE**

**Where to find local building codes and permit requirements.**
You can scan your local rules online from your planning or permitting department. See what type of work requires a permit and what can be done without one. If your work requires a permit, you will likely find that the process varies depending on the scope of the project. For example, major work (like an addition to a single-family house) may require an approved plan, inspections, and a certificate of occupancy, while minor work (like building a deck) may require only a quick over-the-counter permit. Be sure you have the right permits, if required, before starting any work on your rental.

## Time Is an Issue

Even if you could conceivably complete a task safely and efficiently, it still may not be prudent or efficient to do it yourself. Time is money in the rental business, and it may make good sense to hire an outside contractor if you are stretched thin.

For example, if you rent out a single-family home at $1,500 a month, every day without a paying tenant costs you roughly $50 dollars. So you want to minimize the number of days a rental is vacant. But as a part-time landlord, you may only be able to devote time to painting the bedrooms and other such work on weekends. The result may be a delay of a week (or $350 dollars) before you can even start painting. Along with the $350 in lost rents, you still have to buy the paint (say for, $150) and expend your labor. So if a painter would do the job for $500 or less, you are probably much better off going that route.

Time is especially crucial when handling repairs in occupied units. A project that might be fine to handle intermittently over several weeks in your own home, such as upgrading your kitchen (if your family does not mind the inconvenience), won't work for renters. They will not stand for you dismantling their kitchen, disappearing and reappearing, for a week or two.

Also, your state may require that you respond to a tenant's repair-related complaint within a specified period of time (such as ten days, perhaps depending on the nature of the problem) or face the possibility of a tenant withholding rent or pursuing other legal options.

A quick, professional solution may be your best bet in these kinds of situations. A paying tenant rightly expects to have the job scheduled and done on time.

**TIP**

**Cut down on service calls with preventive maintenance.** See Chapter 5 for advice, Including on how to develop a seasonal inspection checklist and perform maintenance that will go a long way toward preventing later calls for repairs.

## Heavy Materials or Appliances Are Involved

Consider your abilities and the weight of materials or appliances involved in any task before you take it on yourself. It typically makes sense to hire a contractor or arrange delivery if:

- you have to carry anything heavier than a bucket of paint up a ladder
- you can't get an item safely into your current vehicle, and you don't want to buy or rent a truck, or
- you can't carry an object, such as a stackable washer dryer, safely around or into a unit, especially an upstairs one.

Whether it's a load of sheetrock or a new refrigerator, you can still play a key role in managing the process when heavy items are involved. You'll manage costs by making a good initial purchase, coordinate a smooth delivery by informing tenants, protect the unit (by covering the floors with padding and tarps), and clean up. Being a manager, not a human forklift, will extend your longevity as a landlord. Plus, a landlord recovering from back surgery is seldom an effective one.

When I started with my first property in my early 30s, I had a truck and sufficient energy to move appliances, lumber, and landscaping materials. I don't do this any longer. Instead, I look for efficient delivery as an important component of any appliance, lumber, or material purchase. In retrospect, I realize I was not saving much, if any, money. It was also too much wear and tear on me and the vehicle.

## Your Joint Health Is at Risk

While you may figuratively bend over backwards to keep your best tenants, don't literally endanger your health with awkward positions or repetitive motions. Your and your tenants' safety is priority one. Be realistic about your abilities with respect to a potential task. In addition to issues regarding heavy materials (discussed above), the type of movement or body position required in a task may be awkward. Are you really ready to stay on your knees on a hard floor for a full day installing flooring, crunch into a tight crawlspace to fix a leak, or balance on the roof for hours to paint hard-to-reach siding? Not only might the movements be unnatural, you could have to deal with extreme summer heat or dangerous winter ice.

And, yes, you could encounter critters under houses and on roofs and attics (mice, snakes, spiders, or worse). The risk may not be that these normally peaceful creatures will attack you (most rodents or insects are more afraid of you), but that the fright you get when something moves out of a dark corner causes you to panic and hurt yourself.

> **TIP**
>
> **Protect your knees.** Many landlord tasks are taxing on the knees, low back, and ankles. Wear kneepads (and take frequent breaks) while crouching on hard surfaces. Pack these with your turnaround and repair tool supplies.

## The Repair Is Dangerous or Unsafe

Realistically assess the risks in any job and whether it makes more sense to hand it off. The Safety First Checklist (see below) will help you make this decision.

## Safety First Checklist

These safety prompts should help indicate whether hiring a contractor is the safest course of action.

- ☐ Do you know where to start with the task, or is it totally new? New tasks present new risks, so beware.
- ☐ Does the job involve electric, gas, or water shutoffs that you are unsure about (or that have seized up), which could pose risks?
- ☐ Can you safely access the area (attic, crawlspace, roof) in order to make a repair? If you can't get there, you can't fix it.
- ☐ Do you own the tools required and can you safely, competently use them?
- ☐ Is extreme weather a problem? Heat exhaustion is a very real threat in summer in many areas. Similarly, in winter a deck or roof that is wet or slick with ice could be a deadly risk.
- ☐ Are the size and weight of the materials you need to move feasible and safe? Hauling sheetrock upstairs alone can court physical injury or property damage.
- ☐ Is there any risk of a gas leak or an electric fire?
- ☐ Is special safety equipment required or recommended?
- ☐ Are there any toxic or environmental hazards (asbestos, lead, dangerous mold)?

# Guilt by (Condo) Association

Another situation where I would recommend a contractor nine times out of ten involves significant work on a condominium. First make sure it's a repair that is not already covered by the association (check its bylaws, rules, and declarations). Owners often own and are responsible from the walls inward. So the average leaky faucet or new dishwasher is up to the owner. But a plumbing or electrical issue inside the walls will be up to the association. Calling a licensed contractor for interior work on any condominium can give you added insurance and peace of mind. Also, you will definitely want the consent of the condo board or the association property manager. The repair may require their approval, and even it doesn't, you are better off keeping them informed.

Even if you have the skills and the repair is simple, imagine yourself called before a group of angry condo board members who are sticklers for the rules. They may feel you were not qualified and should not have done the work. It is a no-win situation. Even if you fixed something correctly and saved the association money, you'd still be in the wrong. Worse yet would be if, say, your undersink p-trap repair leaked and flooded the unit below. You could end up paying for an expensive contractor just to repair the unit below—not your own! Remember, if you make a major repair, you open yourself up to responsibility for problems that arise later. If you change a light fixture, and an electric fire occurs years later, the insurance adjustor or condo board could point the finger at you, even if your guilt is unclear.

## It's Cost-Effective to Hire a Contractor

As a landlord, you are a manager, not a specific tradesperson. You are a generalist, so your expertise should be in managing the property and people you work with regularly. Know what you can do and know what you can't do efficiently. The costs of a computer programmer trying to reroof a unit or a nurse battling to replace her rental's windows may be higher than first thought.

Consider a routine plumbing repair that might cause you some delay, potential leaks, and stress. A plumber could do it in an hour. In terms of cash outlay, you might save $100 or $150 by doing it yourself. But what if it takes you three hours? And what if your hourly rate (at your job) is $60 an hour? Quickly, you begin to see that you may have lost $20 to $80 by doing it yourself. This is what economists call "opportunity costs."

This book is designed for part-time landlords, people with day jobs, folks with more human capital than real estate. You no doubt want to be an effective landlord—but without negatively impacting your primary source of earnings (your day job). If the time, stress, or potential injury of handling a repair job might impact your main employment, that's another good reason to call in a pro.

## With Exterior Condo Work No Good Deed Goes Unpunished

Condominiums present a challenge for the highly skilled landlord with the ability to do a job on the exterior of a unit or a common area. While you might like to handle a quick touch-up paint job or even do some landscaping, it may not be feasible or even allowed. Much will depend on the association's written rules, as well as its culture, policies, and practices. There is often a collaborative, planned process for any work done on a condo complex (think meetings, budgets, reports).

Here's one example I recall: An experienced tree service professional lived at a condo complex where I was president. He took it upon himself to top some trees to provide owners in his area a clear water view. While he saw his good deed as adding value (and a good view does often help properties sell and add to owners' enjoyment), I got angry calls from people who felt this renegade "scalped" the precious trees. I had to ask him not to do it again—an uncomfortable situation. However, I seem to recall the association then trimming the trees in the rest of the complex (because others then wanted the unobstructed water view!).

Even benign activity, like trimming high weeds in the area in front of my unit, has brought in odd responses about why I didn't do the entire complex. One person summoned me to her unit, unaware that I was a volunteer.

That said, I have yet to find an association that would oppose activities such as picking up trash on grounds, sweeping walkways, and cleaning your windows and door(s) (if easily accessible). Beyond that, it will really depend.

## The Contractor Can Do the Job Faster and Better

A major reason to use contractors to make repairs and do related work in your rental units is simple: They are faster. Good contractors move with speed and purpose through the mazes of electrical wiring and the mountains of sheetrock. They should be able to do a job in half the time you'd take (or less). Comfortable with their high-quality tools, experienced contractors can move without hesitation or wasted motion. They've done this type of job hundreds—if not thousands—of times before. They see the pitfalls ahead and already are thinking of the second step. Good contractors know the tricks of the trade and the small details that often make all the difference. In short, they specialize in this task; it is what they do best.

Similarly, what you do best is probably your day job (and part-time property management, of course). You will need to be a jack-of-all-trades in some respects (cleaning, painting, record keeping, making minor repairs, showing units—which you'll do as well anyone after a few years). There's no need to become a specialized construction tradesperson on top of it.

CAUTION

**Discover how much time a repair really takes.** Many popular home improvement books give wildly optimistic time projections for different repair tasks, such as replacing a sink or patching a large hole in the wall. They do not include time for studying and researching a problem, moving furniture, buying and mobilizing the materials, gathering the tools, driving to the location, and thoroughly cleaning up debris and dust. And they usually give a best-case scenario—one without any errors or difficulties. If a home repair book says that a common task will take just one to two hours to do, don't count on it until you've tried it. A job may take longer than you estimate just to prepare everything you need, schedule the repair with the tenant, and get to the unit.

For most part-time landlords who are full-time professionals with a high hourly rate, "doing it yourself" on most major repairs and construction projects will not pencil out financially. There are also other very real costs. Part of the learning curve in working with new tools and materials may mean you buy the wrong ones, install them incorrectly, and possibly have to redo the entire project. Online sales boards list whole categories of materials that do-it-yourselfers mistakenly purchased. And our landfills have considerable materials from projects gone wrong. Thinking about the total costs—the opportunity costs, the environmental costs, and the risks a project may go wrong (with the property damaged or you injured)—often leads the efficient landlord to search for an experienced contractor for major projects.

## You Plan to Sell Soon

Whether you are selling or just rerenting your property will also also be a factor in deciding whether to use a contractor for something like flooring. For example, a handy landlord could install a laminate floor on a groundlevel unit and easily rerent it for many years. However, if you are about to sell the rental unit, definitely call in a professional and think about higher-end flooring and fixtures to make your unit competitive in the sales market. This is an exception to our goal of achieving "fair rental condition" with your rental properties.

## Your Gut Instincts Say to Hire Help

A major theme in this book is that landlords can and should strive to grow their understanding and skills in many areas. However, there's a fine line between pushing your comfort zone to learn something new and getting in too deep. Trust your gut instincts. If a project seems wrong, dangerous, or too unfamiliar, then call for help. If you're feeling like MacGyver, wondering whether you should cut the red or blue wire, or when something might possibly explode, flood, or flame, then call in help. In addition, read "Watch and Learn" later in this chapter to find out how you might tackle the issue next time. In the worst case, you can write off the amount of the pro's bill—just save your receipt. (Chapter 12 covers tax issues for the part-time landlord.)

By the same token, your gut should tell you when you *are* the best person to do a particular job. Sometimes the urgency, oddness, or type of task just makes you the best person to do it. Just a few examples I can recall from my own experience:

- a tenant's cat lodged a dead bird under the refrigerator (hint: a high-powered vacuum works)
- a neighbor complained about a large yellow jacket nest next to the unit I was showing the following day (at dusk, try the foam spray designed for wasps and yellow jackets, after wrapping yourself in multiple layers of protective clothing), and
- the classic clogged toilet call in the middle of the night (but try my tenant clog script in Chapter 3 before driving over).

## Choosing Contractors

Contractors come in all types, business sizes, skill levels, and trades. Your choice (or lack thereof) will depend greatly on the size and economic conditions of your community and the local services and housing market. Whether you own rental property in a small rural town or a big city, you'll want to consider:

- state rules and regulations for hiring contractors
- the scope of your project
- which contractors come highly recommended, and
- how much you can find out about each prospective contractor's experience, skills, availability, number of employees, and valid license.

### Find Out Your State Rules on Hiring Independent Contractors

State regulations vary extensively when it comes to contractors. Many states set licensing requirements that require a minimum level of training, experience, or passage of an exam, say for a plumbing license, and require a license for work over a certain dollar amount (such as $500). State agencies often provide useful guides on how to hire and work with a local contractor and describe the relevant rules. This is a great way to get started. The California Contractors State License Board's website, for example, (at www.cslb.ca.gov) offers such resources as a general guide, *What You Should Know Before Hiring a Contractor*, and publications on specific types of work, such as landscaping and asbestos removal.

To find the agency that oversees contractors and the regulations for your state, check out the National Association of State Contractors Licensing Agencies (NASCLA) at www.nascla.org.

## Define Your Repair Needs or Construction Project Up Front

Who is the right contractor? Well, it depends. An ideal contractor to fix your fence is probably not the same one you want to reroof your rental. And the general contractor you use for a one-time major remodel probably won't be the same one you use for routine door and window repairs. So the fit between your project and the contractor is key. This is why you need to get a good understanding of the work to be performed before even contacting or screening contractors. Factors such as the job size, number of required workers, and length of time it should take to complete will make a big difference in which contractors are appropriate, available, or even interested in the job.

Probably the three most important words in a landlord (or anyone's) interaction with contractors are "scope of work." These magic words describe exactly (not as a broad outline or vague idea) what you want done. The scope of work will help direct you to select the proper contractor. If, for example, your scope of work requires a particular type of roofing, you probably want contractors who have recently done a similar application (ideally to the satisfaction of the client). A clear scope of work should guide your entire project, including your contractor selection.

Of course, you are not locked in on finishing the job exactly as specified, no matter what you agree on for the scope of the work. One of the most common phrases in the contractor vocabulary is "change order," meaning the process in which the owner (here, the landlord) and the contractor agree to depart from the scope of work—often to add a higher-grade material, extra feature, or another option (likely at additional cost).

## Get Recommendations From Satisfied Customers and Identify Likely Prospects

Sometimes your best source for a particular type of contractor is the network of people you work with as a landlord, such as other rental property owners, legal and financial professionals, general contractors, or even materials suppliers (see the discussion of landlord networks at the end of Chapter 11). Ask who they think is doing the best work in whatever field you are looking for, be it concrete or carpentry. I sometime find this prompt useful, "Who would you use if you were going to (insert the scope of work, be it landscaping, remodeling, or replacing your windows and doors)?" This can get you some great leads.

> CAUTION
> **Be wary of unsolicited bids or estimates from contractors who come to your door (or through mail, phone, or email).** If these contractors have this much free time, they probably don't have anyone calling them (perhaps for good reason). Your ideal service provider will have a loyal clientele and active calendar (a good sign) but won't be so booked as to be unavailable.

## Carefully Research Each Prospective Contractor

Once you have one or more solid leads, check each contractor's website, online reviews, the state licensing board (for details on the contractor's license and any complaints about shoddy or incomplete work), Better Business Bureau complaints, or even court records for recent lawsuits. Ask about the contractor's reputation among others in your network and community. Do all the detective work you can.

The contractor's skills, experience, and availability are the most important factors in getting the job done. Focus on researching these three things to determine whether a prospective contractor is right for your job. Obviously, cost will be a factor, but you'll want to start by making sure you have a qualified contractor.

> CAUTION
> **Keep an eye out for red flags.** Be wary of contractors whose projects ended up in litigation or allegedly failed to meet workmanlike standards. These red flags could mean anything from a communication issue to a serious construction defect. Remember, going to court would have been the last resort, if the client brought the lawsuit (many contracts require mediation and arbitration). Of course, other types of lawsuits may not be problematic (for example, where the contractor was in a lawsuit related to a car wreck off the job).

## Check Out a Contractor's Skills and Experience

The most important things to find out about a contractor's abilities are:
- Does the contractor seem to have the skills and time to do the job?
- What kind of work does the contractor ordinarily or regularly do?
- How long has the contractor been in business?
- Does the contractor do similar work to the type and scale you want done?

If you're looking for work on a residential property (four units or less), a contractor who routinely handles smaller-scale projects is ideal. The major companies that focus on luxury homes and larger-scale new construction probably aim for larger high six-, seven-, or eight-figure jobs. So your $1,000–$10,000 repair will probably be viewed as a nuisance rather than an opportunity.

## Look Into the Contractor's Availability

Good luck explaining to a tenant that the plumbing hasn't been fixed because you're waiting for a contractor to finish with another, larger job. It's crucial to find out how busy or available any contractor that you intend to use will be.

I like a contractor who is reasonably busy (being in demand is a good sign), but not too busy to value my business or keep in touch regarding availability. If it is a nonemergency, I like that the contractor can come by next week for a bid (not next month). Honest contractors will simply tell you they are not taking on new work. Have them call you when they can—but don't waste time chasing after contractors who never call back. No matter how good a contractor is, he or she won't be of any help if unable to show up.

## Find Out Whether the Contractor Has Sufficient Employees

Once you find a contractor, whether it's a plumber or electrician, take a look at the number of employees on staff. An ideal company would be a small to midsized firm. With one- or two-person companies, you may have problems if they have other work and get behind or booked solid. There is also a more limited skill set to draw on and less backup if a worker gets injured or sick, quits, or retires. There is nothing worse than having a project left undone because your contractor's firm is understaffed. To avoid this potential issue, a contractor with a handful of high-quality full-time employees who have a close working relationship is often ideal for the small-time landlord.

## Confirm the Contractor's License, Bonding, and Insurance

Is the contractor "licensed, bonded, and insured?" While the requirements vary by state and by type of contractor, here are some general guidelines:

**Licensed.** Make sure your contractor has the required license in your state for the type of work he or she will be doing, such as electrical, plumbing, or structural. Get the contractor's license number; many states allow you to check it online (including any consumer complaints).

**Bonded.** A contractor's license bond may provide some protection (for example, if work is improperly done) and recourse, by guaranteeing the contractor won't violate the license laws in that state. Get the contractor's bond number and certification, with which to check the level and type of bond. The dollar amount of bonding should be commensurate with the volume of work being done by the contractor. There are various types of bonding, so check your state rules or get professional advice if you have questions about bonding or a potential claim against a bond.

**Insured.** The contractor should have bought adequate liability and worker's compensation insurance. Customers can ask to see a certificate of insurance.

### Examining the Contractor's Resources and Responsiveness

Make sure your contractor has what it takes to both get back to you and show up for the job in a timely fashion. That means multiple vehicles, an established location (not just a garage at home), and adequate means of communication. From early on, pay careful attention to whether the contractor answers the phone or calls back in a reasonable time, or responds promptly to your emails, and whether its billing and accounting practices are professional. Your first interactions can also be a way of screening a contractor's ability to communicate, a key component in any project.

## Check References

If you're satisfied with the answers you get by talking with a contractor, ask for and check references (as to the quality of the work and any problems such as cost or time overruns) from customers (ideally, landlords or homeowners with properties similar to yours). I prefer recent and relevant references. I would check with the last three recent clients who had a similar type of work done. If you find all three have favorable reviews, you have a good prospect.

## Hiring a Handyperson

You may be interested in hiring less skilled or more general helpers, such as a handyman (or woman) for small jobs such as painting a rental unit, hauling trash, or making a minor repair. Be sure to comply with any state rules or restrictions when doing so. Some states may require that the worker have a license (such as for electrical or plumbing work), while other states may not require any license for jobs below a certain dollar limit (sometimes called a "minor work" exemption or exception). State law in California, for example, allows someone to do a job without a license, provided the job is worth less than $500 (including labor and materials). Other states, such as Alaska, have a specific license for handymen, and the total project must not exceed $10,000 and the worker must carry liability and property damage insurance and a $5,000 bond.

CAUTION

**Breaking up the job may not be a legal way to take advantage of your state's minor work exception or handyman license limit.** For example, if the minor work limit is $1,000 in your state, and you've got a $2,000 job, don't try getting clever by offering two contracts to the same person for $1,000 each.

All the rules and best practices on hiring contractors described in this chapter apply to hiring a handyman or less skilled worker, as well. Screen your handyperson candidates closely, check their references and insurance, get written estimates, and make sure they have any required business license and no outstanding complaints.

CAUTION

**Beware of casual day labor.** This can take many forms. It may be a neighborhood kid, a local chore fundraiser for the swim team, or noncitizens standing outside home improvement centers. Casual labor arrangements come with various risks. For starters, you lack a way to screen the workers, so you have no way of determining their skills or even their background (such as criminal behavior). In addition, the IRS could construe this as being an employer/employee relationship, triggering tax and filing requirements. And if a worker is injured on the job or hurts someone else, you could be fully liable—people doing casual day labor are unlikely to carry their own insurance. Instead of using random day labor, try and find a contractor who can take on the same task.

# Making Sure the Worker Is an Independent Contractor (Not an Employee)

Small-time landlords don't typically have the resources or scale to hire employees, or enough work to keep an employee busy every day. The paperwork and liability would be a hassle, too (not to mention the additional expenses, such as payroll taxes and workers' compensation insurance premiums).

Using independent contractors helps landlords get help without this hassle or the oversight responsibilities of having employees. Even more important, landlords can use independent contractors without getting into two of the most burdensome parts of having employees: (1) legal liability, and (2) tax withholdings. Let's examine these two factors, and make sure you won't get into IRS trouble by treating your independent contractors as employees.

**Legal liability.** If you hire an independent contractor and something goes wrong and the contractor hurts someone or has an accident (causing a tree to fall on the neighbor's house or crashing into a bicyclist on the way to the job), you are not generally liable for the damage or injury (the contractor is). However, you would be on the hook if the contractor could be considered your employee. Employers are generally liable for the damages (or torts) of their employees committed on the job (also called the scope of employment). So for risk management, all landlords should hire independent contractors and make very certain the roles are clear.

**Tax and withholdings.** If you hire an independent contractor, you do not have to worry about withholding state and federal taxes or paying for the worker's Social Security, Medicare, or workers' compensation. Just pay the contractor's bill and wave goodbye. (The one exception is that you may have to file IRS Form 1099-MISC if you pay over $600 to an unincorporated contractor.)

In short, properly hiring independent contractors can help steer you clear of both liability and tax headaches. It is the most efficient and safest way for part-time landlords to get help on their properties.

## Characteristics of Independent Contractors

Because you want to make sure to hire independent contractors, it's important to understand the way they differ from employees. Both the IRS and courts in all 50 states will use a multifactor test to make this determination. The factors listed below (or some close variation on this theme) are commonly used across the U.S. (for the tax or liability context) in determining whether someone is an independent contractor or employee.

Generally, independent contractors:

- work by the specific job for a finite, set time frame (rather than long-term, without set start and end dates)
- are paid by the job (instead of receiving a set salary as would be paid to an employee)
- provide their own tools, equipment, vehicles, and place of work (if you are supplying these, the relationship looks more like you are an employer)
- are separately licensed and insured, and
- work without the control or supervision of whoever is paying them.

The type of work being done may also be relevant in distinguishing an independent contractor from an employee. An independent contractor is more likely to have a distinct occupation (rather than be considered a generalist). What the parties perceive about the relationship can be relevant. The IRS may also look at additional financial factors, with an independent contractor having a significant investment, opportunity for profit and loss, and unreimbursed expenses, for example.

If the people you hire meet all or almost all the criteria above, you should be in the clear and can go forward with the certainty you have an independent contractor (and a well-screened one at that if you follow the tips in this chapter!). You will not be liable for a contractor's actions if he or she hurts someone, and you don't need to worry about employee tax withholdings.

In most cases, it should be clear whether someone is an employee or independent contractor. If not, structure the relationship to clarify the roles in light of the factors above. It's possible to get into trouble. Say, for example, you find an ideal handyman and decide to hire him on an hourly basis every few days for several months; closely direct him on jobs, and provide him some of the tools. You may well have an employee/employer situation under some definitions—and you might find out the hard way (perhaps in the form of a lawsuit if your handyman hits someone with his truck on the way to get the lumber you sent him to buy).

There is no exact formula for when someone is an employee or independent contractor. The court or the IRS would weigh the factors above and make a decision, so make sure yours is not a vague or close case that could go either way. Some courts have stated that one factor—control or who's in control—is especially important. If you control how your contractor does the job and when he or she does it, then the relationship may be construed as employer/employee in nature. (Besides, such need for supervision may be a clue that you should hire a more qualified contractor.)

## Avoid Contractors That Mainly Do Commercial Work

Many larger contractors deal primarily with major commercial projects (think new schools, stadiums, and big box stores). Unless these contractors have a residential division, you will be wasting your time contacting them. Your rental will be considered residential (if four units or less). If a contractor uses the language "residential" in advertising, that's good.

An ad that says "residential and commercial" could also be a good sign, but check the contractor's website or any online information (building permits, reviews, advertisements, and the like) for the scale of projects the firm is working on. Is it building huge apartments, or doing John Doe's kitchen remodel? Some firms list both, but in practice focus on one or the other. A contractor who is currently or often tied up on major jobs is probably not for you. If, for instance, the contractor has several $100,000 projects and one $1,000 project (yours) on the calendar, yours will likely be a low priority. You may not get the contractor's best people or most timely service. But if you hire a smaller firm, with several $300 minor repairs on its calendar, your $1,000 job may be its number one priority that day!

To avoid problems, remember that you are a client (not the supervisor or employer). Give precise goals or outcomes (for example, in the scope of work, discussed below), but not the means to that end.

> **TIP**
>
> **It doesn't matter what you call your worker.** Don't be too clever and try to disguise an employee by labeling him or her an independent contractor. Just calling someone an independent contractor is not enough. What's important are the actual facts of your working relationship.

## Where to Find Legal and Tax Rules on Hiring Independent Contractors

The IRS's detailed rules for classifying independent contractors are covered in IRS Publication 15-A, *Employers Supplemental Tax Guide* (Supplement to Publication 15 (Circular E) *Employer's Tax Guide*). Or, you can just search "employer or independent contractor" at www.irs.gov. Also, be sure to check your state tax agency for any relevant rules; some states' rules are more stringent than or differ from the IRS rules.

You'll also find useful articles on hiring independent contractors in the Employment Law section of www.nolo.com. These cover a range of relevant topics, such as documents to gather and issues to consider on your first meeting with a potential contractor (to make sure someone is an independent contractor for both tax and liability purposes); IRS paperwork (Form 1099-MISC) you must file when you pay an unincorporated independent contractor more than $600 over the course of a year; and how to avoid classification problems.

Finally, for detailed information on tax, liability, and other related issues, see *Working With Independent Contractors,* and *Every Landlord's Tax Deduction Guide,* both by Stephen Fishman (Nolo).

# Getting Bids and Estimates From Contractors

When interacting with contractors, it's best to eliminate any vagueness. The initial bid or estimate is the best spot to begin seeking clarity—especially because either of these might soon form the basis of a written contract or agreement with your (aptly named) contractor.

While the terms "bid" and "estimate" may be used loosely or interchangeably, the difference is important and highlights the two main types of arrangements landlords will have with contractors. A bid is generally associated with a fixed-price agreement (sometimes called a "lump sum" agreement), and an estimate with a cost-plus arrangement (which you may also hear called "time and materials"). In the fixed-price arrangement, a contractor bids a job and then (ideally) completes it for that amount. In a cost-plus scenario, the contractor tracks all the time and materials spent on the project (plus overhead and profit) and calculates the bill.

Depending on the job, you'll want to get written bids or estimates from two or three contractors—perhaps more for larger, more costly jobs, such as a new driveway or reroofing. Figuring out who's offering the best value may be difficult if you don't know the exact scope of the work (explained below), but starting with highly recommended contractors (someone with strong references and past work experience) and asking for lots of detail will help.

It's important to remember that a bid or estimate is just an opener, an offer by the contractor to do the work. But depending on the level of detail and the format, you might be a few small steps away from signing off on the bid or estimate and turning it into a binding contract.

CAUTION

**Don't abuse the bidding process in order to get free advice.** Screening and meeting with contractors is a prudent idea, and a helpful way to get information on pricing and tips for projects. But remember that it costs contractors time and money to do good bids and estimates—and it's unfair to ask for free bids if you are not committed to a project (or are unlikely to accept a contractor's bid).

## Key Terms to Understand When Working With Contractors

Here are some of the most basic terms that you may see in written bids or estimates provided by contractors; and which should definitely be included in the contract or agreement that you eventually sign with your chosen contractor. But you'll want to do your own homework or consult experts (covered in Chapter 11) for more guidance—the more you understand the process and ask questions, the better your odds that the final bill won't shock you and the end result will be your desired one.

## Scope of the Work

Next to the all-important selection of the contractor, agreeing on the exact scope of work to be performed is probably the most important concept to address. Without a clear, written scope of work, covering key aspects such as the materials, tasks included, and timeline, neither you nor your contractor can be sure what the job entails. A contractor can't give you an accurate estimate or bid without knowing this (saying you want something "fixed" is not sufficient). And you can't compare bids or estimates from different contractors without knowing the scope of work.

More detail—such as plans, specific sizes, types, brand, model numbers, colors, and gauges—are better than less. On a roof bid, for example, never accept just "shingles" but insist on "50-Year (Brand Name), Type, Description, Amount, Color." A careful contractor will note a second color choice and include a provision for handling gutters, cleanup, and more.

Check if any items are left out expressly and for specific exclusions that may add costs—for example, demolition, trash removal, permits, taxes, or options, such as higher-end or different construction materials. These could all add up if not included in your agreement.

## Cost and Payment Arrangement

Your method for payment is also important to get clear on in advance. This will typically be either a fixed-price or a cost-plus agreement. Below are some very simple descriptions. If you want to get a better understanding of the key differences between fixed-price and cost-plus agreements, do some online research, focusing on the pros and cons and most common practices for jobs like yours, and check resources, such as the American Institute of Architects (www.aia.org) for sample contracts of both varieties.

### Fixed-Price

The most familiar working arrangement is the flat or fixed-price contract (also called a stipulated or lump sum), in which you agree to pay a flat price for the total job, including all labor and materials (although the final cost may be higher, depending on change orders—discussed below).

Fixed-price contracts are easy to administer, require less accounting and billing detail than cost-plus agreements, and provide more certainty when it comes to cost. That said, you could actually overpay for a job that turned out to require less time and materials than projected. Still, this method works best for most types of projects.

### Cost-Plus

Under this arrangement, a contractor charges you for hourly services and for every item (down to the last screw or 4x4), all marked up and itemized in the final bill, typically with a set percentage (such as 20%) for contractor profit and overhead. Rather than start out with a fixed-price bid for the job, the contractor will give you an estimate, but you won't know the exact cost until the work is done.

Without a limit on project costs, you may feel you're writing blank checks. But the cost-plus arrangement can actually work for both parties in some situations. It may be ideal if you have a highly trusted contractor. And it can also eliminate any incentive to do rush work or use lower quality materials.

It may be most useful with unforeseeable or concealed aspects of a job that may make it difficult for a contractor to provide a firm bid. For example, work involving rot repair within walls or under shingles or searching out leaks, sources of moisture problems, or anything that involves underground work, is almost always done on a cost-plus basis. The cost-plus arrangement also means more detailed and (you hope) transparent billing.

## What's Best—Fixed Price or Cost Plus?

Truth be told, the cost-plus and fixed-price agreements are not as distinct as they appear, or don't have to be. For example, most fixed-price agreements contain some allowance for time and materials (for example, on how to handle concealed conditions like rot repair). Similarly, you can ask for a "not to exceed" amount (sometimes called an "upset price") in a cost-plus contract, giving it some fixed (or at least maximum) price limit. Finally, even in a cost-plus arrangement, you might use a flat contractor fee (as opposed to, say, a 20% percentage profit and overhead) to eliminate a contractor's incentive to increase the overall project costs. There is room for the creative landlord who understands both types of agreement to use them both, depending on the situation.

Most importantly, starting with a detailed description of scope and covering key issues in a written agreement can minimize problems. And if you understand the ins and outs of fixed-price and cost-plus agreement, you will already be among the most knowledgeable users of contractor services.

> ! CAUTION
>
> **Jumping right on the lowest bid or estimate, especially if it significantly less than the others you get, can be risky.** In the best case, the contractor could have low overhead or be very efficient. Or maybe the contractor uses less skilled labor or cheap construction methods. And what seems the cheapest can end up being more expensive in the long run if the contractor's work is defective and you need to hire someone else to correct the mistakes. So before going with the contractor who offers the lowest price, check references (for quality work) and other details, such as materials used in project.

## Schedule and Key Dates

Along with the exact scope of work to be performed, your agreement should specify commencement and substantial completion dates and other due dates; payment terms (discussed next); and how deadlines will be enforced and the contingencies that can extend them (such as change orders, discussed below).

## Payment Terms

Look closely at payment terms (dates, deposit amounts, payment methods, and the like) in your agreement; the details will vary depending on whether you have a fixed-price or a cost-plus agreement. Ask any questions, especially about the timing of payments. A reasonable up-front payment (such as 10% or an amount equivalent to material costs) is fine, but the larger your up-front payment and progress payments along the way, the less leverage you have to insist on timely, high-quality completion. I also favor contractors who allow credit card payments, for ease, rewards/miles, and tracking. This is also a way to screen for more sophisticated, tech-savvy contractors.

## Change Orders

Depending on the job, unforeseen or concealed conditions, such as rot, termites, or asbestos, may result in contract changes or added expenses, even with a fixed-price bid. For example, if you are remodeling an old house or replacing a roof, you will not know exactly what you face until you tear off the old roof or begin demolition. Less reputable contractors may actually give you a low bid up front, knowing they can make a profit on unforeseen or concealed issues (like rot repair).

Your contractor should spell out the procedure and rate for handling extra work in such situations. Often the best way to deal with a concealed condition, even in a fixed-price contract, is on a time and materials (cost-plus) basis. Putting an exact figure on a condition or problem you haven't yet seen is nearly impossible.

Also, the procedure for change orders, where the parties decide how to handle a deviation from the scope of work, should be discussed up front. All change orders should be set out in writing, and signed by both you and the contractor, before the relevant work begins.

## Dispute Resolution

If the wheels fall off the deal, how to handle your dispute is an important decision to work into the contract. The options include mediation, arbitration, small claims court, and civil court. For reasons of time and expense, many homeowners as well as contractors prefer the agreement to require that you start with mediation instead of rushing straight to court. Also, your state may have required steps for handling disputes with licensed contractors, often giving the contractor a chance to cure the problem.

# Signing a Contract

Once you have a chosen a contractor and have a clear scope of work, make sure all the key terms of your agreement are accurately expressed in a written document. The amount and type of paperwork will vary by contractor, project, and whether it is a cost-plus estimate or a fixed-price agreement. Most contractors will have their own form agreements. Some have all the key terms included in the bid and you can simply sign to accept them, while larger projects have multi-page contracts. Study the paperwork. Look up unknown terms and seek professional advice or references where needed. The websites of material manufacturers are ideal, too, for looking up products, materials, and their application.

As you review the agreement, look at key terms discussed above, especially scope of work. You may need to negotiate certain items and tasks at this point—for example, you might agree to a lower grade of material or ask that some of the "not included" items be included; or you may decide to take on a particular task yourself, such as hauling away trash.

CAUTION

**The contractor's agreement may also be telling.** A contractor who doesn't have his or her paperwork in order, or who is unclear about key terms, may not be quite ready for your business. If the contractor can't put the project and terms clearly on paper, how will he or she be able to execute it in reality?

## Insurance May Dictate Your Contractor and Contract

Was your home project necessitated by recent damage (from a storm, pipe break, or the like), which you've called upon your insurance company to cover? If so, realize that working with insurance adjustors poses special challenges and can impact your choice of contractor. First, you'll want to use a contractor experienced in handling matters where an insurance company is involved. Insurers often have exacting standards for payment.

If the insurance company is paying the bills, it will not pay a penny more than its estimating program provides. Much will depend on the terms of your homeowners' policy and the condition of your property before and after the damage.

But all the same rules about scope of work, contractor selection, and documentation apply—except multiplied by ten. You will need a contractor who can communicate verbally and in writing the costs of the project down to the square inch and last nail. Everything will need to be documented and justified.

Some insurance estimating programs may miss (or humans may not enter) key details on trim, square footage in closets and entryways, municipal code requirements, proper materials grades, and current market costs.

If you are up against a multibillion dollar insurance company, a superb contractor—one who excels in building skills, industry knowledge, communication, and billing savvy—will be your ace in the hole. You can level the playing field with the right person working for you.

# Your Role While the Work Is Being Done

Your duties as a landlord do not end after you have arranged for a contractor to work on your rental unit. In fact, they intensify. The risks of injury, property damage, and upset tenants is at its highest during projects involving contractors.

Keeping alert and educated about the process can also make for a smooth working relationship with the contractor. If you are able to converse about procedures, specifications, and products, you are less likely to get into a dispute about billing issues or workmanship. So be available and present when needed.

## Tenant Safety Coordinator and Communications Director

You, not your contractor, know your tenants and can best inform and direct them. It is your job to communicate and protect them and their property during any type of job—be it a simple leaky faucet or complete remodel. The most important thing is to get everything set up with your tenants ahead of time.

If the work will be done *inside* the tenants' rental unit, provide them proper notice of the contractor's entry (your state's law will probably define reasonable notice, such as 24 hours). Pets may be a special issue, so be sure they are put away in a room or the backyard so they won't escape or get frightened. Also, make sure the tenant does whatever's necessary to prepare the work site—for example, if a contractor is installing a new garbage disposal, ask the tenant to clean out the entire area in, around, and under the sink.

If the work will be done *outside* the tenants' rental unit, make sure you alert tenants in writing (email, text, phone call, or note on the door) about any significant work that may affect them or require special action. For example, if you are having the roof repaired or the exterior painted, you should advise the tenants to park away from the building (both to avoid damage to their cars and provide access for the contractor), and remind them not to touch the paint or allow a dog into the yard during the hours the paint will be drying. Or if a landscaper is doing work in the backyard of a single-family rental home, you may want the tenant to leave the driveway free for the landscaper's truck and supplies.

Whether the work is done inside or outside of the rental unit, give your tenants timelines of what to expect (estimate on the high side), and provide updates as the work progresses. If the contractor thinks it will be an hour, plan for three; if the job is for a week, plan for two or three. You will be the conduit between the tenants and the contractor.

## Watch and Learn

You can learn from watching your contractor at work—if he or she is willing. Some contractors may want to be left alone. And that's fine. Others will talk your ear off and are eager to share information. If you can find one open to having a customer watch and learn, here are some of the benefits:

- You may be better able to maintain your rental with the contractor's insights and guidance. Many contractors are glad to show you how to perform preventive maintenance.
- You will gain a better awareness of what a task entails, how long it should take, and what it should cost.
- You could build rapport and trust with a potential long-term contractor.

While you shouldn't expect to learn all the intricacies of plumbing or carpentry, your interactions can take the mystery out of the project. The contractor may even give you money-saving tips or ideas, like the right caulk to use on a shower or how to finish drywall. Also, if you are on site and watching, the contractor can immediately ask about anything unexpected that comes up.

190 | EVERY LANDLORD'S GUIDE TO MANAGING PROPERTY

> ⊘ **CAUTION**
>
> **Be especially alert if the work may involve asbestos or poses any kind of environmental hazard (like lead, asbestos, or mold).** For safety and economic reasons, it's best to hire a contractor to deal with vinyl asbestos floor tiles, older acoustic ceiling tiles, vermiculite or asbestos insulation; and lead paint. Many of these can be encapsulated or are only harmful when disturbed (such as by breaking them up in demolition)—all the more reason not to go poking around yourself. Use qualified firms for detecting and testing for such hazards and only those certified for abatement of hazardous building materials for removal or remediation. Some of these may even require rooms or an entire unit be vacated until deemed safe.

Probably the most challenging processes involve work on areas with lots of foot traffic. This includes projects on stairs, walking paths, or involving doors and windows. Plan for safe temporary access or alternate routes around wet concrete, removed steps, or wet paint. Send tenants periodic construction updates. It will help ease their tension and let them plan their days. Remember, although it is a work site, it is still the tenants' home.

## Gofer, Traffic Cop, and Dust and Mop Brigade

There are typically many tasks that landlords can help with on a job being handled by an outside contractor (depending in part on what you've agreed with the contractor ahead of time). Start by asking the contractor if there is anything special you need to do to prepare the property for the work—such as roping off areas around your duplex or putting up a warning sign, or saving street parking space if parking is difficult in your neighborhood. This will save time and make it easier for your contractors to get the job done. On a more mundane level, you may help speed the work by getting items that a contractor needs from the store, such as an extra piece of lumber or special screws.

Your contractor may prefer you well out of the way, but it is your building, and if you know enough not to actually interfere, the contractor will eventually appreciate your presence.

After the contractor leaves, you can probably find plenty to do in terms of sweeping, dusting, and picking up debris. (Ideally, the contractor will do a good cleanup job, per your written agreement, but something always seems to get overlooked.) And you can always arrive beforehand and put up plastic or lay tarps to manage the dust and debris. I've never had a contractor complain about me covering floors, masking off areas, or getting tenant vehicles out of the way.

When on a job site, be especially vigilant about nails and nails sticking out of boards. These can flatten tires or, worse, injure tenants. Another benefit of being on-site is that you can monitor progress on the project, inspect the materials being used (type of shingles, paint quality, or color codes). Ask for leftovers or at least get the vendor, brand, and color codes.

Of course, if nothing else you can be a highly engaged client, interested, positive and can always be a cheerleader with food and beverages. It can go a long way to keeping contractors at peak performance and grateful.

## Letting Contractors Know You'll Go the Extra Mile to Keep Costs Down

During a recent roofing project, I kept busy on site, sweeping up loose shingles and nails on the ground and laying out tarps to cover plants and lawn areas. Having built rapport and cut down the workers' hours, they thought to mention that the bath fans at the nearby hardware store (where they had an account) were high-end $200 dollar units that would require new framing to install, taking another hour (at $50 per hour). But they also said I could get some that would fit right in at the local big box home improvement store. Off I went and got two for $50; these fans fit right into the existing opening and were installed in minutes. I saved $150 on the fans, and at least another $50 on installation—for both units. This was just one of several times when I was able to make a quick decision that lowered costs—all because I was on the spot.

TIP

**Keep an occupied unit clean.** Proper mats and dust barriers (like a wall of plastic Visqueen) combined with frequent sweeping and vacuuming can keep tenants and workers from tracking dust and debris into units. If it's wet or snowy outside and workers are going in and out (common in construction), consider buying a pack of protective shoe booties for workers to simply slip over their boots upon entry.

## All Around Good Customer

Put yourself in your contractor's shoes. A good contractor has plenty of other customers, and can choose one of them over you next time, so it's in your interest to have someone who's happy to do the next job for you. Here are some of the things you can do to make the contractor's job more desirable:

- pay immediately
- be reasonable in your requests
- be openly appreciative of quality work done on time (in other words, say thank you, post positive reviews online, and so on)
- have the job site prepped and accessible
- establish rapport (maybe you have shared friends or colleagues or have a common interest or background), and
- let the contractor know when you will have additional work in the immediate or longer-term future.

Think about all these from the first meeting, when you can drop some names of mutual friends or other common points of reference. And before you part ways at the end of a job, mention a possible future project, even if it is distant.

## Team Photographer

Try to capture before, during, and after photos of your projects. Really well-organized contractors will do this—especially if they find rot or the two of you agree on a change order, but you can do it as well. A paper or digital file of work done and in progress provides a reference for the future. They can also become "Exhibit A" if a question arises about the work from a future buyer, an insurance adjustor, a city inspector, or in any legal dispute about the work. Photos may even come in handy in a tax audit, if the IRS asks about an expense or repair.

Even if all goes well, some day in the future, you may want to show a potential buyer all phases of what was done. This can help market the property and show transparency and confidence. If you remove sheetrock, consider taking photos to show your framing and pipe and electrical layout. You may not ever get a chance to see behind the wall again.

## Keep the Big Picture in Mind

Your goal is to keep and retain great tenants for the long term. Contractors can help keep you safe and sane in this endeavor. You can easily get worn out physically and psychologically by regularly taking on building problems that are over your head. A nagging property problem can cause sleepless nights. Bending into a dark crawlspace with a sharp tool for hours could leave a landlord physically injured. So, find good contractors and cultivate good working relationships with them. You may get taken a time or two by an unskilled or dishonest contractor, but that is just a minor bump in the road to finding good ones. If you follow this guidance and act honestly and reasonably, good contractors will add a great deal of value to your property and help you keep your best tenants longer. In the big picture, how you manage your contractor relationships will partly determine your success as a landlord.

## What's Next?

The goal of all of the work done by you (in Chapters 3 and 4) and your contractors in this chapter is to offer a desirable product to your tenants; a clean, well-maintained rental unit. The next chapter covers how to find the ideal tenant for your well-prepared rental unit.

# Getting Great Tenants

This chapter (and the three that follow) shifts the focus from managing the rental property to managing the relationship with your tenants. We'll cover the basics of finding, screening, and choosing tenants—from writing an effective ad to showing your property to prospects to setting criteria for and choosing the ones who will live in your property. It includes strategies that will help you build trust and set the stage for a successful tenancy, as well as comply with the maze of federal, state, and local regulations that affect tenant screening and selection.

Once you've chosen a tenant, Chapters 8 through 10 take you through the next steps: signing a lease, ongoing communication through the tenancy, and move-out.

## Developing a Tenant Screening and Selection Plan

Before you write your first ad or schedule a showing with prospective tenants, it's crucial that you make some initial decisions about who you want living in your unit, on what terms you're willing to rent to them, and exactly how you'll go about choosing them. This early planning will make the process of screening and selecting tenants run more smoothly and ensure that you treat all applicants the same. You'll want to start by mapping out all of the following factors (be sure to review these periodically, whether it is your first or 50th time renting a unit):

- what you will include in your lease or rental agreement, such as the amount of rent, the limit on number of occupants, and your policy on pets (see Chapter 8 for details on setting lease terms)
- how you will handle initial inquiries (by phone and/or email), and how you will track and respond to them
- what type of information you'll collect in a rental application, and the specific form you will use, whether online and/or paper
- whether or not you will require a credit report, and what fee (if any) you will charge for this
- how you will show the rental (by appointment or open house), and

- your key criteria for choosing tenants, such as sufficient income to pay the rent, rental history, employment record, and credit profile.

Read on to learn how fair housing laws may restrict how you screen and choose tenants and for advice on landing great long-term tenants.

## Complying With Antidiscrimination Laws

While you are legally free to set legitimate business criteria (such as positive references from previous landlords) for screening and choosing tenants, it is illegal to refuse to rent to someone for a discriminatory reason. The federal Fair Housing Acts (42 U.S. Code §§ 3601–3619, 3631) prohibit discrimination on the basis of race, religion, national origin, gender, age, familial status, or physical or mental disability (which includes recovering alcoholics and people with a past drug addiction). These are called protected categories. Many states and cities also prohibit discrimination based on marital status, sexual orientation, source of income, or gender identity. Knowing and following these laws is crucial to avoiding discrimination complaints and lawsuits.

**RESOURCE**

**Information on antidiscrimination laws.** The U.S. Department of Housing and Urban Development (HUD) website (www.hud.gov) includes federal fair housing rules and a list of state fair housing agencies. You can also get information by phoning HUD's Housing Discrimination Hotline at 800-669-9777.

Here are some tips on complying with fair housing laws.

**Be consistent and treat all applicants equally in all phases of the tenant screening and selection process.** Don't set tougher standards, such as a higher income, or refuse to show the unit to someone, simply because of the person's race or disability.

**Avoid discriminating in your ads or conversations with prospective tenants.** Don't refer (directly or indirectly) to preferences for tenants based on their children/familial status, gender, age, race, number of occupants, or even drug or alcohol use.

**Play it safe even if your property is exempt from federal laws.** Federal fair housing laws exempt owner-occupied properties with four or fewer units, and single-family houses rented without the use of ads or agents (provided you own no more than three rental houses at a time). Even if your rental property is exempt, you should still follow federal fair housing guidelines. Here's why:

- State and local laws may still apply. For example, owner-occupied buildings with four or fewer units are not exempt under California law (while they are exempt under federal law).
- You could still be sued under other federal laws (such as the Americans with Disabilities Act), plus any applicable state or local laws.
- It could be costly even if you prevailed. With legal fees running into the tens of thousands of dollars, you could spend a small fortune just to try and prove that a loophole applies to you. And even if you win, good luck trying to get part of your legal fees paid by the other party when you have an unsympathetic case like one where you are alleged to have discriminated against tenants.
- Refusing to honor federal discrimination laws could be bad public relations and a poor business practice. Word is bound to get out, which could be bad for business long term.

CAUTION

**Don't get analysis paralysis.** Be aware of the groups protected under fair housing laws, but don't be paranoid. Focusing on the protected categories is less helpful than looking at the wide range of legitimate and neutral business criteria that affect a prospect's fitness as a tenant. Gender or ethnicity can't predict a person's ability to pay rent or future behavior. The legal risks are real, but so are the business risks if you are too fearful to screen and select a tenant promptly.

# Managing Prospective Tenants' First Impressions

You and your rental will get just one chance to make a good first impression on prospective tenants. It is a good idea to manage this early tenant selection process closely—from your ads and initial phone contacts through in-person showings. I'll explain this process in detail and its tremendous benefits in helping you secure the best tenants possible.

## Differentiate Your Rental

The rental market can be competitive, so think about how you can set your rental apart and attract the best long-term tenants. This requires both selling the unit *and* your services to a customer (the future tenant). The guidance in Chapters 2 through 6 on choosing and maintaining your unit should give you an edge, with a clean, well-maintained unit in a good location. But your rental is still just a building. If there are many comparable units on the market, then the differentiating factor could be the unit with the most diligent and competent person managing the relationship—namely you.

I have had several great long-term tenants who told me they turned down another unit (even one that may have had a better view or was newer) because I was the first to contact them, show them the unit, lay out the terms clearly, and answer all their questions. Even a perfect property can be flawed if it doesn't have the right landlord. Make sure you have both a great property and the best service.

## Under-Promise and Over-Deliver

Renting real estate is different from selling in many ways. When real estate agents sell houses, they paint visions of perfection and domestic bliss, and then they close the transaction and the parties never see each other again. In a rental situation, you and the tenant will be in an ongoing relationship, perhaps for years. You need to establish good communication and trust from the beginning, because the tenant will expect you to fulfill any promises you made. Whatever terms, conditions, or expectations you set will be part of the ongoing relationship with the tenant.

Often tenants are most dissatisfied if their expectations do not meet reality. If you advertise a "serenely quiet" or "peaceful" place, or overuse terms like "security" and "safety," consider whether you can control and meet these expectations. If not, leave words like these out of your ads or conversations. Claiming that the neighborhood is very quiet when it isn't, or is in a "safe neighborhood" when crime levels are on the rise, for instance, might not only violate consumer fraud laws, but also undermine the foundation of honesty and trust in a successful landlord-tenant relationship. Such statements could be used against you in a legal dispute if a tenant relies on them and then finds the unit is in a very noisy area or is a crime victim on the property.

Give the most honest description or answer to a tenant's question you can, let prospective tenants know your management philosophy, and offer total property transparency. Someone who becomes your tenant will know the limits of what you can and cannot do and adjust their expectations accordingly. See "Answer Prospects' Questions Honestly," below, for more on this.

Similarly, if you fail to deliver on something you promise, a tenant will not only be unhappy, but may have grounds to terminate the tenancy early. Let's say, for example, you get caught up in the moment and tell a prospective tenant that you'll install a new lawn and a new fence for his dog and children if he signs a one-year lease for your single-family home. He relies on that oral promise in signing the lease. But you never follow through, and point out that it's not required in the lease. Your tenant may be able to get out of the lease or pursue some other remedy based on his reliance on your statement, even though it wasn't in writing.

# Crafting Your Advertisement or Posting

Browse your local rental ads and you will likely see a range of quality. Some ads will likely be professional and precise, giving a clear picture of the property and how to proceed. Other ads may read awkwardly and neglect to include some basic information about the rental unit and lease terms.

Experienced landlords and managers likely placed the higher-quality ads. They have the experience and communication skills to effectively convey the features and terms of their rental. Your goal is to craft a similarly high-quality ad with the right amount of information, designed to target the tenants who are seeking exactly what you have to offer.

## Decide Where and How to Advertise

There are a range of methods to let people know about your rental—from old-fashioned newspaper classifieds and fliers posted at the local laundromat to online postings on Craigslist and other social media. How you post and market your rental begins your process of sifting renters. If you use print newspaper, you will reach a different audience than if you post online. Your choice of advertising depends on several factors.

**The audience you want to reach.** Landlords who mainly rent to students will want to sign up with college housing offices, while those hoping to attract tech industry workers should post online.

**Your advertising options.** Free and popular online advertising services like Craigslist are common in most areas.

**The location and type of rental.** Posting a "for rent" sign in front of your fourplex may be just fine if you think neighbors or passersby may be a source of leads but less useful in a secluded area.

Current tenants, say in a multiplex, can also be a good resource for filling vacant units. Next to you, they have the most at stake in getting a good tenant (a quiet, agreeable neighbor). If the current tenant is a good one, there's a fair chance that their friends and acquaintances will be suitable, too. Do all the same screening and use your same criteria, and if your current tenants' recommendations are suitable, you may not even need to advertise.

> **CAUTION**
>
> **Bad guys read "For Rent" signs, too.** If you hang one in a window or front yard, and the unit is clearly vacant, it could be an invitation for vandalism or theft. In some neighborhoods, you might even lose home appliances and housing components like copper pipe. So gauge whether it is worth the risk. Also, if you hang a sign on an occupied unit, protect tenants by listing your phone number and email plus a "Please don't disturb occupants" note.

## Tailor Your Ads for Maximum Impact

Wherever you advertise, your ad should include key terms and details of your rental—the location, rent amount, pet policy, and anything else that will attract the largest pool of highly qualified applicants. While new landlords tend to write a short story about their place and large property managers just give a sentence or two, you might look for a happy medium. See "Sample Rental Ad," below, for a good model.

The poetic language of real estate and rental ads ranges from the clever to the bizarre, sometimes masking the truth. For example, a "small study" is often just a walk-in closet, and I have seen some "peaceful settings" adjacent to cemeteries. Make sure the reality of your unit matches its advertisement. You could mention one or two of the property's most favorable features in a factual way ("fenced backyard" or "close to parks and trails"), but let your ad stand out in terms of price, terms, and clarity.

In the past, the per-character or line charges of newspaper classifieds gave landlords a financial incentive to be concise. Today, Craigslist and online media have freed you to write more—but don't overwhelm readers with volume.

Sometimes the ads for rentals provide unwitting clues about who is a novice, a pro, or simply in trouble. First-time landlords often write an essay about their unit in loving detail. They include esoteric building and construction information, and even occasional terms or comments that run afoul of landlord-tenant laws and fair housing guidelines (excluding children or expressing a preference for single people, for example). If you stick to the facts of your rentals, you can avoid such problems.

Keep in mind that your advertisement can do much of the screening for you by eliminating people looking for more bedrooms, shorter leases, and different locations. This can save you many wasted contacts and phone calls. The advertisement is also your very first communication, and can set the expectations of the tenancy.

**TIP**
**There's no need to talk to everyone in your area looking for rental housing.** It will wear you out and drive you crazy. You want to have contact only with those looking for a unit like yours, in your price range and location. Further, they should be amenable to the other terms in your ad.

## Determine How You Will Handle Inquiries

Use a level of technology and method that is comfortable for you in communicating with prospective tenants. If you're a phone person, that's a fine way to receive calls and get prospects. Your openness to texts, emails, and other forms of communication will set your level of technology usage as a norm for later in the tenancy. As a small landlord, you probably don't need a website. Unless you own over eight to ten rental units, you probably won't have enough vacancies to justify it. Plus, you can post the same information online for free, and simply email prospects your rental application.

## Sample Rental Ad

Below is a generic example of an ad format I have successfully used in the past. Posted in the proper category (*apt/housing for rent*) on Craigslist, it could include photos as well as a mapped address. If you are advertising on Craigslist, be sure to check the correct posting detail boxes on pets, laundry, smoking, and parking. This will quickly convey your policies and rental features to prospective tenants. But also include the rental terms and more details in the body of the post, to reemphasize, for example, that pets are allowed "on approval." Also, you can use the optional map function at the bottom of the page so that you don't have to write out driving directions.

If you use traditional classifieds or another online site, the same general rules listed below apply. Here is a sample.

---

**Available Now! 2BR/1 BA.** $1,000/mo. Lower level unit in fourplex in College Park neighborhood. Pets on approval. 6-mo- or 1-year lease. $1,000 deposit. 2 designated parking spots. Rent includes water and trash, washer/dryer in unit. Contact Mike by phone (555-1212) or email (mike@mike.com) for a showing or rental application.

---

Let's dissect each part of this ad and think about the significance of the words and terms. Don't forget that you can add anything else that might be especially important to renters, such as a yard for pets, partial furnishings, or a garage or storage area.

## Available Now

The key here is that you want people who are ready for a place now —like today, not in a few months. Ideally, post on a Friday, before the weekend, or a time when you'll be available to show the place to prospective renters. If you have a conventional weekday work schedule, try and post your ad Friday night; that way you can take calls all day Saturday and even schedule showings later that day or on Sunday. Weekends and after work are when many tenants are free to search for rentals, too.

Advertising the immediate availability of your rental unit distinguishes it from those about to be vacated or those still being cleaned up or in the turnaround process. You'd be surprised how many landlords advertise places that will be ready at some vague date in the future or are still occupied, only to have to turn away people who need to move in pronto. See "Avoid Showing an Occupied Unit," below, for more on the subject.

## 2BR/1BA

Renters shop for housing primarily based on the number of bedrooms and baths. Logically, they should also consider size (square footage), but many don't. In most cases, renters think in terms of bedrooms and bathrooms because they need a separate bedroom for each roommate or family member, or don't want to share a bathroom. I always have the square footage available for any inquisitive tenants, but leave it out of the rental ad.

## $1,000/mo

As a small landlord, I would use a straightforward, no-gimmick rental rate, unlike some of the off-combinations (such as "free first month's rent") you'll see in ads for rentals in large complexes. Ideally, your rate will say it all— being just below the market rate. That gets the emails rolling in and the phone ringing better than a free toaster oven or complicated pricing scheme. See Chapter 8 for advice on setting rent.

## Lower Level

Here, I signal that someone would not need to navigate the stairs daily or move furniture up steps. This can be a real draw for people who want to avoid the inconvenience of climbing a lot of stairs with bags of groceries, older pets, or toddlers in a stroller. However, "lower level" also signals to prospects that they may have a tenant above them (in a multilevel unit), which is a common source of foot-traffic noise. While mentioning the level of the unit can give prospective tenants clues about the fitness of the rental for their lifestyle and for convenience, you also need to be wary of disability discrimination or illegally "steering" people away from a particular unit, such as one on the second floor of a building without an elevator, based on disability.

## Fourplex

The building style matters to many renters. Some renters have a clear preference for a single-family home, a townhouse, or a standard apartment. In this case, the smaller multiplex signals that this is not a single-family home, but it is not a 100-unit apartment complex, either. You may also have to describe it to a new tenant over the phone, or simply have an exterior building photo available with the ad or on request.

## College Park Neighborhood

Location should be prominent in your ad, to separate out people who don't want to live where your rental is located. You could list a particular neighborhood, area of town, district or suburb, or a major street or cross streets. Many renters are looking for a distinct area or neighborhood, so having that in your ad gets your rental on their list. If your rental is too remote from a person's workplace or out of their children's school district, or doesn't fit their lifestyle, it's probably not a good fit.

## Pets on Approval

Here, I have advertised pets are a possibility. Due to the high numbers of pet owners in this country, this feature of the rental will set it apart from the majority of large complexes that have strict "no-pets" policies. It drives up the interest in your unit exponentially. But notice I am not automatically saying "yes" to all pets of all types and numbers. The condition "on approval" is very important, and this topic and pet policies are explored in depth in Chapter 8.

## Six-Month or One-Year Lease

The goal here is to aim for long-term tenants, while simultaneously screening out short-term tenants. If you forget to list the desired tenancy length, you will get a barrage of short-term tenants, even those asking for weekly rates. Also, advertising two options, six months or one year, helps you appear flexible. As mentioned in Chapter 4, almost all your work as a landlord will be in turning around units—preparing and rerenting them. You can reduce your tenant turnover dramatically if your ad helps screen for long-term renters from the outset.

## $1,000 Deposit

A common security deposit level—both provided by law and rental markets—approximates one month of rent. This amount passes muster in all 50 states, and it provides some level of security in the event of nonpayment of rent.

It is not uncommon to see ads where landlords ask for unreasonable and even illegal deposit amounts. Even if your state has a higher limit, however, you'll want to make sure you have a valid reason for requesting that amount, and that the market will bear it. For example, you may require a higher deposit for pets or if offering a high-end rental. See Chapter 8 for more on the subject of deposits.

## Two Designated Parking Spots

Americans coast to coast are attached to their automobiles. Your prospective renters will therefore want to know about your unit's parking, including the number of spots. Also mention whether parking is off-street or on-street, if it is covered, and if it is designated (as opposed to first come, first serve). People also covet garages, both for their cars and storage. So mention all these aspects if you have them. It may also be important to list parking for recreational vehicles and boats in some communities.

## Rent Includes Water and Trash

Be clear about what the rent payment includes. If you scan rental ads in your area, you may notice that some are cryptic about what they actually include. Some rates may look low, but come with high utility bills and add-ons. Extra expenses from unexpected utility bills are a common tenant complaint, so disclose what your rent includes and what the tenant can expect to pay for utilities.

Get estimates or past bills for the unit from utility companies, and have these on hand at the showings (or send scanned bills to interested tenants). Be prepared to tell prospects that utility bills may vary based on usage and the number of tenants. If utility bills aren't available, do your best to come up with an estimate (you should be able to get information from tenants who are moving out), and err on the side of higher estimates; this way, tenants will more likely be pleasantly surprised rather than upset when the first bill arrives.

## Washer/Dryer in Unit

In the old days, this would be abbreviated w/d and that still may be used in your area, but I would avoid an ad that appears in code or uses too many abbreviations. Many new renters will not understand them.

> **TIP**
> **Don't write in code.** It was not uncommon 15 or 20 years ago to see a newspaper ad saying 2BR/1BA, Close In, w/d, d/w, incls w, s, g, h, pet on app, 700/mo +700 dep, crd and back chk. Even if you use a newspaper or weekly circular, today's renter may not understand all the lingo, and may not call.

## Contact Information

Your ad should clearly say how to contact you by phone or email for additional information. (And make sure it's a realistic way to reach you.)

# Should Your Ad Include Exact Street Address and Photos?

When crafting your ad, you'll want to consider how specific to be about the rental location, and whether to include photos. Your decision may depend on your particular rental unit and the overall rental market.

## Address of Rental

Including the exact street address may be useful to weed out uninterested tenants, but there can be downsides, too, particularly in metro areas where the address may bring too many onlookers. As with posting a "For Rent" sign, you may encounter problems with vandals, or face complaints from current tenants if the property is still occupied.

You're often better off listing the general area in the ad, and then giving a more specific address only to those who contact you and want to see the place. Not listing an exact address also prevents someone else from using your posting, photos, and address in a rental scam (called "scraping") to collect money from interested tenants. (See "Avoid Online Rental Scams," below.) If you don't want to give the exact address on Craigslist (viewable to anyone in the world), you can streamline giving directions to prospects with a pattern email script that you can simply cut and paste for those who want to do a drive by or see the neighborhood.

## Photos of Rental

Whether you include photographs may depend on several factors. Photos can be helpful for prospective tenants, but they also have risks. Photos can over-idealize a unit if they were taken when it was newly remodeled five years ago, and a tenant may be let down if the reality does not measure up. On the flip side, photos can look underwhelming, depending on the lighting, angles, and other factors such as your skills as a photographer and your camera.

You can find great tenants with or without photos in your ads. Think about what works best for you and the particular unit. Some units, like people, are just more photogenic. Others, like a lower-unit corner condo with few windows, may not photograph well at all but look great in person. If you browse your local rent ads, you will find some photos may actually be a deterrent. Looking at standard empty rooms is often not that compelling. You can always offer photos on request. And much of what will distinguish your unit may not be available through photos. The prospective tenant can't get a full picture of the cleanliness or pleasant smell, or even get to meet the very reasonable landlord from just a few photos of rooms that look like the rest.

More enticing than photos are your rental terms. If you are at or below market rents, in a fairly convenient neighborhood, and you allow pets, then in most markets your phone will ring regularly and your email will get plenty of reply messages with or without photos.

**TIP**

**Take photos at move-in time.** Whether or not you post photos with your ad, you should take some photos of all the rooms just before you begin showing the unit, to record it's "before" condition. You could use these to show interested prospects who ask for photos, or keep them should your tenants dispute your evaluation of the condition of the unit at move out. See the discussion of move-in checklists in Chapter 8.

# Making Initial Contact With Prospective Tenants

Ideally, your advertisement will greatly reduce the pool of potential renters down to those truly interested in the size, price, location, and terms you are offering. But your first contact, whether by phone or email, is also a chance for another level of sifting. You will be finding out about the applicants and they will be finding out about you and the unit.

## Handle Phone Calls and Emails Promptly

Once you have your advertisement up, do your best to keep your cell phone on and take the calls and texts as they come in. If you have a day job, you can let the messages build up until you take a break or get off work; then just go through the numbers in your list and call them all back in order. Email also works well. Keep a list by name and number to track all your prospects and communications. Send everyone interested a rental application, answer any questions, and see if you can schedule a showing (more on this later). Be sure you've had some communication with the prospect before scheduling a showing, to make sure you've discussed the terms of your rental and clarified their interest level in your unit.

 **TIP**

**You can set up a separate email address (for free) solely for rental contacts and your rental business.** It keeps the prospective tenant contacts separate from your home email and may reduce spam or unwanted solicitations. I made my email include my city and the word rental (yourtownrentals@email.com), a professional touch. I give tenants my other contact info once they sign a lease. Also, if you just have few rentals, you probably won't have the volume of calls to justify a separate cell phone; but if you use your personal cell phone for business, you may be able to deduct part of the cost (as discussed in Chapter 12).

Tracking and responding to calls may be challenge for the part-time landlord with a day job. Don't try to field these on your employer's time. Instead, plan to post your ad in the evening on a night before you are off work for at least a day or two.

It will make a strong first impression if you pick up the phone or get back to people right away. In busy rental markets, tenants learn not to expect return calls the same day or even at all. I try to get back with everyone the same day. People are often surprised and mention I am the first or only return call. Such a practice not only sets the tone for responsive management, but results in more leads and more applications, increasing your chances of getting the best long-term renter possible.

## Be Prepared to Answer Common Questions

As you answer phone, email, or text messages, you'll often find that what you are getting are questions. This is a good thing. Some people will simply ask whether the rental unit is available and when they can see it. Others will be trying to find out if your unit fits their particular needs. Be ready for such questions, but don't try to oversell the property—there's no sense wasting either of your time if it becomes clear that this will not be a good fit. Many times your dealings with prospective tenants will end when they hear your answers to their questions or learn more about your unit or terms.

People will commonly ask these types of questions by phone or email:

- Do you take Section 8 (see below for more on this)?
- Do you have room for boat or RV parking?
- Do you allow certain pets (*insert exotic breeds or large number of pets*)?
- Will you allow a shorter tenancy?
- Will you hold a unit for a set time (*insert number of months*)?
- Does your unit have a certain feature (*insert dishwasher, garage, storage space, or yard*)?
- Can we do a certain activity (*insert day care, car repair, pet sitting, home business*)?
- Can I pay the first month's rent and deposit in installments?
- Do you limit the number of people who can live there?

Ideas for helping you craft policies, lease terms and rules related to many of these questions are found throughout this book.

## Make a Plan for Dealing With Out-of-Towners

Technology has made it possible for landlords to get calls from around the country and even the world. While I'm always glad to tell people about rentals on the phone or to arrange a showing when they arrive in town, I don't accept a deposit or close rental transactions at a distance—even if I have a completed rental application and a promise to pay rent in advance. I insist on meeting my tenants and showing them the unit first. (Being a landlord is a different legal relationship, for example, from a short-term online vacation rental, so you want more information for both parties.)

Trying to explain a unit to an out-of-town tenant just leaves too much possibility for later misunderstandings. If you have a quality unit at the right price, you will have plenty of strong renters in town, so go with the people who have seen it and inspected it closely. Of course, I sympathize with someone who does not want to arrive in town homeless, so I answer questions and suggest moderately priced extended stay hotels (even ones that allow pets) or short-term vacation rentals. I let callers know I will show them the unit if it is still available when they arrive in town. Ironically, I almost never hear from these people again, making me wonder if their relocation plans fizzled or my rental was not really a good fit—in which case it's really a good thing we weren't locked in to any legal lease or relationship.

While I don't take money at a distance from someone who wants to rent sight unseen, I have closed deals at a distance—but only if the person has actually seen the unit beforehand. You can easily do the rental forms online or via fax.

## Avoid Online Rental Scams

The Internet is ripe with scams of all types, so don't become a victim or embroiled in one. If you show enough rentals, someone will show up with a story about how they experienced a scam or wanted to make sure your unit was really available and that you were the actual owner. One of the most common and easiest scams for con artists involves using a real ad for a vacant unit in the area and then getting people to contact them about it. Then the supposed rental property owner claims to be out of town and not have the key and attempts to get a holding deposit or even the rent and a deposit wired to them. By not taking money at a distance from people you have never met in person, you distinguish yourself from these scams right away.

TIP

**Be a landlord, not a one-person welcoming committee.** My first few years as a landlord, I spent hours talking to out-of-town prospects who had hundreds of questions about my community, moving there, and everything from shopping to entertainment to recreation. In retrospect, none of these people ever panned out as a renter. Rather, they were just seeking general information about housing, the city, climate, and moving logistics. So I realized eventually that I could not be the source of inside community and rental market information for everyone coming to town. Your cell number makes you a public resource in some prospective renter's eyes.

## Communicate Directly With Tenants (Not Their Parents)

From time to time, someone will call about your unit on behalf of another person—the most common situation being a parent calling on behalf of a son or daughter. The parents may want to know if you are willing to have a cosigner on the lease or rental agreement. This may not be a problem in the case of college students or first-time renters (see the discussion of cosigners in Chapter 8). But I want to make sure that the son or daughter is driving the bus—not the parents. The prospective tenants need to be motivated enough to call and make the appointment, come to the showing, ask me questions, and answer mine. Having a solid cosigner is not enough.

I had problems (late rent and an unusual numbers of guests) two times (early in my landlord career) renting to young couples who were living at a parent's place before moving into my rental. In retrospect, I realized the parents were driving the process and the tenants probably never wanted to move away from the free rent and comfort of Mom and Dad's. No wonder they never took responsibility for the rental and its terms.

Today, if a parent calls me about a place for a failure-to-launch son or daughter, I tell them to have the son or daughter call me. They never do.

# Emailing Rental Applications to Interested Parties

When I started in the landlord business, I would print dozens of applications for each vacancy. A stack would disappear after every showing. But in the last few years, probably 90% or more of applicants prefer that I email the application.

There are several advantages to using email. I can give the application to people on the first communication when they contact me in response to my advertisement. I can email it to a prospect's address when they arrive at a showing, and never run out. I can store rental applications without printing any paper or taking up a file cabinet. Easy, secure delivery is another bonus of email. Applicants can just type in the answers and mail it back. It saves paper and hassle.

Also, I think you get more accurate applications through email, because people have time to look up their information, such as references' phone numbers. They don't have to scramble to quickly fill out the application on the kitchen counter at the end of the showing. This speeds up the showing process, too. If they like the place, the application is in their inbox and they can fill it out at their home on their time.

You can still have a few paper applications on hand at showings. A few people may fill an application when they see your place. Be sure to give others an option to drop the application off with you at a later time or leave it in a secure designated spot on the property. Tracking people down or working out the logistics of dropping an application off is always a challenge for people who can't fill it out on site at the showings. See "Great Screening Begins With a Thorough Rental Application," below, for details on the contents of rental applications and using them to screen and select tenants.

> ⚠ **CAUTION**
> **Avoid fair housing complaints by giving everyone who's interested a rental application**—even if you don't think the person can meet your criteria. And be sure that each adult who will be living in the rental unit completes an application.

# Final Steps in Preparing Your Rental for Showing to Prospects

All your efforts to get your rental in top condition, covered in Chapters 3 through 5, are designed to help you attract tenants. But even after you've done the important maintenance and turnaround work, you still want to put your unit in an ideal state to stand out.

## Easy Ways to Add Wow Factors to Showings

Chapter 4 explains how to get your unit in show condition for a new tenant. Here are some additional small touches (fairly simple and low cost) that can help your unit stand out, and impress the prospects viewing it:

- Add live flowers in pots at the front entry and on the back porch in spring and summer.
- Paint the exterior door and trim (and mailbox, if any).
- Add new doormats (just inside and right outside the front door) and put a new bath mat and shower curtain in the bathroom(s).
- Add new window curtains if yours are dated (get them on sale in the discount aisle and save them for the next eventual vacancy). Use simple-to-install curtains that slide on a rod. Then make sure to pull the curtains back or leave them open to let in light.
- Bring in a tasteful standing floor lamp with high-wattage bulb. Place it in any dark corner or area.
- In landscaped areas, add new mulch.
- If you have a single-family house or multiplex with a lawn, make sure it has been mown within the last few days, and sweep away any grass clippings or leaves on the walks.
- Make sure the interior temperature is comfortable. Arrive early to cool or warm the unit for the showings.
- Place an attractive bowl of higher-end candy (not Halloween leftovers) on the kitchen counter.

## Make Sure Your Unit Passes the Sniff Test

The first smell the prospective tenant gets when entering your unit is as important as the visual impression. Aim for either no odor at all (some tenants even have sensitivities to fragrances) or a natural scent. You don't need to be an expert in aromatherapy, but imagine the prospective tenant has just visited several malodorous units and now walks into one where the landlord is more attuned to smell. Here are a few ideas on using the sense of smell to your advantage.

**At a minimum, make sure your turnaround process has vanquished bad smells or lingering unpleasant odors such as from tobacco or pets.** It may take intensive cleaning, sealing, or even removal of offending areas of carpet, but it's worth it. For more on cleaning and removing odors see "Pet, Tobacco, and Other Odors" in Chapter 4.

**Avoid air fresheners and synthetic products that mask odors.** Masking an odor with an arsenal of sprays, plug-ins, and other products does not help build a long-term relationship with tenants. They will discover the odor within a few days of move-in. It's better to eliminate odors before showing a unit and then use scents to enhance the showing.

**Bring in fresh air.** If you won't be letting in nearby street traffic or noise, open a window and air out the unit when you arrive if the weather allows.

**Go for natural aromas.** Use a citrus or pleasant-smelling cleaner in the prepping process, and go over surfaces right before or in between showings. Some of the best smells conjure up baking or the holidays. Add a teaspoon or two of vanilla to a small warm pan, or add a few cinnamon sticks to boiling water.

> **TIP**
>
> **Small, lightweight metal pans designed for backpackers are handy for creating natural aromas.** Place the vanilla or cinnamon stick and water in the small pan, and put it on a hot burner a few minutes before a showing. As the pan cools, place it in the under-oven drawer, out of sight, but still emitting a pleasing smell. Keep it there and repeat the process until all your showings are done.

## Avoid Showing an Occupied Unit

While some landlords show occupied units, I wouldn't unless absolutely necessary. Here are just a few reasons why:

- the unit may be a mess
- a disgruntled tenant may make a negative comment, and
- scheduling a time that works for everyone is challenging, especially since you may need to follow proper notice requirements in your state and listed in your lease (typically 24 hours).

While you may think you can reduce vacancy time between tenants, you may simply be wasting your time, and worse, losing good prospects whom you could have landed with a clean, vacant unit that you have turned around properly.

Not only will you want the current tenant gone before showing a unit, you will likely need some time to do your regular maintenance and cleaning (see Chapter 4) between tenancies. If your previous tenant is still packing boxes (or is not even at that stage), you've lost control of the unit's cleanliness, appearance, odor, and presentation. So don't even schedule showings until you have been through the unit and have it in good condition. As a small-time landlord, you have the luxury of fewer vacancies and you can take the time to get one tenant out smoothly, do your turnaround properly, and prepare for the next tenant.

But what if you must show an occupied unit—whether because of logistics, economics, timing, or some other necessity that requires you to show it? Consider prepping both the old and new tenant. Ask the current tenant to make the unit as presentable as possible and to put away pets. Tell the tenant you won't ask him or her to comment or engage with the prospective tenant ("We won't bother you with any questions; all you have to do is open the door").

Then make sure to tell the prospective tenant to use some imagination and picture the unit vacant. Bring along a measuring tape and ask the prospective tenant ahead of time about the amount and size of furniture they will be bringing. Focus any time in the unit on dimensions and square footage, the number and layout of rooms, and facts about the unit. This may pull the attention away from the outgoing tenant's personal property or cleanliness. Also, tell the prospective tenant about your turnaround process (cleaning, painting, and so forth) and what you will do before turning the unit over. Then hope for the best.

> **CAUTION**
> **There are situations in which a landlord can show an occupied unit successfully**—for example, if you have a neat-as-a-pin tenant who hasn't started packing and doesn't mind the showings, (especially if the tenant's furnishings and design are appealing); or a friend or acquaintance of the departing tenant is interested in renting the unit, having already seen it on prior visits, and the current tenant is happy to cooperate.

## Prepare for a Safe Showing

Locations vary widely in regard to crime and safety, and you never know who may call you for a showing. Here are some tips for a safe showing.

**Only schedule daylight showings.** The tenant really needs to see the place in the light anyway. Use this rationale if someone insists on a night showing.

**Find out all you can about the prospect ahead of time.** Get the full name, phone number, and email. Text or email your application and ask the prospect to return it in advance. Be on the alert for anything troubling about the person or circumstances. You can use the Internet to find out more about the person for your safety and his or her fitness as a tenant, but don't decline a showing for discriminatory reasons (the person's age, gender, race, and so on).

**Always bring a fully charged cell phone.** You may need it to take calls from prospective tenants to schedule showings or guide lost prospects to the rental property.

**Bring someone along if it is prudent based on your area or your circumstances—particularly if you're holding an open house and expect a crowd.** Have a friend or spouse doing odd jobs around the unit (even if just for a presence).

**Have a "Plan B."** If your comfort level or suspicions are aroused, call the prospect and say you had a scheduling issue. Call off the showing. Reschedule when you can bring someone along.

**Have an exit strategy.** Leave the front door and back door unlocked for the showing, all lights on and the curtains open, in case you want to get out quickly.

**In a marginal situation, take a phony call in the parking lot or from your car, or have someone call you at a set time.** Let the prospective tenant look inside alone.

**Develop an emergency script to end a showing before it even starts.** If someone appears intoxicated, unstable, or threatening, have a quick explanation of why you can't go inside the unit together. Stay in your car or a publicly visible area and tell them the exterminator got mixed up and just visited so there are toxic fumes for 24 hours. Make sure you aren't basing an emergency simply on any discriminatory factor, like race or gender, but on some neutral characteristic like threatening behavior or intoxication.

## Setting Up and Staggering Your Showings

Once you have interested prospects who understand the terms of your rental and are interested in seeing the place, it's time to show it. You have several options: individual appointments at a time convenient to a prospect; an open house when you show the rental to everyone who's interested; or a staggered showing, when you make appointments in 15-minute increments.

What will work best depends on many factors, including your market, your schedule, and what the prospective tenants prefer. In some areas, tenants may be accustomed to traditional open houses and come en masse. In other areas, you may not get much interest in an open house. My preference is for the staggered showing. This is a hybrid option that consolidates the timing like an open house, but lets you provide individualized attention. It avoids crowding and the stress that this puts on neighbors or other tenants (in a multiunit complex).

## How to Stagger Appointments

By simply modifying the traditional open house, small-time landlords can get more control, offer better service, and create less stress for prospective tenants (and you). Rather than have all prospects show up at one time, try to individually schedule them in a block of time, about 15 minutes apart for several hours on a weekend afternoon or early evening.

Setting up a staggered showing is easy when you have interested prospects. After you've been in contact with someone and answered any questions, simply provide the address and when you can show the place: "The apartment is at 33 Park Lane, I can show it to you tomorrow at 1:30 p.m." If the person doesn't already have your cell phone number, provide that, too, and get theirs. Then tell the next prospect you can show the unit at 1:45 p.m., and schedule successive callers in increments for whatever time block you have allowed.

### Winning the Phone Tag Game

Ideally, you'd want to answer every call and talk with your prospects a bit before scheduling a showing. But the reality for part-time landlords is often some phone tag. I've gotten over 100 inquiries in a day on a single unit at peak times of the year. If you've gone back and forth and a particular prospect is clearly interested, you can cut through some of the back and forth by leaving this type of phone, text, or email message: "I can show the rental at 33 Park Lane at (*insert date and time*). I'll expect to see you then, unless I hear from you otherwise." Then you can answer questions at the showing. Suggest a time after work or early evening, when you can consolidate showings. Otherwise, if you wait to hear back or until you can actually talk to everyone who's left a message (and only schedule a showing time during a phone conversation), you will have a time lag, which can be a day or two (and you could lose prospects).

Staggering each appointment should give you a steady but not overwhelming flow of prospects. You could start with scheduling people every 30 minutes if you think more time will help, or if you have a larger property, such as a two-story single-family house. But 15 minutes should be more than enough time for prospects to look around and ask questions; if not, someone could keep looking while you greet the next appointment if they are keenly interested, but most will have decided whether they want to submit an application after a few minutes. Just stick to your schedule and politely start on the exterior or parking area toward the end of your time frame to transition out of the unit.

As you get the routine and rhythm, you can reduce the time and stagger prospective tenants in a way that fits your property and showing style. The key is that everyone gets the same treatment and time to view the unit and ask questions. Offer everyone a paper application or email one if you haven't already.

Of course some prospects will not be able to come in at the time you initially suggest, so as slots open up, you can pencil in later inquiries. The key is to make one trip to the unit and show it to several tenants in one time block. If you get a prospect who can only see the unit at a certain time, then try to schedule some subsequent showings around that same time. I try to block at least three to five showings together.

> **CAUTION**
>
> **Knowing that there's competition adds urgency.** You don't need to crowd 20 people into a one-bedroom apartment to make them see that they're not the only ones hoping to move in. With staggered showings, they will see the other prospects leaving just as they are arriving, and others arriving just as they are leaving. Many prospective tenants also ask about the level of interest in the unit, and I simply tell them the number of showings or calls I've received on the unit. The process is always competitive for well-priced, clean units in good markets.

## Why Staggered Showings Can Give Small Landlords an Edge

Remember, part of your differentiation strategy is personalized service. If you are doing your job properly, you won't have many vacancies and can afford to go all out when you have one. A busy property manager with several hundred units and perpetual vacancies can't do that.

You wouldn't really be able to demonstrate personalized service in an anxious crowd of 20 applicants at a traditional open house. Staggering your showings to have time with each legitimately interested candidate lets you match names (from online applications) to faces, address individual needs and questions, treat all applicants equally (thus avoiding discrimination complaints) and ultimately see who's the best fit. Because one of the prospects will likely move in, the time you've spent orienting that person to the property will not have been wasted.

## Dealing With No-Shows and Drive-Bys

There are few inevitable quirks of the showing process, such as no-shows and people who drive up but then drive away. These are just part of the business. If their mind was that made up they are probably not tenants who would have worked out anyway. Besides, those who don't bother to call are probably not the conscientious sorts you want as long term renters.

In preparation for the inevitable no-show and drive-by prospects, gather contact information ahead of time. It may be that the person is simply lost or couldn't read the house number. Also bring along a book (like this one), an e-reader, or paperwork, or a list of light tasks to do just in case someone is a total no-show. You will be even more ready for the next showing in a few minutes!

If someone arrives so late they missed their time slot, greet them and invite them to look around and take an application, but stick mostly with your on-time prospects. If you notice an inordinate number of drive-bys, consider whether there's a reason. Is your curb appeal up to par? If so, it was probably something about the location or even the prospective tenants. Or maybe your unit was so nice they knew they'd never have a chance to store their three junk cars or to let their pet goats inside. Count your blessings. You will have great prospects coming by in a few minutes.

> **TIP**
>
> **Encourage a preemptive drive-by.** I encourage callers who want to know more about the area or building to do a drive by *before* scheduling the showing. If they like the neighborhood, layout, and look of the place from the outside, they can arrange to have a look inside. This prevents the awkward moment when I look out and wave at people as they duck in their car or quickly drive away.

## Closing the Door on Traditional Open Houses

Consider whether the traditional open house fits with your overall strategy to offer personalized service and to set your unit apart. A standard open house, where you show the unit for a set time to the public in a "come one, come all" format has many drawbacks and may not be ideal for the smaller landlord who has fewer vacancies. There are a number of logistical issues and risks involved in a traditional open house showing.

### Traffic and Parking Associated With an Open House

With an open house, you don't know how many people will show up or exactly when they will show up. The traffic and parking could cause issues by taking up a current tenant's parking spot or filling the street and annoying neighbors. If you are doing a showing at a condo or a property in a tightly controlled homeowners' association (especially one with strict street parking rules or a gated entry), you can count on ruffling some feathers if you try to bring in ten or 15 cars at a time on a Saturday morning.

Condo or homeowner association (HOA) scenarios call for tact and consideration. Consider doing quiet, one-person individualized showings during the weekday, if possible, when fewer residents are around. If you have to cross a common area, like a lobby, elevator, or gate, be sure and find out your association's rules and guidelines for this process.

## Noise, Damage, or Theft at an Open House

Open houses present risks for all types of rental properties. These include neighbor complaints, owing to the increased noise levels and possible damage to other cars or property as the various vehicles pull in and out. Within your unit, it's harder to make sure nothing gets broken, with many hands trying all the knobs and fixtures. If you have a multiplex, you also could risk a theft in another unit or from porches and yards.

## Inability to Connect With Prospects

Even if you can avoid a traffic jam or other problems, the traditional open house may not let you connect one-on-one with the prospects and get to know their needs and answer their questions. There may be an ideal long-term renter at an open house who needs a place that day, but the neighbor who came looking for the free snacks is taking all your time. With a large group, you will find it hard to know who is truly in the market for your unit and who is just browsing.

## Inefficiency

Part of the allure of the traditional open house is consolidating all the showings and prospects into one time slot. And if the traditional open house approach works for you and your situation, that's great. It may fit certain personalities, properties, or landlord styles. But purely on an efficiency basis, it may not be the best choice.

Putting all the interested people into a short open house can mean just one showing time, one trip, and one event. But the quality of interactions suffers. You may not be able to recall who came by and what they were like. You will probably need to follow up with more interactions with serious applicants, so that you can find out later what you would have learned right away in a staggered showing. Plus, an open house may not be much more efficient at all, due to your lack of control. If you have a two- or three-hour open house, and everyone comes in the first 20 minutes, you may find yourself sitting alone for a few hours. Worse yet, some prospects who came during the initial rush may leave frustrated if they can't get your attention or answers to their questions. So your open house may have closed off some prospects.

## Legal Risks

Consider the risks if you can't talk to everyone at an open house, and some people in protected classes feel left out or neglected. In the worst case, the result could be a fair housing claim.

# Your "Sales Pitch" During Showings

You don't need to take any sales courses or read any books on personal selling to be effective. Ideally, the unit, the price and terms, and your management should sell the place. Your job is more about demonstrating what you have to offer, listening to the prospective tenant's needs, and answering questions.

In fact, a soft-sell approach is probably the superior tactic with a rental property. You can show the features and walk through the unit, so that people can visualize whether and how their furniture and lifestyle might fit the unit's dimensions and layout. Don't over-sell or get pushy; if it's not a good fit, and you get people into a unit they don't really want, this will only lead to trouble later.

> 💡 **TIP**
>
> **Try a counterintuitive sales pitch.** Some of the best sales involve not selling at all. You actually can do more listening than talking. Your job is to try and find a prospective tenant's needs and fill them. If your unit works well for the tenants, they will talk themselves into it far better than you ever could. I often leave prospects with this statement: "If you can find a better unit for your needs for the money, please rent it." I actually want them to be sure they got a good value and ideal fit. Otherwise, they will be gone when the lease is up, or earlier.

## Answer Prospects' Questions Honestly

People will ask lots of questions about your rental at showings, many of which will be easy to answer (such as the rent and your policy on pets). Here are other common questions I'm frequently asked. Whether these or others, be sure to tell the truth. Misleading statements, whether in advertising or in person, will only cause you problems down the road.

### Noise

I would guess over half your prospects will ask about noise. I never make assurances about sound or noise. Instead, I disclose what I have heard while working at the unit, give my impressions, and invite people to come back (actually urge them back if it's a concern) at a different time, especially at night. I agree to meet people at the rental at a different hour, or suggest they come by at night and sit in their car in the driveway. (If you arrange this, be sure to tell any other tenants in the rental property about it, so they don't get suspicious.)

### Other Tenants and Neighbors

I take roughly the same approach to questions prospective tenants ask about neighbors, with some variations. In a duplex, triplex, or fourplex, I let applicants know we have a high level of control over the neighbors. I mention if I have gotten any complaints about noise or tenant behavior, explain what type or frequency, and describe my policies for dealing with these kinds of complaints.

If it is a condo, I outline the process for complaining to the association board and the fines for noise violations. (Condos can actually be quite effective at controlling noise, in my experience.) If it is a single-family or multiplex property and neighboring property owners cause noise problems or other concerns, I let prospects know if I have complained to the city/police and the effectiveness (or lack thereof) of my complaint; I also make clear that I cannot control the neighbors' behavior.

### Your Approach to Problems and Philosophy

Many applicants may want to know a bit about your management and role as a landlord. This is an important factor in choosing a rental. But at this short initial meeting, you probably can't answer detailed questions about every policy or scenario (that could come later if someone wants to sign a lease).

You can, however, give any prospective tenant a broad outline of your general landlording approach to major issues and general philosophy. For example, you can let the prospect know that you allow pets on approval (and stress that the pets just can't bother other tenants or damage the unit and must be allowed under your insurance policy); that you have an active maintenance program (mentioning any recent improvements); and that you generally strive to get good tenants and leave them alone, but will respond promptly if there is a building issue or problem with another tenant. A summary of what you do and how you manage the property, without overwhelming prospects with detail, can be part of an honest sales approach.

## Point Out the Property's Flaws, Too

While not the first thing to point out, do mention any downsides to the property. Almost every rental unit has a drawback of one kind or another. It is better that someone knows now (rather than after signing a lease) that a loud train comes by a few times a day or the house two doors down has a barking dog. Take a full-disclosure approach and comply with your state disclosure rules (see Chapter 8 for details).

## What to Cover When Showing a Rental Unit

While you will mostly listen and answer people's questions, be sure to cover the basics when doing a showing. I allocate approximately 15 minutes, which is usually more than enough time to accomplish the following:

- Walk through every room and open all closets, drawers, and cupboards.
- Show the kitchen and bath(s) and turn on and off faucets so they can see the water pressure.
- Let people see the yard, if your property has one.
- Point out parking, storage, trash, and mail.
- Mention nearby features of the area such as parks, bus stops, shopping, or hiking trails.
- Have copies of your lease, policies, and utility bills on the kitchen counter, as well as extra copies of rental applications.
- If it is a condo, cover any association rules, guidelines, or policies.

## Useful Icebreakers

Just as the prospects are screening you and the unit, you are also screening them. Their current living and working situation are always relevant and fairly easy to fit into small talk. (These topics may be covered in your rental application, but there's nothing like hearing it straight from the prospect.)

After you greet the prospective tenants, think about some simple conversation starters. Some of these can lead to more information-rich areas about an applicant's needs and situation:

- So, where are you living now?
- What brings you to town? Why are you interested in moving?
- These units work great for someone who works near (mention a nearby geographic area).

The key is to break the ice and then stop. Let an applicant fill in the blank space. For instance, when you ask where someone is living now, he or she will often tell you a great deal—both favorable and frightening. What a prospect volunteers by way of likes or dislikes about a current living situation can help you determine how well the person would fit your unit. Tenants are often looking for a new place for a reason. For example, if someone tells you he lives in a tiny loft in downtown, your larger suburban unit may be ideal to help him out of the cramped arrangement.

For people who are new in town, it is usually a job that brings them there, which they will soon mention, given a subtle prompt. Another helpful work-related conversation starter is asking about a tenant's commute. You can find out if this location will be convenient and why the person may be leaving his or her current place. Listen closely, and ask follow-up questions.

> **CAUTION**
> **Avoid topics that touch on protected classes or could be interpreted as discriminatory.** These can include any reference to disability, family status, race, gender, and other areas not relevant to the unit or landlord-tenant relationship. Also, avoid any topic that may cause problems later (such as saying you plan to do something like update the kitchen, when you really are not serious about the project in the near term).

## When to Start Screening Prospective Tenants

You are showing your unit, getting great feedback, and growing a list of prospects. Are you ready to choose an applicant, keep showing the place and taking applications, or some combination of these? My preferred approach is to take applications for a set time or until I get a substantial pool of qualified applicants, then do an initial screening of them.

The final decision, however, depends on the market. In a hot market, you may have 20 solid applications within the first few days, which provides a critical mass with which to start screening. There is no legal rule about when you have to start screening tenants, but don't delay long, or prospects could lose interest.

Also, be ready to defend your process—be it a "first qualified" applicant gets the place system, or one in which you build a pool of prospects and rank them based on your screening criteria (discussed below). I believe in markets and letting the process work at least a week or two. Give the best candidates a chance to find your rental. You simply don't know who is out there looking for a place unless you advertise and show your rental for a meaningful amount of time.

**TIP**

**Don't be tempted to fill a vacancy with an iffy tenant.** Absolutely 100% percent of the time, you are better off with a vacancy than with a problem tenant. Consider that with a vacant unit, you are not disturbing other tenants, the unit is still in ideal condition, and a suitable tenant could respond to your ad at any moment. Your only stress may be a mortgage payment to cover if you run past the month. A problematic tenant can disturb others, damage your unit, and still not pay—so you are in the same boat in terms of covering the mortgage, but you also face losing other good tenants, having your unit damaged, and maybe a costly and stressful eviction process.

# Developing Your Screening Criteria and Procedures

One theme in this book is to give the small-time landlord some options and ideas to structure in a way that best fits your situation. Just as you will develop your own turnaround routine with your units, involving some combination of painting, cleaning, and minor repairs, you will develop a process for screening tenants using some combination of the neutral and legal business criteria described below for selecting tenants. The goal is to choose tenants who will pay their rent on time, keep the place in good condition, not cause you problems (such as excessive noise or unpermitted guests), and stay a long time.

Because tenants' backgrounds and rental histories vary a great deal, they don't lend themselves well to a quantifiable, numeric approach. You are probably best off looking at the totality of the facts you gather on each prospect using rental applications and credit reports (discussed below) in order to make a well-informed decision.

In many markets, prospective tenants face a range of screening processes. They may experience everything from no real screening at all (problematic) to extensive (and expensive) vetting using third-party services, which can take a long time. As a part-time landlord, you may need to adopt a workable system somewhere in the middle, one that allows you to screen effectively without being unduly burdensome.

Whatever system you develop, your screening should meet these criteria.

**Legal and ethical.** Use neutral business criteria to choose tenants, such as a satisfactory credit report, and uniform screening that complies with antidiscrimination laws and is fair to all tenants.

**Economical, in terms of the money and the time you spend screening tenants.** If your process is too burdensome or costly, you won't be able to sustain it long term or with all of your prospects.

**Practical, in terms of the realities of the rental market.** In the rental game, if you snooze you may lose (good tenants will move on to other units). If you take a week to try and track down a long-lost landlord reference, your top prospect may have already signed a lease elsewhere. There is some advantage to being the first mover, able to screen quickly and painlessly. This may be your advantage as a small-time landlord. Similarly, if your process wears you out or thins your pool unnecessarily (because even good prospects find it too daunting), it is probably not sustainable. While you want some functional barriers that screen out problem tenants, too many barriers, forms, or screening levels could shrink your tenant pool down to nothing, or worse yet screen out good tenants, too.

**Reliable.** Make sure your system works. It should be getting you trouble-free tenants who pay rent on time and stay through the lease (and even renew). There may be some orthodoxy in tenant screening that may or may not work for you and your situation. Adapt your system if need be to develop a reliable process.

---

### Actually, You've Already Been Screening Tenants— Without Looking at One Rental Application

With a stack of applications from interested prospects, you are ready to start your screening process. But remember, you have actually already been screening. For example:

- Your carefully worded advertisement screened out some renters who were not seeking your price, terms, size, or location.
- Your thorough application and insistence that all interested prospects fill it out screens problematic tenants who either won't fill out an application or know it will highlight past issues.
- Your initial communications with people on the phone and at showings screens out prospects who find that that your rental is missing a certain feature they want, that you really do require the deposit and first month's rent (prorated) in full, or that your pet policy would not allow an ostrich or pack of sled dogs in the apartment.

---

## Great Screening Begins With a Thorough Rental Application

Your rental application is your most important tool in selecting good tenants, and your first line of defense against poor tenants. After you've met a few hundred prospective tenants, you will see very clearly the power of a good rental application. In fact, you can see potentially problematic tenants—especially those with a very poor rental, employment, or criminal history—recoil when you hand it to them. They may not even fill an application out even if you urge them to.

See the sample Rental Application, below, for an ideal format for a short but thorough rental application. It includes key information about a prospective tenant's rental and employment history; financial obligations; previous evictions; bankruptcies; and criminal history.

**RESOURCE**

**Where to find rental applications.** You can find rental applications from many sources, including office supply stores and landlord associations. The sample shown below is from Nolo's *Every Landlord's Legal Guide* and an online form is also available for purchase from the Nolo website.

# Top Criteria for Choosing Good Tenants

By now, you may be worried that screening tenants presents a legal minefield. While you want to be aware of the types of criteria you cannot use (protected classes), don't panic. A wealth of neutral, useful criteria *can* be legitimately used to screen tenants, as follows.

## Sufficient Income to Pay the Rent

The landlord-tenant relationship simply will not work out if the tenant doesn't have the financial means to reasonably cover the rent. Verifying an applicant's income (both from employment and sources such as Social Security) and major financial obligations early on is crucial. A classic ratio used by government agencies is that rent should be within 30% to 40% of household income. Still, people differ, and you have to look case by case. Use common sense and simple math.

**TIP**

**Allowing someone to rent a place he or she can't really afford doesn't actually help.** You are just getting the person into a financial bind. Make sure the income-to-rent ratio works out with some margin of safety. Young people and new renters, in particular, often underestimate how much taxes, insurance, and car expenses take out of their paycheck and budget.

## Sample Rental Application

### Rental Application

*Separate application required from each applicant age 18 or older.*

Date and time received by landlord _____

Credit check fee __$38_____ Received _____

---

**THIS SECTION TO BE COMPLETED BY LANDLORD**

Address of Property to Be Rented: __178 West 81st St., Apt. 4F_____

Rental Term: ☐ month-to-month ☑ lease from __3/1/20xx__ to __2/28/20xx__

Amounts Due Prior to Occupancy

First month's rent _____ $ __3,000__

Security deposit _____ $ __3,000__

Other (specify): __Broker's fee_____ $ __3,000__

TOTAL $ __9,000__

---

### Applicant

Full Name—include all names you use(d): __Hannah Silver_____

Home Phone: __609-555-3789_____ Work Phone: __609-555-4567_____

Cell Phone: __609-987-6543_____ Email: __hannah@coldmail.com_____

Fax*:_____

Social Security Number: __123-00-4567__ Driver's License NumberState: __D123456/NJ__

Other Identifying Information:_____

Vehicle Make: __Toyota__ Model: __Corolla__ Color: __White__

Year: __2008__ License Plate Number/State: __NJ1234567/New Jersey__

### Additional Occupants

List everyone, including minor children, who will live with you:

| Full Name | Relationship to Applicant |
|---|---|
| Dennis Olson | Husband |

---

\* By providing this fax number I agree to receive facsimile advertisements from the landlord or management company.

**Source:** *Every Landlord's Legal Guide,* by Marcia Stewart, Ralph Warner and Janet Portman (Nolo). Copyright Nolo 2014

## Sample Rental Application, continued

### Rental History

FIRST-TIME RENTERS: Attach a description of your housing situation for the last five years.

Current Address: _39 Maple St., Princeton, NJ 08540_

Dates Lived at Address: _5/2008–date_ Rent $ _2,000_ Security Deposit $ _4,000_

Landlord/Manager: _Jane Tucker_ Landlord/Manager's Phone: _609-555-7523_

Reason for Leaving: _New job in NYC_

Previous Address: _1215 Middlebrook Lane, Princeton, NJ 08540_

Dates Lived at Address: _6/2003–5/2008_ Rent $ _1,800_ Security Deposit $ _1,000_

Landlord/Manager: _Ed Palermo_ Landlord/Manager's Phone: _609-555-3711_

Reason for Leaving: _Better apartment_

### Employment History

SELF-EMPLOYED APPLICANTS: Attach tax returns for the past two years

Name and Address of Current Employer: _Argonworks, 54 Nassau St., Princeton, NJ_

Phone: _609-555-2333_

Name of Supervisor: _Tom Schmidt_ Supervisor's Phone: _609-555-2333_

Dates Employed at This Job: _2000–date_ Position or Title: _Marketing Director_

Name and Address of Previous Employer: _Princeton Times_

Phone: _13 Junction Rd., Princeton, NJ_ _609-555-1111_

Name of Supervisor: _Dory Krossber_ Supervisor's Phone: _609-555-2366_

Dates Employed at This Job: _6/1996–2/2000_ Position or Title: _Marketing Associate_

ATTACH PAY STUBS for the past two years, from this employer or proir employers.

### Income

1. Your gross monthly employment income (before deductions): $ _8,000_

2. Average monthly amounts of other income (specify sources): $ _____

   _Note: This does not include my husband's income._ $ _____

   _See his application._ $ _____

   TOTAL: $ _8,000_

**Source:** *Every Landlord's Legal Guide,* by Marcia Stewart, Ralph Warner and Janet Portman (Nolo). Copyright Nolo 2014

## Sample Rental Application, continued

### Bank/Financial Accounts

|  | Account Number | Bank/Institution | Branch |
|---|---|---|---|
| Savings Account: | 1222345 | N.J. Federal | Trenton, NJ |
| Checking Account: | 789101 | Princeton S&L | Princeton, NJ |
| Money Market or Similar Account: | 234789 | City Bank | Princeton, NJ |

### Credit Card Accounts

Credit Card: ☑ VISA ☐ MC ☐ Discover Card ☐ Am Ex ☐ Other: _____

Issuer: __City Bank__  Account No. __1234 5555 6666 7777__

Balance $ _1,000__  Average Monthly Payment: $ _1,000_

Credit Card: ☐ VISA ☐ MC ☐ Discover Card ☐ Am Ex ☑ Other: _Dept. Store_

Issuer: _City Bank__  Account No. _2345 0000 9999 8888_

Balance $ _2,000__  Average Monthly Payment: $ _500_

### Loans

| Type of Loan | Name of Creditor | Account Number | Amount Owed | Monthly Payment |
|---|---|---|---|---|
|  |  |  |  |  |
|  |  |  |  |  |
|  |  |  |  |  |

### Other Major Obligations

| Type | Payee | Amount Owed | Monthly Payment |
|---|---|---|---|
|  |  |  |  |
|  |  |  |  |
|  |  |  |  |

**Source:** *Every Landlord's Legal Guide,* by Marcia Stewart, Ralph Warner and Janet Portman (Nolo). Copyright Nolo 2014

## Sample Rental Application, continued

### Miscellaneous

Describe the number and type of pets you want to have in the rental property:

None now, but we might want to get a cat some time

Describe water-filled furniture you want to have in the rental property:

None

Do you smoke? ☐ yes ☑ no

Have you ever:   Filed for bankruptcy?   ☐ yes ☑ no   How many times _____

Been sued?   ☐ yes ☑ no   How many times _____

Sued someone else?   ☐ yes ☑ no   How many times _____

Been evicted?   ☐ yes ☑ no   How many times _____

Been convicted of a crime?   ☐ yes ☑ no   How many times _____

Explain any "yes" listed above: _____

### References and Emergency Contact

Personal Reference: Joan Stanley   Relationship: Friend, coworker

Address: 785 Spruce St., Princeton, NJ 08540   Phone: 609-555-4578

Personal Reference: Marnie Swatt   Relationship: Friend

Address: 82 East 59th St., #12B, NYC   Phone: 212-555-8765

Contact in Emergency: Connie & Martin Silver   Relationship: Parents

Address: 7852 Pierce St., Somerset, NJ 08321   Phone: 609-555-7878

### Source

Where did you learn of this vacancy? Ryan Cowell, Broker

I certify that all the information given above is true and correct and understand that my lease or rental agreement may be terminated if I have made any material false or incomplete statements in this application. I authorize verification of the information provided in this application from my credit sources, credit bureaus, current and previous landlords and employers, and personal references. This permission will survive the expiration of my tenancy.

_Hannah Silver_                                   _February 15, 20xx_

Applicant                                          Date

Notes (Landlord/Manager): _____

_____

_____

Source: *Every Landlord's Legal Guide,* by Marcia Stewart, Ralph Warner and Janet Portman (Nolo). Copyright Nolo 2014

## Will You Accept Section 8 Vouchers?

If you haven't yet, you will be asked as a landlord (perhaps many times): "Do you take Section 8?" This is a government-subsidized housing voucher program where tenants find housing on the private market and pay part of the rent themselves (for example, 30%), while a local housing agency pays the remainder. Tenants qualify by demonstrating a certain income, and landlords have to agree to participate. So if you signed up for the Section 8 program, you'd get part of the rent from a check from the local housing agency and part from the tenant. You will even see some rental advertisements that list the landlord's openness (or lack thereof) to the program.

While landlords have been free to participate or not in the past, there are statutes and cases in some states that do not allow landlords to refuse to rent to those who will be paying with a Section 8 voucher. Even some cities prohibit landlords from discriminating against Section 8 tenants (often called "source of income" discrimination). If you are averse to the program and wonder if it applies to you, see a landlord-tenant lawyer in your locality.

Laws or no laws, this often ends up being a market decision. For example, your rent amount may be well in excess of what the tenant and Section 8 will cover. In this case, it is not really an issue. However, if every other caller is asking about Section 8 and all the other properties in your neighborhood are Section 8, it is likely you will fill that unit with a Section 8 recipient. Of course, if you chose the property correctly and studied the market and renter demographics, as mentioned in Chapter 2, Section 8 may have been part of your strategy.

If you are interested in Section 8, sign up with your local public housing agency. It will inspect your unit and direct Section 8 applicants to you. You will screen these applicants in much the same way as you would other tenants and sign a lease with the one you approve. Then you will also sign a housing assistance payment contract with the public housing agency. For more information, see the Housing Choice Voucher Fact Sheet from The Department of Housing and Urban Development, available on the HUD website at www.hud.gov; simply search "housing choice vouchers" or Section 8 housing."

> **TIP**
>
> **Even if you take Section 8, you can still be selective.** However, your tenant profile will generally be different in terms of income and credit-worthiness, so you may have to adapt your procedures to focus on issues like rental references, employment history, and criminal background checks.

## Positive Employment History and References

Someone's paycheck from a job is often your rent check, so a tenant's job stability, career trajectory, and employment patterns are highly relevant. A tenant who has difficulty holding a job is often one who has difficulty paying the rent. But also consider other forms of verified income (indeed, you can't discriminate on legal income sources in some states).

In addition to verifying employment history and income, you'll want character references from the current employer, describing the applicant's ability to get along with coworkers and supervisors.

## Positive Rental References

The best predictor of what kind of tenant someone will be is usually the type of tenant he or she has been in the past. Focus on getting rental references from landlords and managers. You'll want to find out if the applicant consistently paid rent on time and respected the rental property and other tenants. Think twice about renting to someone with a recent termination or eviction.

Try as you might to track down rental references, sometimes you are just not a priority for a busy landlord or property manager. Other times the person may have nothing positive to say. After a few attempts, you may receive a message stating only that the person was or was not a tenant. This lack of positive feedback can also be telling. If the major property management firms in your area (and most of your applicants' rental references) only verify that the tenant lived at the unit, or they do not reply at all, you may need to focus on other factors like the length of tenancies, employment references, or income, or rely more on the credit information, including past history of evictions, from an applicant's credit report.

 **TIP**

**Develop a short, factual script when checking references.** Be consistent and ask the same questions every time you call a former landlord or employer to check out a potential tenant. Keep notes of all your conversations, so that you have a written record if a rejected applicant files a fair housing complaint.

## Satisfactory Credit Record

You'll want to check out the applicant's debt level and bill-paying history. Some of this information may be available in a rental application, but a better source is a credit report. See "Pros and Cons of Credit Reports," below, for more on the topic.

## Clean Criminal Record

Here's my simple rule on criminal records, which I probably could have figured out without having gone to law school: no felony convictions. Renting to someone who is a direct and current threat to persons or property is a major risk. And it is unlikely you would be found in violation of fair housing rules for excluding felons. There is a need for housing to reintegrate people into society, but as a small-time landlord, you probably don't have the resources or training for that role.

If an applicant has a misdemeanor on record, you may want to consider the facts of the case. A driving under the influence (DUI) conviction from ten years ago may not have much relevance to the current tenancy. But a series of recent misdemeanor assaults is certainly relevant—you don't want to risk more violence on the premises.

You can always be open to the tenant's explanation of the violations and potential for rehabilitation. Consider, on the whole, whether the crime impacts someone's ability to be a respectful tenant and pay the rent on time.

CAUTION
**Refusing to rent to a drug addict may be legally prohibited.**
Addiction status is protected under federal fair housing law. But the sale
of illegal drugs, or violence associated with drugs or alcohol, is likely not
protected. For example, you could not exclude someone for past or current
addiction to illegal drugs, but you could for a felony conviction for drug
trafficking.

## A Policy Fit

Make sure applicants fit your rental policies. You may screen prospects
who ask unusual questions or have unique needs in your initial contact
(as long as you comply with antidiscrimination laws). They may get
your answer and not bother with an application. Or, you may be surprised to see in the application a large number of pets, a need to park a
semi tractor-trailer, or seven intended occupants for a small two-bed-
room unit. These would all very likely violate your stated policies and
lease terms, (covered in Chapter 8), so screen people out on that basis.

CAUTION
**Be especially careful with condo rules and policies.** Make
sure tenants fit any association rules. For example, some condominium
associations are 100% nonsmoking properties, some place strict weight limits
on dogs, and many have specified limits on number of cars allowed in parking.

## Screening for Pets

As part of your "pets on approval process" you will also want to
gather and verify some information about a prospective tenant's pets.
You don't need to be an animal behavior expert to select pets. Like
bad tenants, bad pets can drive off other good tenants and destroy
units. In my experience, responsible owners often have responsible
pets—so, if you have screened your tenants well, then you're halfway
through screening the pets.

When screening pets, start by making sure the species, breeds, sizes, and ages fit your parameters and requirements (see Chapter 8 for advice on setting your pet lease terms and "pets on approval" policy).

Check with previous landlords to find out whether the tenant has had the same (or other) pet a long time—this is important to see if the tenant lived successfully with the pet for an extended time (because we like long-term tenants). Also, ask whether there were any pet problems or issues, such as damage or excessive barking that bothered neighbors.

Even the tightest-lipped landlord reference will talk about pets. Listen closely. If the previous landlord never noticed or heard from the pet and the unit was in okay shape, this is positive and what you hope to replicate—a quiet, well-behaved pet that no one really notices (if someone notices a pet it is often due to a complaint about barking or something someone stepped in). Occasionally, I find the tenant had a pet against the landlord's policy. This is a red flag, indicating a tenant who does not follow pet policies, and might not follow other rules, either.

You can also ask the tenant's personal references what they think of the pet. And don't be afraid to meet the pet or ask the owner for photos.

Keep in mind you must accommodate a person with a mental or physical disability whose pet serves as a support animal.

## Pros and Cons of Credit Checks

Credit checks, done through credit reporting agencies (CRAs), can provide a rich source of information on the applicant. They offer neutral, data-driven business criteria, covering the person's payment and financial history (and possibly past evictions).

Their downside is the cost, as well as the accompanying reporting requirements (which are triggered under the Fair Credit Reporting Act (FCRA) 15 U.S.C. Section 1681), if you reject someone based on the contents of their credit report. And if you are targeting lower-income tenants (who may be credit challenged) or students who have not built up a credit history, the report will be less useful, or they'll simply have no credit history available.

## Financially Fragile Renters

Make sure your policies and standards are realistic in light of the economic realities of your market. A recent report states the majority of renters in America (58%) are "financially fragile" (defined as not being able to come up with $2,000 in 30 days). The FINRA Investor Education Foundation report, entitled *American Renters and Financial Fragility*, summarized the precarious financial situation of renters in the U.S. based on 2010 demographic, income, and housing data. The full report is available at the FINRA Investor Education Foundation website, www.finra.org (search for the name of the report listed above).

If you decide to require applicants to provide credit reports as part of your screening process, be sure to figure out how you will pass on or eat the costs. Set standards so that you require the report and use the same numeric thresholds for all applicants. When deciding whether or not to require credit reports, keep in mind the following:

**A prospect's credit information won't tell you whether this person will be respectful or quiet, only whether he or she has a pattern of making payments on time.** It is possible that someone has a great credit score, but plays loud music all night or has a dog that barks all day.

**Someone with a poor credit score may still be an acceptable tenant.** For example, someone with one large uninsured medical bill or a former homeowner who went through a foreclosure in the financial crisis may have a negative credit history but otherwise be a solid prospect. If you are housing low-income or Section 8 tenants, the majority may be credit challenged or have no credit, so the credit scores will be less useful than rental history (if useful at all). Housing references may be more important in this case.

**You can evict for nonpayment—and tenants know it.** Many tenants will prioritize their rent payment first and foremost, so they may be able to maintain a long record of timely rent payments despite falling behind on consumer debt or other bills. As a landlord, what you *really* want to know is not whether tenants will pay their student loan or car payment on time, but whether they will pay the *rent* on time, in full, every month.

I have had long-term tenants with such ingenuity that despite collections actions from lenders and even vehicle repossessions, they have not missed their rent payment or been late.

---

### State Court Records: Additional Screening

If your state has a court system database showing all legal actions—civil and criminal—that is easy to access, quick, and free, then you may consider screening applicants using this public database (likely possible with full name and birth date). This gives you an idea about the veracity of an applicant's statements, and can give you a fuller story. A surprising number of applicants are untruthful on some questions, especially about having been evicted, sued, or convicted. Of course, this service may only turn up information from within your state. You will need to figure out the codes for the type of cases and know whether the person was a plaintiff or defendant. If your applicant sued someone for running into his or her car, it is not an issue. But if the person's last two landlords filed eviction cases, you should run.

Be sure to be consistent in your use of any public or court records in screening tenants.

---

# Guidelines for Evaluating Rental Applications and Credit Reports

Setting your criteria for choosing tenants is just part of the screening process. You will also need to use the criteria to develop standards and apply them equally.

## Develop a Few Hard-and-Fast Rules

Whether it's "no felonies" or "monthly rent must not exceed 40% of the tenant's gross income," you should figure out ahead of time which of your rules are nonnegotiable. Your application may allow for an applicant to explain any facts that could let you consider whether to make an exception to a particular policy. Absent some very compelling circumstances or mitigating facts, however, you won't need to make exceptions.

One definite bright line is a clear fabrication or misrepresentation on a rental application, such as a made-up address or a greatly inflated income. The only exception, of sorts, is when applicants make honest mistakes. There may be cases where someone gets dates wrong on a tenancy, so check before jumping to conclusions. The landlord-tenant relationship is built on trust and you can't move forward safely if the applicant is not truthful in initial interactions with you.

## Adopt Accepted Standards Whenever Possible

Selecting tenants will always involve some level of subjective judg-ment. But I also try to identify and rely on clear objective criteria. This provides legal protections. In a landlord-tenant dispute, judges will look for established regulations, policies, and practices to justify behavior (or not). Below are several examples of objective criteria.

### Occupancy Limit

You clearly have a legitimate concern when five people want to rent and live together in your one-bedroom unit. You know the wear and tear and traffic are probably more than the unit was meant to handle. What's more, you can point to the fact that the federal Department of Housing and Urban Development (HUD), sets a standard of two people per bedroom, depending on the size of the unit and other factors (like not discriminating against families).

You also have to consider the configuration of the units, the limitations of the building, relevant legal or safety codes, and ages of children. You probably would never exclude a couple and new baby from a one-bedroom under the standard, for example. But you could certainly note the standard if five adults were applying. See Chapter 8 for more on occupancy standards.

### Income Limit

The amount of income that can be spent on housing and still be considered "affordable" for the tenant has varied some over time in the U.S., but today you generally see it in the 30% to 40% of income range. It can vary by location. You might want to set a figure. This makes sure the tenant is not overextended every month.

Of course, you should examine an applicant's individual circumstances, and look at outstanding debt (or lack thereof). But even if debt-free, a rent amount approaching half of someone's discretionary income becomes difficult for even the most thrifty tenants.

Also be sure and consider all sources of income from all listed occupants that can be verified, and don't discriminate against any legal source of income.

### Dangerous Dog Breeds or Prohibited Activities

Another source of objective criteria can come in the form of insurance restrictions or activities prohibited by a homeowners' association or local government. If you can point to the fact you will lose your insurance by housing a particular dog breed or that no smoking is allowed anywhere on the complex, these are clear standards justifying your refusal to consider these applicants. You will likely have clarified the allowed dog breeds or smoking rules before the person submitted the application, but sometimes tenants fail to mention such facts and you find them as you read closely and follow up.

## Require Complete Applications— And Ask for More Information If Necessary

You can't do a thorough screening with an incomplete rental application, such as one that leaves out addresses of past residences. What people leave out of their applications is often telling. Sometimes an applicant will conveniently skip the part of the application on criminal or rental history. I always follow up just in case someone overlooked some questions. But most of the time, you won't hear back from the person. You can't really go forward with a partial application.

Be on the alert for tenants who do not list their current landlord or ask that you not contact the current landlord. This could signal that the tenant has not given proper notice, is not on good terms with the landlord, or—worst case— is in a current dispute or eviction process.

## Will It Stand Up in Court?

While picking tenants will never be an exact science, throughout the screening process you can be thinking about how you would rationalize or articulate why you picked or preferred a given tenant. It's typically quite clear which tenant has the best rental and employment history and income. You may have competitive situations, but it is not like you are sifting through Ivy League college applications.

Suppose after the staggered showing one afternoon, five prospects show up and fill out applications. Four are marginal, but one stands out. Think how it would play out if a rejected applicant sued you for discrimination: "Well, you see, your honor, I had the showings, met with each person, took applications from these five people who submitted them, (here they are). I studied them closely and the applicant I chose had the best rental history and references, highest income, and no criminal or negative legal history. I verified her employment and talked to two satisfied past landlords. She is clearly above the others in all the categories (your applications being exhibits "A-E"). So I offered her the place and she took it. Been great ever since." If you can articulate something like that, odds are you won't be sued, and if you are, you should prevail.

# Choosing a Tenant

Once you have selected the best tenant, offer him or her the place. Be sure to hold the offer open for only a set amount of time (for example, 24 hours). This is not so much to pressure the tenant as to make sure you can quickly move on to the next candidate if your first choice defers. It also makes sure that the tenant doesn't stall or shop your offer around, looking for other places or delaying you.

Here's my typical message: "Joan, I have reviewed your application for the unit at 33 Park Lane. Let me know if you are still interested and when we can set a time (at least an hour) to meet and sign the lease. I will go through the unit, cover our rental policies, and answer your questions. We can exchange the keys for the first month's rent (prorated) and deposit for a total of (*list amount*). I will hold this offer open for 24 hours from the time of this email. It will expire at (*day/time*). If I do not hear from you by then or we are unable to set an exact time for the transaction, I will offer it to someone else or continue showing the unit. Thank you."

Chapter 8 covers signing a lease or rental agreement and provides an effective process for getting the new tenancy off to a good start.

Make sure you time and structure your offer so as to never offer the same unit to two people. Also, never let a tenant string you along. My longer-term tenants have always accepted the place with noticeable joy—not equivocation.

If your prospective tenant is tentative and still shopping but wants to try and lock in your unit just in case, this may not be the tenant you want. Tell the person to look around and come back when ready to sign the lease. If the unit is still available, the person can do so then. If someone needs more time to get the rent and deposit together, remember that the money you require up front is one of the most important screening criteria. Will this prospective tenant really be able to pay the rent each month? If the person doesn't want to sign and take the unit in the time frame you outline in your offer, odds are it won't work out for the long term. In the meantime, keep showing the place or offering it to the next tenant who meets your criteria.

## Avoid Taking a Holding Deposit or Other Arrangement That Limits Your Options

You may be contacted by someone who wants you to hold a unit or enter some form of option contract, in which a prospective tenant puts some money down in exchange for you not renting the unit for a specified time frame (giving the prospect the exclusive option to rent it during that time). I recommend you politely decline. If you offer that applicant the unit and he or she wants it, then sign the lease. If not, thank the applicant and keep looking. Agreements to hold a unit can create uncertainty. They can take your unit off the market at the worst possible time—right when it is ready to rent and being advertised, and while (hopefully) you are getting many inquiries. I am not sure why some landlords or tenants use these agreements. Few tenants (and landlords) understand how a holding deposit option contract or agreement to hold a unit works, and they can create more problems than they solve.

# Rejecting Applicants

Once you have decided on your most qualified tenants, you still have a stack of applicants who were not offered the unit. They did not meet your criteria or present a strong enough employment, income, or rental history profile. Or perhaps they had a felony or poor credit score. It is a good idea to note the reasoning behind your rejection of a prospective tenant on the person's application, for future reference. There are really two types of rejections in my opinion: easy ones and hard ones.

## Easy—Nothing Is Required

If you study the rental application of someone who simply doesn't fit your rental terms, you don't have to send a letter or contact the person. Perhaps he or she did not meet your employment and income requirements, have a good rental history, or even fit the terms of your rental (like having six dogs when you allow two). Based on the application (and your verification of the information on it), these prospects don't meet your standards.

In this case, I don't even contact the applicants unless they continue to contact me. Ninety-nine percent of people understand that when they are not contacted, they were not selected. They applied and you screened them, so it ends there. If applicants do check back, I simply thank them for applying, tell them how much I enjoyed meeting them, and let them know it was a very competitive process and I wish them all the best (read: be nice). You could send all the unqualified applicants a rejection letter, but I find it awkward and unnecessary and don't do it unless it's legally required, for example, because of one of the reasons below.

## Harder—Adverse Action Letter Required

There are a few instances in which you will want to send a more formal letter to rejected applicants. The main one is if you've used credit reports, in whole or part, to reject an applicant. Also, if you use any kind of tenant screening service that may have used a credit report, you should send an adverse action letter. If you use credit reports, study the exact requirements for adverse action letters and develop a form letter or use an existing one. The exact requirements for adverse action letters and rejection letters across the U.S. are beyond the scope of this book.

**RESOURCE**

**More about adverse action requirements.** Check the website of the Federal Trade Commission (www.ftc.gov) and search for the report *Using Consumer Reports: What Landlords Need to Know.*

## What's Next?

With an excellent tenant selected, you are poised to move forward with signing a lease and getting the tenant introduced to your rental policies and the practical considerations of living in the unit (like parking, trash, rules, and more). Once you have the lease signed (the main topic of Chapter 8), be sure and take down your ad and prepare a form email to send all future inquirers, to the effect that the unit has been filled. ●

# Starting the Tenancy Right:
# Lease Terms and Onboarding Process

Once you've selected a new tenant, it's time to take care of some paperwork. By signing a lease or rental agreement, and presenting your new tenant with a move-in checklist, you'll get the tenancy off to a good start. Providing everything in writing is crucial to avoiding problems later, such as misunderstandings about your policies and terms. It's best to over-communicate on key issues such as how your deposit process works, what your late rent policy is, and how you handle visitors and unauthorized occupants.

Along with introducing your rules and expectations, you will also want to introduce the new tenant to the actual rental unit and all its features (appliances, mail, trash, parking, storage, and so on). With a thorough onboarding process, you can set the stage for a successful tenancy.

> **TIP**
> **Don't assume that your tenant will actually read and remember every word of the lease.** See my advice under "Signing the Lease or Rental Agreement," below, on how to make sure new tenants understand your key rules and your roles and expectations.

## Key Terms to Include in Your Lease or Rental Agreement

The lease is easily the most important document in the landlord-tenant relationship. It should encapsulate all the important terms and conditions of the tenancy and set out both your and the tenant's rights and responsibilities. If a term or condition is not in the lease, it will be hard to enforce—so, effective management begins with the lease terms.

Here are several key clauses that will help you better manage the people and the property.

> **TIP**
>
> **Make sure your lease terms comply with state law.** Many of the issues you will cover in your lease (late fees, security deposit rules, notice required for landlord's access to rental property or to terminate a month-to-month rental agreement) are regulated by the laws of your state. To find yours, see the Landlords section of Nolo.com, which also includes articles on other lease-related issues, such as federal and state required landlord disclosures.

## Term of the Tenancy

The length of time that you and your tenant will be bound to the lease or rental agreement will be among your most important early decisions. You'll want to decide whether to use a month-to-month rental agreement or a fixed-term lease. There are pros and cons to each.

### Month-to-Month Rental Agreement: Pros and Cons

Month-to-month rental agreements provide flexibility for you and the tenant. You can increase the rent or end the tenancy on relatively short notice, typically 30 days' (subject to any rent control rules). Month-to-month rental agreements may be standard in your market, for example, if you're in an area where vacation rentals (summer beach houses or winter ski cabins) are the norm. Actually, many of my very long-term tenants (several years or more) prefer to rent on a month-to-month basis because of the flexibility. However, we initially started with a longer-term lease and renewed it several times.

On the other hand, starting out with a month-to-month agreement will usually result in more tenant turnover, with all that's involved in preparing a rental unit for new tenants, finding new renters, and so on. If you advertise for a month-to-month rental, you create a self-fulfilling prophecy, in which the tenants who respond are those specifically looking for a shorter-term rental. This is the prime downside.

However, the short-term orientation may also match your goals. If, for example, you think you may do a major remodel or move into the place yourself, you'll get the flexibility of ending the tenancy fairly easily (for example, with 30 days' notice).

> ### TIP
> **Month-to-month agreements may also be useful if you're thinking of selling a multiunit property.** Many homebuyers want to live in residential rentals (they get much better financing terms due to the owner-occupancy). With a month-to-month agreement, you could give the current tenants a 30-day termination notice when you get an offer on your property (which often takes 30 or more days to close), allowing the new owner to move in or find a new tenant right after closing. Also, some buyers—even if they aren't moving in—may want the flexibility to choose their own tenants. Contrast this situation with trying to sell a property with a tenant who's locked into a one-year lease; the new owner would have to wait until the lease expires to move in or choose new tenants, both of which could limit the marketability of the property and the pool of buyers.

## Fixed-Term Leases: Pros and Cons

Most landlords in business for the long haul will want to target long-term tenants. The most surefire way to do this is to advertise and allow only longer-term leases. Leases obligate you and the tenant for a fixed period of time, such as six months or a year, during which time you can't raise the rent or end the tenancy (unless the tenant has violated a lease clause, such as by failing to pay rent).

The one-year lease is a staple across the U.S., but as a small-time landlord, you can be more flexible and nimble. So also think about offering the option of a shorter fixed-term lease, such as for six (or even nine months), if there is a market in your area for such terms.

While leases restrict your flexibility, there are many pluses to having long-term tenants—especially if your rental unit is in a community with high vacancy rates. And since the most labor-intensive part of being a landlord is turning around a unit and finding new tenants, you can reduce your workload greatly this way.

## Number of Occupants

You can limit the number of people who live in your rental as long as you comply with all relevant housing codes. The two-person-per-bedroom standard mentioned in Chapter 7 is the most likely limit to plan around. It follows some HUD (Department of Housing and Urban Development) guidance that also directs landlords to consider the facts in a given situation, such as square footage, children and their ages, and the limits of the building (water, sewage, electricity). Also look at any local or state housing codes, including fire or safety regulations, that relate to occupancy standards; these may be more liberal than HUD standards. You can avoid the perception that you're discriminating against families by simply and clearly using government standards for occupancy as a criterion. You probably want to be flexible and reasonable when looking at the occupancy standards in close cases, however, especially with families.

Most importantly, be sure that all adults who will be living in the rental unit, including both members of a couple, complete a rental application and sign the lease or rental agreement. Also, make sure all minor children are listed on the lease. You simply cannot be an effective landlord if you don't know who is living in the unit. You can't communicate with and manage your tenants (the theme of this book) if you don't know who they are or how to contact them (handling unauthorized occupants is covered in Chapter 9).

## Guest Policy

Another common area where a lease term can help landlords manage their property relates to guests or long-term visitors. Setting a written limit on guest occupancy of a unit can help you enforce your rules and policies and know who is living there. A good clause will put a limit on a visitor's stay. For example, consider a 14-day occupancy limit on any guest not on the lease. This is a reasonable limit, which lets tenants have guests and some freedom, but allows you some control. Before letting a guest stay continuously for more than a few weeks, the tenant will need to get your written permission.

A visitor who stays more than a month is, for all practical purposes, living at the unit. At that point, assuming the person meets your tenant criteria, and you're fine about adding a new tenant, you probably need to add this person to the lease (see the discussion of lease renewals and amendments in Chapter 9, for more on this). The person has already been in your unit for a recognized landlord-tenant lease period (as long as a new month-to-month tenant, for example).

You will also need to make sure the new tenant knows the rules, which the lease can help communicate (along with an in-person meeting). The best way to get information about the prospective new tenant is through your standard rental application and tenant screening process (covered in Chapter 7).

## Rent: How Much, and How It's Paid

In most areas of the U.S., you may charge as much rent as the market will bear, within any rent control limits. I try to examine my local rental market (not only when first renting, but at each turnover or renewal) and gauge exactly what the closest comparable units are being rented for. I look closely at the classifieds and rental listings to find a similar-sized unit in my area and I check what features and utilities are included or excluded. Finally, I try to exclude from my analysis any wishful one-off ads by novice or misguided landlords who have set the price abnormally high or abysmally low. Professional property managers tend to set the most realistic market rates. They have the most information about the rental market and know what it will bear.

Once you know the market well, I suggest aiming right for the market rate or, to get an even larger pool of applicants, trying just below market rate. For example, if you think the market-rate rent is around $1,000 a month for your unit, you could set your rent at $975. The larger pool created by this minor reduction may help you rent the unit faster and get a better quality, longer-term tenant.

> **TIP**
>
> **Are you limited by local rent control ordinances?** Communities in five states (California, New York, Maryland, New Jersey, and the District of Columbia) have passed rent control ordinances (although some of these exempt landlords with four or fewer properties). If you own rental units in a community with rent control, check the local ordinance to see if it affects your property.

All landlords want to receive their rent on time and limit hassles collecting it from tenants. Choosing good tenants who have a solid history of paying rent on time is key to doing this. But also make sure your lease is crystal clear on all rent-related details, especially late fees (discussed below), as well as the following:

**What forms of payment you accept.** I prefer the simplicity of a check or money order. It creates a record, is safer than cash, and is easily written and transferred. I have also had success with tenants using auto-pay options, where a check is mailed automatically to me by the tenant's bank every month. Different forms of electronic payment are changing all the time, so use what works best for you and your tenants.

**How and where tenants must pay the rent.** I give my tenants a supply of self-addressed stamped envelopes (SASEs) with "Forever" stamps for monthly rent checks. SASEs are a good investment: They make sure there is no question about your address, and avoid insufficient postage issues. I've found that using the postmark date of the mailed rent check is a simple and fair method to determine whether or not rent is late.

**How returned (bounced) checks are handled (the charge and other consequences).** Consider imposing a charge for returned checks in an amount that reasonably approximates your costs to deal with the issue, and meets any state limits on bounced-check charges. I simply pass on the same fee my bank charges (with no markup). You may also require that, after one returned check, subsequent rental payments be in the form of a cashier's check or money order.

---

💡 **TIP**

**The more specific your rent clause, the better.** Some of the terms described here may be considered minor housekeeping, but they're very important. Spelling out your rental policies will help make your payment process (and the tenant's rent responsibility) completely clear, helping you collect your rent on time.

## Late Fees and Policies

Along with how you collect the rent, how you follow up if a tenant pays rent late is a key policy to cover in your lease. Not only will chasing late rent make it hard to manage your rentals, you may not even be able to stay in business if you can't collect your rent on time.

If you're like most landlords, you'll have a mortgage on your property, and your bank will be swift and ruthless in assigning late fees for nonpayment. If you can't pay the monthly mortgage bill out of pocket, you're especially reliant on the tenant's rent check. You could damage your credit or even lose your property if you can't collect rent on time.

> **TIP**
>
> **As a backup, keep some cash in reserve.** You'll want to set aside enough to cover the mortgages on your rental properties, for the rare occasions when a tenant—or possibly two tenants—are late with rent payments. Even if your finances are tight, you can save your credit and avoid late fees (and stress) with this advance-planning measure.

Make sure your late-fee structure is reasonable, legal, and provides adequate incentive for on-time payments. Parse your late-fee clause and terms to ensure it squares with your state's late-fee statutes; these may set specific limits or simply prohibit late fees that are excessive or punitive.

Here are some additional tips on setting late rent fees in your lease:

**Set a day by which rent is considered late (and a fee will kick in).** While you can legally charge a late fee one day after the rent was due (except in the few states that require you give tenants a few days' grace period), I recommend adding a bit of leeway. My leases require that rent be paid on the first of the month, but that late fees will be charged after the third day. (I originally used the fifth of the month as a trigger date for late fees, but went to the third of the month as I got more rentals and more mortgages in my name.) Just a few days' leeway is realistic and acknowledges that neither the mail system nor your tenants' memories are always perfect. This prevents you from nickel and diming tenants for a minor infraction, a behavior that may erode trust.

**Set a reasonable flat late fee.** Avoid late fees that take too much time to explain or are hard to compute. Consider a flat amount, say $10 to $25, that is triggered if the rent is mailed (has a postmark date) past the cutoff date (such as three days after rent is due). No matter what state you live in, make sure your late fee relates to real costs associated with the delayed rent payment, such as penalties you will owe for not paying your own mortgage on time, your time spent contacting the tenant who's late with rent, and your transportation costs for extra trips to the bank or post office.

**In addition to the flat late fee, include a per-day amount (such as $5 per day) after the cutoff date.** Say the rent is due on the third, at which time you charge a late rent flat fee of $25, plus $5 per day for each day the rent is late. A tenant who pays three days late would owe $40 ($25 for the flat late fee and $5 for each of the three late days); if the tenant pays five days late, he or she would owe you $50. Charging an additional per-day fee should motivate the tenant to pay sooner, rather than later. Tenants will generally act in their own best interest and try to avoid such fees.

**Consider capping your total late fee at 5% of the monthly rent.** Particularly if your late fees escalate day by day, it's worth trying to prevent a claim that the total is excessive or punitive. For example, if you charge $1,000 per month rent, and you cap your total late fee at 5% of that, the total late fee would be $50. Be sure to set the cap within any applicable statutory late-fee limits or guidelines in your state.

Chapter 9 provides some communications strategies and ideas for the inevitable late-rent situation. But to be effective and even proactive, you want to start with clear late-rent guidelines in your lease. Also, explain the terms and give examples for tenants, so they can see how the late fee works and avoid it. Your goal is to get the rent in on time, not collect late fees.

## What's the Worst That Could Happen If You Charge an Excessive Late Fee?

A desperate tenant who is buying time in an eviction case and grasping at any possible legal arguments, could allege your late fee was excessive, punitive, unconscionable, not calculated properly, or violates state laws on usury or public policy. Your state may even have an express rule on late fees. One of those arguments might well stick, such that your late fee would be unenforceable.

A high late fee not only puts you in legal peril, it could be bad for business. If the tenant is unable to pay the late fee, you will have to resort to eviction or abandon any hope of collecting the money, making this lease clause toothless and destroying the tenant's incentive to pay on time. Your odds may not be good in enforcing an excessive fee in court, either. A tenant who has paid the rent in full (just not the full late fee) may make a more sympathetic litigant than a landlord demanding a high late fee. Also, courts may be reluctant to uphold excessive late fees if they could lead to evictions (and hence homelessness), so you may find your late fee structure getting close scrutiny for reasonableness.

If you are intent on charging the maximum legal late fee allowed in your jurisdiction, consider having an experienced landlord-tenant lawyer draft this provision of your lease to make sure it fits within your state's laws. (Finding a landlord-tenant lawyer is discussed in depth in Chapter 11.) But even with legal advice, you may still be taking a large risk for a relatively small amount of money if your late fee structure could be considered excessive. An excessive late fee could cost you more to defend than you'd ever collect.

To avoid problems, you should be able to show that your late fee is clearly within legal requirements of your state and provides incentives for tenants to pay rent on time, while reflecting your actual costs and the time value of money. Be realistic about whether your late fee is really reasonable and enforceable in light of your tenant demographic. A tenant who can't come up with $1,000 for rent probably can't cover a $200 late fee, either.

## Pets Policy

You may prohibit pets on your rental property, or limit the type you accept—except for properly trained service animals needed for a person with a disability, such as a guide dog needed for a blind person.

A short lease clause on pets should allow service animals but prohibit other pets except as approved by you and under the conditions listed in your lease. This lets you take a middle ground approach, allowing pets that you have screened (as discussed in Chapter 7) and approved, rather than sticking with a black-and-white, "no pets" rule. Tenants will recognize the language "Pets on Approval" when they see it in the rental ad, understanding that you are open to the idea of pet ownership—but not wide open. That is, you won't accept all sizes, types, and manner of animals (including dog breeds that are not covered under your insurance company or that are not allowed by a condo association). You can and should be selective regarding pets and their owners' ability to control them.

Allowing pets on approval makes good business sense to me, by widening the potential market for the rental unit. Despite the high percentage of pet-owning tenants in the U.S., many landlords, and especially large apartment complexes, do not allow pets. A pets-on-approval policy also helps bring in long-term tenants who will want to renew their lease, given the scarcity of pet-friendly rentals. You may even be able to charge more rent or a higher deposit (within state limits).

But there are drawbacks to allowing pets. They can create noise, smell, and property damage, and add to your management duties and work when turning around units. Some pets pose risks to other tenants or visitors (or even you) from dog bites. Consider all of these factors in making the best decision for your situation.

Once you've settled on a pets policy (whether to prohibit them or accept them on approval), express it consistently within your rental ad (covered in Chapter 7) and your lease or rental agreement for a particular rental unit. Include any condo association pet policies (such as maximum dog weight or a cats-only rule) in your written materials as well, such as tenant rules and regulations (discussed below) if these are applicable. See Chapter 9 for dealing with pet issues that arise during the tenancy.

 RESOURCE

**Useful resources on pets and pet policies for property managers and tenants.** Check out the websites of the San Francisco SPCA (look for "Tenants & Landlords" under the "Resources" tab at www.sfspca. org); also see the "Pets" section on the website of the Humane Society of the U.S. (www.humanesociety.org) for resources for property managers (note that the latter says that 72% of renters have pets!).

---

### Bright Line Rules When It Comes to Pets

I am open to pets, but not wide open. Here are my three bright line rules:

**No dogs that my insurance company will not allow.** Dog bites are a major source of insurance claims, and some insurance policies won't cover them at all, or won't cover injuries by certain breeds of dogs. I can't take that risk. Check with your insurance agent regarding any restrictions and make sure all prospective and current tenants are aware of them. I also would not allow exotic pets that were not legal in the U.S. or locally, or that require special permitting or pose risks to humans (such as large snakes and venomous spiders).

**No pets that aren't housetrained.** Immature pets (in particular, puppies and kittens) can create a mess and a serious maintenance issue. I prefer they learn to be house trained in someone else's house. They're also an unknown quantity, still requiring a good deal of training before they're calm and sociable (or at least nondestructive) canine and feline tenants.

**No pets that violate community restrictions.** If the unit is a condo or under the governance of a homeowners' association, I defer to the community rules. These can run the gamut from no pets to detailed weight, number, species, and breed rules.

## Security Deposits

The purpose of a security deposit is to give you some "security" for any incidental damages at move out and also to cover unpaid rent if you have to evict the tenant or he or she skips out while owing rent. Try to collect a deposit that is a meaningful, but not prohibitive amount. Also keep it separated from your other accounts or accounted for as required by your state's laws.

About one month's rent is usually considered an acceptable deposit and should provide incentive for your tenant to keep (and return) the unit clean and undamaged. Also, remember that your rental could be more appealing if your up-front costs (deposit and first month's rent) are just below market rate. But if you charge too low a deposit, you will have less money to cover repairs or any damages the tenant causes.

Think about whether your deposit could cover the lost rent for a standard eviction (which could take several weeks). And even with a security deposit approximating one month's lost rent, you will still need to act quickly in late-rent scenarios (a topic covered in depth in Chapter 9).

### Spell Out Key Security Deposit Details

Whatever amount you decide on for a deposit, your lease or rental agreement should clearly spell out the following (in compliance with your state and local laws):

- security deposit amount
- when and how you will return deposits
- what deductions you may take
- how you will account for the deposit
- whether or not you will be paying interest on the tenant's deposit, and
- whether you require an additional pet deposit (although you can't require these for a trained service companion animal or, in many states, if the additional pet fee means you'll exceed the state's deposit limits).

In settling on these policies, you'll need to find out your state's precise rules on deposits and follow them to the letter. Be aware of any cases or judicial opinions interpreting your state law on security deposits.

> **TIP**
> **Think twice about charging any nonrefundable fees, such as for cleaning.** Some states, such as California, specifically prohibit nonrefundable fees, so if you plan on charging one, make sure they're allowed under your state law.

## Avoid Deposit Dustups by Starting Right

Maybe nowhere is there more potential for problems between tenants and landlords than with the security deposit. To set expectations at the outset and increase the chances of a smooth transition and deposit return when that time comes, make the deposit a topic of conversation at the lease signing, when you accept the deposit check. Also explain to the tenant how move-in procedures, such as filling out a move-in checklist at the start of the tenancy, (a topic discussed later in this chapter), can help the tenant get the full deposit returned.

## Don't Get Creative With Deposit Terms

Landlords consistently post rental ads with all sorts of problematic (and even illegal) deposit terms. Some get creative and accept the deposit in installments, others try to make portions of it nonrefundable. Some charge too much, while novices may forget about the deposit altogether. And, of course, tenants routinely complain about that one time they didn't get their full deposit back (many times, probably with good reason).

Security deposits are not a place for ingenuity or creative thinking. Use those skills in marketing and preparing your unit. Make your deposit very simple—a set amount (like one month's rent). Make it fully refundable, and set a procedure for returning it, including an itemized list of any deductions after your inspection and the tenant's move out. When I return deposits, I like to use certified mail to provide proof of mailing within the required time. For details on itemizing deductions and returning deposits, see Chapter 10.

## Other Common Lease Terms

The lease touches on every aspect of the landlord-tenant relationship. Here are additional terms typically covered in leases and rental agreements:

- landlord and tenant responsibilities for repairs and maintenance, including what tenants can and cannot do themselves (see Chapter 5 for more on the subject)
- condition of rental at move-in time, incorporating tools such as a landlord-tenant checklist (discussed below)
- restrictions on tenants running a business on the rental property
- details on how and when landlords may enter the rental unit (most states require 24 hours' or reasonable notice, and specify acceptable reasons for entry, such as to make necessary repairs or to send in a service contractor)
- prohibition against assigning the lease to someone new or subletting it for a time without your permission (within the limits of state law), including renting out the place on a short-term basis or through an online home rental site (a particular concern if you're in a popular vacation area)
- who's responsible for paying various utility bills
- prohibitions against tenants causing any disturbances or violating the law, such as by dealing drugs or creating a noise nuisance
- requirement that tenants notify you if they will be gone for an extended period of time
- statement that landlord's insurance does not cover tenants' belongings (and that tenants are responsible for insuring their personal property)
- any special policies or rules (see "Tenant Rules and Regulations," below)

- consequences, including possible termination of the tenancy, for violating a key term of the lease, and
- financial consequences of actually breaking the lease (a topic discussed in detail in Chapter 9).

## Tenant Rules and Regulations

Unlike rental property managers in large apartment complexes, many small-time landlords may not need to issue a detailed set of rules and regulations. You aren't managing several hundred people at once. This ability to customize your service and conditions may help set you apart from large complexes. For example, you might allow three small dogs upon approval, or allow tenants to cook with barbeques (a designated distance from the building). Some of these activities are strictly prohibited at one-size-fits-all apartments.

But you will still want to have some rules to help regulate your tenants' behavior (and their guests' behavior) and prevent later disputes. Whatever rules or policies you decide on for a unit, be sure to spell them out in writing. This doesn't mean giving tenants a thick packet of policies or a rule book; they won't read it. Try to provide one page of clearly written bullet points; something the tenant can put on the refrigerator. Attach this document to your lease and make sure it is incorporated by reference there. In other words, put a box or line in your lease where the tenant initials and signs that he or she has read and will comply with the attached rules.

Make sure your rules cover:
- pet policies
- your policy on smoking in individual units and/or common areas
- quiet hours (I designate these as 10 p.m. to 8 a.m.)
- permitted use of the yard, garden, or common areas
- lost-key charges
- authorized vehicles that may park on the premises (license number, make, model, and color), and
- details on storage, parking and recycling.

Having these rules incorporated into your lease gives you the authority to evict a tenant who persists in seriously violating your policies. More about communicating with tenants to prevent and respond to issues that arise in the tenancy is in Chapter 9.

> **CAUTION**
>
> **Any condo or homeowners' association rules should be included in your lease.** If your property is in a community governed by a condominium association or HOA, this is actually a scenario where you *should* give the tenant a heavy load of information. You'll want to make sure the tenant receives the full policies, regulations, and rules of the association. You don't want both the tenant and you to be fined by the board because, for example, the tenant put up a laundry line or flew a flag where it wasn't allowed. One association where I have a rental condo has a large packet of rules just for pets. I also share with long-term tenants the association meeting minutes, future construction project information, and any issues that the association is dealing with. In short, everything I get as an owner, I pass on to the tenant.

## Disclosures About the Property You Must Make to Tenants

Federal law requires that you inform new tenants of lead paint hazards in the rental unit, using a lead disclosure form (for details, search "the lead disclosure rule" on the HUD website at http:// portal.hud.gov). This federal disclosure rule affects all landlords, with a few exceptions, including those renting out housing built after January 1, 1978, homes certified lead-free by a state accredited lead inspector, zero-bedroom units (like studios, efficiencies, and dorms), some rentals in retirement communities, housing for disabled, and short-term rentals.

In addition, many states require that landlords disclose information to new tenants, such as any shared utility arrangements or known radon risk hazards.

# Where to Find Lease and Rental Agreement Forms

Apartment associations, law libraries, and commercial publishers have developed some strong forms for most situations you encounter in landlording. Products are also available at office supply stores, but these are not always up to date and legally accurate.

Nolo includes plain-English, legal lease and rental agreement forms in its books, such as *Every Landlord's Legal Guide* (and the *California Landlord's Law Book: Rights and Responsibilities*), and also offers interactive online forms. These can all be found on the Nolo site (www.nolo.com/products/leases/residential).

If you get an idea or concept that you would like to add when creating your ideal lease or other landlord documents, you can have a lawyer do a professional review for a reasonable fee (Chapter 11 discusses how to find and work with a landlord-tenant lawyer); having a lawyer involved is especially important if you want to make a substantive lease change. The most cost-effective approach is to start with an established proven form first, and see whether you can make it work (and meet your state's legal requirements) with small adjustments.

Once you have a solid document, simply make many copies or use it online and in your email correspondence with tenants and prospects—until such time as you find out that your state laws have changed, or you wish to make another alteration.

 **TIP**

**Amending or ending a lease by mutual agreement or eviction?** Chapter 9 includes details, including how to prepare a new lease when a current tenant wants to add a roommate, and circumstances, such as tenant nonpayment of rent, that justify a lease termination or eviction.

# Signing the Lease or Rental Agreement

Once your lease is ready, set up a time for the tenant(s) and any cosigners to meet with you and each sign it. Sending the tenant a copy of the lease ahead of time will help speed up the signing process. I even make a copy available to all prospective tenants at the showing.

Ideally, your lease-signing meeting (allow at least an hour) will take place at the rental unit, at which time you can do a walkthrough (as discussed below) and give the tenant keys to the rental. Besides, as a part-time landlord, you probably won't have a rental office (or need one). But despite the casual setting, this is a serious event. Keep your tone professional, so as to convey the fact that you are both taking on a significant contractual obligation.

Ask the new tenants to bring a check or money order for the first month's rent (prorated if necessary) and the security deposit. Be sure and tell the tenant the exact amount.

As with the rental application, every person you have approved to live in the rental unit, including both members of a couple, as well as any cosigners (discussed below), will need to sign the lease or rental agreement.

I lay out (on the kitchen counter!) the lease, the SASEs for rent checks, the move-in checklist (discussed below), the keys, and any written rules and policies. I also give tenants a new manila envelope for all their paperwork.

Review every part of the lease with the tenants. Give them time to read (or reread) the lease and ask any questions. Explain which state laws affect the contents and the practical impacts. Read the key parts aloud and explain every term. Make sure that the tenants clearly understand all legalese and jargon like "joint and severally" (which basically means that each person is fully liable for any damage, unpaid rent, and possibly even legal fees). See Nolo's free Law Dictionary on Nolo.com, for plain English definitions of common legal terms.

TIP

**Check your state rules regarding translation of leases.** California, for example, requires landlords to translate a lease into Spanish, Tagalog, Korean, Chinese, and Vietnamese, if it had been negotiated primarily in these languages. The exception is if the tenant has supplied his or her own fluent translator at the signing.

Why all the fuss about the details in the signing process? You may never be in a legal action. But the goal here is precisely that—to help you avoid legal problems. Think of your lease, cosigner agreements, and all your processes as insurance. They give you peace of mind, greatly increasing the chances that the tenants will fulfill their obligations to care for the rental unit and pay rent on time.

Sign the lease at the end of your discussion of terms and only when the tenant hands you a check for the full amount due—the first month's rent (prorated if the tenant is moving in on a date other than the first of the month), plus the deposit or whatever other fees you have agreed on. New renters will need a hint to realize this is the part where they hand you the check. I like to say something like: "So, with the deposit and prorated rent, $1,200 gets you the keys. Just sign right here." (Then you swap the keys for the check.)

Execute (create signed originals of) two copies of the lease: one for the tenant, one for yourself. You and each tenant should sign both copies. If there is more than one tenant, they can make copies for the signed original for themselves. This is one of the best feelings you get as part-time landlord: You completed a laborious turnaround and matched a deserving tenant with a safe, clean home. The tenant is delighted. You get a sense of accomplishment, and checks in your pocket and a long-term lease in your hand.

Keep your copy of the signed lease with other important tenant documents (discussed below).

> CAUTION
> **Do not sign the lease or allow anyone to move into your rental who hasn't paid the first month's rent and deposit.** No doubt, you will eventually come to a situation when a tenant who otherwise made it through your screening process does not bring the required initial payments to the signing. If the person has a legitimate reason for the delay (a bank closure or car accident, for instance), agree to reschedule the lease signing for the next day. But if the prospective tenant simply has a convoluted scheme to pay you in increments or with some other payment plan, say that you are sorry, but you will have to keep showing the unit. Someone who can't pay the first month's rent and deposit will unlikely be able to pay in future months. Requiring the first month's rent and deposit is one of your most important financial screening requirements.

# Making Cosigner Situations Work

A cosigner on a lease is simply another person agreeing to be equally liable for the performance of the obligations in the agreement. After reading all the guidance on selecting tenants in Chapter 7, you may find it odd to consider accepting someone who cannot meet the lease obligations alone. But there are a few common situations where it can work. For example, the vast majority of 18-to-19-year-olds have no credit score, and few have built up any significant rental history; so, if you are housing college students and use credit scores and rental history as criteria (and you likely will), you would want a cosigner (probably a parent) to also sign the lease.

You are, in most cases, under no legal obligation to accept or reject cosigners. You should, however, adopt a policy on this matter and apply it consistently—though limited exceptions exist when you may not be able to refuse a cosigner. For example, if someone with a disability has insufficient income, but a relative or guardian agrees to cosign (and the proposed cosigner is stable and solvent), then in some jurisdictions, a landlord must make this economic accommodation.

## Parents of First-Time Renters as Cosigners

The most common cosigning situation you will face is when parents or guardians cosign for their young adult children—particularly if you live in a college town and target college students. Requiring a cosigner in this situation can be wise for legal and extra-legal reasons. The parents (or their college funds) will often be paying the rent anyway, so they are already involved. Putting their names on the lease (or more literally, on a separate cosigning agreement) solidifies their connection to these obligations. Also, it lets you show the parents or cosigners all the rules, expectations, and (if they are present at the showing or signing), the condition of the unit. In addition, the parents could be another source of leverage encouraging the tenant to clean up the unit and leave it damage-free. They will want their deposit back and the lease to run smoothly.

## Screening Cosigners

Keep in mind the reason you have a cosigner: for added security. If a parent with bad credit signs for a child with no credit, then you aren't getting much added security. Use the neutral business criteria that you've been carefully developing to screen any prospective cosigners. That means asking cosigners to fill out the same comprehensive rental application and undergo the same screening process as the actual tenant.

## Cosigner Paperwork in a Nutshell

Let's say three 19-year-olds wish to rent your single-family home near a college. You could end up with three future tenants and six cosigners (each tenant's two parents), or nine people, if you ask for the maximum number of cosigners. Add in the applications and screening of all the cosigners, and it is a lot of paperwork. Just getting everyone to sign the documents will present logistical challenges.

Of course, the simplest way to handle the transaction is to have everyone at the signing. Then make sure each cosigner has a copy of the lease and cosigner agreement. Keep the original cosigner agreement(s) stapled to the original lease in your file.

However, the parents may be out of town or out of state. In this case, you could approve the tenants conditionally (or contingent on getting the cosigner agreement in the mail). Then mail the cosigner a copy of the lease and a blank cosigner agreement. When you get the signed cosigner agreement(s) in the mail, the lease will take effect. Another option is to ask for just one creditworthy cosigner per student, for example, to streamline the process.

TIP

**If you have an out-of-town or out-of-state-cosigner (or one you do not meet at the signing), consider asking that the signature be notarized.** It can add to the ceremonial aspect of the signing ritual and seriousness of the transaction. Plus, it reduces the chances that someone faked the signature.

## Think Broadly About Other College Student Prospects

The traditional college student may not seem like an ideal rental candidate. Some 18-year-olds away from home for the first time may require more supervision than you'd like to offer, and most will likely move out by summer. The short-term nature of the traditional college tenancy is tough for landlords—often leaving them with an annual vacancy of three months or more in summer.

But there are also nontraditional college students who may be more mature, working at a part- or full-time job. Some even have families. They often need year-round housing. Also, consider graduate students, faculty, and all types of university staff. Many of these applicants will have a more extensive rental background, more stable income, and be more likely to stay for the long term, including summers. Try a lower rate for a year-round tenancy to draw them in, or simply insist on a 12-month lease.

# Tenant Onboarding Process

When scheduling a time to sign the lease, make sure you allow enough time to orient new tenants (what I call the tenant onboarding process). You'll want go over everything and get the new tenants involved in looking at their new home and understanding what it will be like to live there. I don't think you can provide too much detail about the unit, common areas, and procedures. You do not want to field daily questions for the next week or have to come back a few times to show the tenant where the recycling goes. Doing a thorough job of orienting new tenants will help avoid common problems down the road, such as a tenant using the front porch as storage or getting objects stuck in the garbage disposal.

This section covers the key elements of a successful tenant onboarding process:

- doing a thorough walkthrough of the rental unit
- giving the tenant a move-in checklist on the condition of the rental (key to avoiding disputes about security deposits at move-out time), and
- providing a move-in letter covering key information, such as utilities and any lockout fees.

## Tenant Walkthrough

At the lease signing, go through everything from the locks on doors and windows to how the appliances work and where the trash goes—even if some of this seems obvious. A tenant who understands the rental unit and all its moving parts and features is less likely to call you about how to open the window or where to put leftover moving boxes, or to damage something doing it wrong.

Plus, every unit has its quirks and unique features. Don't make tenants guess about how the oven works, where their guests park, or when trash is picked up.

Consider covering the following areas and any others relevant to your unit (such as furnishings) in your onboarding process. Use the Tenant

Walkthrough Checklist (below) as a model in preparing your own checklist, adding anything that's relevant to your particular rental unit.

**Locks and keys.** Demonstrate and test all keys, locks, and doors (both deadbolt and doorknob).

**Storage.** Show all storage, closets, and cupboards and explain not to overstuff undersink areas or in closets with bi-fold or sliding doors. Explain expectations or rules about exterior storage and common areas, if any.

**Windows.** Open and close windows. Show tenants how they lock and how the screens (if any) fit. State your expectations for their condition at the end of the tenancy.

**Appliances.** Explain how to use, set, or maintain all appliances. Be sure to cover the importance of cleaning out dryer lint filters and not overfilling washers. I leave manuals in the units when I get new appliances (manuals can usually be found online, too).

**Water and toilets.** Test the water at each sink/bath/shower and show tenants the on and off handles and any water shutoffs (local valves and the water main). Also show tenants where the hot water heater is. Flush the toilet and remind tenants to contact you if the toilet runs, clogs severely, or has other issues. This is a good time to show tenants where you have placed a new plunger (such as a hot water heater closet) and how to use it. These instructions empower tenants to stop a potential flood before it can start (and can potentially save you time and money—see the tips on plumbing and toilet clogs in Chapter 4).

**Bathtub stopper and shower diverter.** Even though it seems obvious, show tenants how the bathtub and shower diverter work. You never know their exact life experience with various household routines.

**Circuit breaker box.** Tenants should know where this is for their unit and how to use it. Remind tenants to turn off power to any appliance before trying to move it (or better yet, to call you before tinkering with an appliance or moving it).

**Trash and recycling routine.** There is nothing worse than a driveway full of trash that should have gone out on trash day now strewn about by animals. Tell new tenants the days of receptacle pickup and the procedures, the dumpster location, and the general rules.

Explain that setting trash outside for later is not acceptable, as this attracts animals (domestic and wild).

**Alarms, fire extinguishers, and related equipment.** Your unit should have smoke detectors, carbon monoxide detectors, and fire extinguishers. Test them with tenants present. Keep a small portable stepladder (foldable preferred) for this purpose unless you can reach the ceiling. Have the tenant initial your lease and move-in checklist showing the detectors work at the move in.

**Efficiency tips.** Offer tips for energy efficiency. Show tenants how programmable thermostats work, if you have them, and how to adjust the heat or air conditioning in each room. Supply tenants with any info from your local utility on energy efficiency as well.

**Moving tips.** Go over any sensitive areas or cautions to remember when moving in new belongings.

**Pets.** Go over pet areas and your pet rules policy (cleanup, noise) and any issues to watch out for (pets scratching doors or climbing screens, ideas for cat litter box areas, and so forth). Ideally, write these up in a separate document.

**Parking.** Clearly explain where tenants and their guests can (and cannot) park.

**Mailbox.** Explain when and where the mail comes, provide any keys necessary to open mailboxes, and say what to do with the mail for previous tenant(s).

**Exterior items.** Review how to close and secure any gates and locks for the yard (important for keeping pets in and unwanted guests out); and the location and use of exterior lights (front and back), motion lights, or other lighting. Give tenants extra bulbs or have them contact you if one goes out. Make sure you cover how to open the garage door (with a remote or manually) if you have one, and offer any tips for pulling vehicles in and out safely.

**Tenant rules.** Go over your list of basic tenant rules and guidelines as discussed in this chapter.

By being clear about the condition of the rental unit at the start of the tenancy, and about your expectations as to how the unit should be kept, you'll also be less likely to encounter disputes about the security deposit when the tenant moves out. Your move-in letter and rules and policies should provide additional details, such as any lockout or lost-key fees and noise rules.

---

### Tenant Walkthrough Checklist

- ☐ Locks, keys, and doors
- ☐ Closets, cupboards, and other storage areas, including under the sink
- ☐ Windows
- ☐ Lights and light fixtures
- ☐ Appliances and manuals
- ☐ Water, toilets, and hot water heater
- ☐ Bathtub and/or shower
- ☐ Circuit breaker box
- ☐ Trash and recycling receptacles location and pickup schedule
- ☐ Alarms, fire extinguishers, smoke detectors, and carbon monoxide detectors
- ☐ Heating system and air conditioning
- ☐ Parking
- ☐ Mailbox
- ☐ Exterior items, including yard, gates, outside lights, and garage door
- ☐ Pet areas and pet rules
- ☐ Tenant rules, including moving tips

---

## Move-In Checklist

As you walk through the unit, you are also showing the tenants its condition. That makes this a good time to give them your move-in checklist (use the sample Landlord-Tenant Checklist below as a model in preparing your own). The idea is that tenants view and list the condition of each feature of the unit, for referencing back to at move out.

## Sample Landlord-Tenant Checklist

### Landlord-Tenant Checklist

*GENERAL CONDITION OF RENTAL UNIT AND PREMISES*

572 Fourth St.        Apt. 11   Washington, D.C.

Street Address        Unit No.   City

| | Condition on Arrival | Condition on Departure | Estimated Cost of Repair/ Replacement |
|---|---|---|---|
| **Living Room** | | | |
| Floors & Floor Coverings | OK | | |
| Drapes & Window Coverings | Miniblinds discolored | | |
| Walls & Ceilings | OK | | |
| Light Fixtures | OK | | |
| Windows, Screens, & Doors | Window rattles | | |
| Front Door & Locks | OK | | |
| Fireplace | OK | | |
| Other | N/A | | |
| **Dining Room** | | | |
| Floors & Floor Covering | OK | | |
| Walls & Ceilings | Crack in ceiling | | |
| Light Fixtures | OK | | |
| Windows, Screens, & Doors | OK | | |
| Smoke Detector | OK | | |
| Other | | | |
| **Bathroom(s)** | Bath #1 Bath #2 | Bath #1 Bath #2 | |
| Floors & Floor Coverings | OK | | |
| Walls & Ceilings | Wallpaper peeling | | |
| Windows, Screens, & Doors | OK | | |
| Light Fixtures | OK | | |
| Bathtub/Shower | Tub chipped | | |
| Sink & Counters | OK | | |
| Toilet | Base of toilet very dirty | | |
| Other | | | |

**Source:** *Every Landlord's Legal Guide*, by Marcia Stewart, Ralph Warner and Janet Portman (Nolo).
Copyright Nolo 2014

## Sample Landlord-Tenant Checklist, continued

| | Condition on Arrival | Condition on Departure | Estimated Cost of Repair/ Replacement |
|---|---|---|---|
| **Kitchen** | | | |
| Floors & Floor Coverings | Cigarette burn hole | | |
| Walls & Ceilings | OK | | |
| Light Fixtures | OK | | |
| Cabinets/Counters | Stained | | |
| Stove/Oven | Burners filthy (grease) | | |
| Refrigerator | OK | | |
| Dishwasher | N/A | | |
| Garbage Disposal | OK | | |
| Sink & Plumbing | OK | | |
| Smoke Detector | OK | | |
| Windows, Screens, & Doors | OK | | |
| Other | | | |
| **Bedroom(s)** | Bdrm #1   Bdrm #2 | Bdrm #1 Bdrm #2 | |
| Floors & Floor Coverings | OK        OK | | |
| Windows, Screens, & Doors | OK        OK | | |
| Walls & Ceilings | OK        OK | | |
| Light Fixtures | Dented   OK | | |
| Smoke Detector | OK        OK | | |
| Other | Water stains in closet | | |
| **Other Areas** | | | |
| Heating/Air Conditioning | OK | | |
| Lawn/Garden | OK | | |
| Stairs and Hallway | OK | | |
| Patio, Terrace, Deck, etc. | N/A | | |
| Basement | OK | | |
| Parking Area | | | |
| Other | | | |

☑ Tenants acknowledge that all smoke detectors and fire extinguishers were tested in their presence and found to be in working order, and that the testing procedure was explained to them. Tenants agree to test all detectors at least once a month and to report any problems to Landlord/Manager in writing. Tenants agree to replace all smoke detector batteries as necessary.

**Source:** *Every Landlord's Legal Guide*, by Marcia Stewart, Ralph Warner and Janet Portman (Nolo). Copyright Nolo 2014

## Sample Landlord-Tenant Checklist, continued

| FURNISHED PROPERTY | | | |
|---|---|---|---|
| | **Condition on Arrival** | **Condition on Departure** | **Estimated Cost of Repair/ Replacement** |
| **Living Room** | | | |
| Coffee Table | Two scratches on top | | |
| End Tables | OK | | |
| Lamps | OK | | |
| Chairs | OK | | |
| Sofa | OK | | |
| Other | | | |
| **Kitchen** | | | |
| Broiler Pan | N/A | | |
| Ice Trays | N/A | | |
| Other | | | |
| **Dining Room** | | | |
| Chairs | OK | | |
| Stools | N/A | | |
| Table | Leg bent slightly | | |
| Other | | | |
| **Bathroom(s)** | Bath #1     Bath #2 | Bath #1     Bath #2 | |
| Mirrors | OK | | |
| Shower Curtain | Torn | | |
| Hamper | N/A | | |
| Other | | | |
| **Bedroom(s)** | Bdrm #1     Bdrm #2 | Bdrm #1     Bdrm #2 | |
| Beds (single) | OK          N/A | | |
| Beds (double) | N/A          OK | | |
| Chairs | OK          OK | | |
| Chests | N/A          OK | | |
| Dressing Tables | OK          OK | | |
| Lamps/Mirrors | OK          OK | | |
| Night Tables | OK          N/A | | |
| Other | | | |

**Source:** *Every Landlord's Legal Guide*, by Marcia Stewart, Ralph Warner and Janet Portman (Nolo). Copyright Nolo 2014

## Sample Landlord-Tenant Checklist, continued

| | Condition on Arrival | Condition on Departure | Estimated Cost of Repair/ Replacement |
|---|---|---|---|
| **Other Areas** | | | |
| Bookcases | N/A | | |
| Desks | N/A | | |
| Pictures | Hallway picture frame chipped | | |
| Other | | | |
| Other | | | |

Use this space to provide any additional explanation:

_____

_____

_____

Landlord-Tenant Checklist completed on moving in on _____May 1, 20xx_____
and approved by:

*Bernard Cohen* _____ and *Maria Crouse* _____
Landlord/Manager                    Tenant

                               *Sandra Martino*
                               Tenant

                               Tenant

Landlord-Tenant Checklist completed on moving out on _____
and approved by:

_____ and _____
Landlord/Manager                    Tenant

                               Tenant

                               Tenant

**Source:** *Every Landlord's Legal Guide*, by Marcia Stewart, Ralph Warner and Janet Portman (Nolo).
Copyright Nolo 2014

You'll want to use a form or checklist that's fairly comprehensive, in which the tenant inspects and list the condition of each room and it components, such as windows, walls, floors. That level of detail will be important at the tenant's departure, when you will determine whether he or she damaged the unit or whether you're looking at preexisting damage.

This checklist or form also helps create transparency and trust. You are sending a message that you will be fair with the tenant (and not charge for someone else's damage), but that you will also hold the tenant accountable for any damage done during the tenancy.

There's no need to make the tenant fill the checklist out right away. You'll get better results if the tenant fills it out over the coming days after spending time living in and exploring the unit. The tenant can send it back to you with the upcoming month's rent (provide one larger SASE with extra postage if necessary for this purpose).

Some tenants will add more detail than others. I've seen tenants who barely write anything and others who make copious notes and describe every scratch or dent in minute detail. The average tenant will just write "OK," "good," "fair," or "poor," and note larger imperfections. Don't worry too much about the level of detail. The act of providing and offering the checklist is as valuable as the information it contains. The tenant knows you will go back over the unit with the same checklist in hand at move-out time, and expect it to be in the same condition.

## Move-In Letter

I always provide new tenants a brief move-in letter highlighting some of the immediate tasks they need to complete and necessary information they'll want to have on hand, such as their new address, how to get utilities switched to their name, and my contact information (phone number and email). Include any other key information for your rental, such as any condominium association rules or contacts. If you own rental property in a state such as California or Texas that is experiencing a severe drought and water rationing, make sure you give relevant information to your tenants (especially if you are the one paying the water bill).

A sample move-in letter follows.

## Sample Move-In Letter to New Tenants

June 1, 20xx
Tom Tenant
123 Mulberry, Unit A
City, State, Zip

Dear Tom Tenant,

Welcome to your new home!

Once you've signed your lease, here is some helpful moving-in information.

1. **Your new mailing address**: 123 Mulberry Street, City, State, Zip Code.

Your mailbox is located right around the corner from your unit. Be sure to have your mailing address changed as soon as possible.

2. **Utilities**: The contact for our local power company is Big Electric, 123 Lighted Lane, City, State Zip. Its website is www.bigelectric.com, and the phone number is 555-0000. Be sure to tell the company you are the new tenant. If you've never rented before, the utility company will ask that you complete the paperwork necessary to transfer electric service to your name. Do this as soon as possible.

3. **Telephone, Internet, and/or cable:** These services are your responsibility. You may contact either Phone Co. or Phone Inc. if you wish to have a landline. Check its websites for instructions (www.phoneco.com and www.phoneinc.com). Both firms as well as Cable Co. (www.cableco.com) are local Internet service providers.

4. **Our policies:** A few reminders regarding our policies (attached to your lease):

   • Quiet hours are between 10 p.m. and 8 a.m. Please do not run the dishwasher, vacuum, or any noisy appliances or play loud music during these hours.

## Sample Move-In Letter to New Tenants, continued

- Park in your designated spot. If you have visitors, have them use the visitors' parking space. Approved pets are allowed in the unit but dogs must abide by local pet leash laws in common areas.
- Keep your porch clear of clutter. Break down boxes before throwing them in the dumpster. There is also a large recycling bin near the dumpster. Smoking is not allowed inside the premises. If you or your visitors smoke outside, please keep the area clean and free of cigarette debris.

5. **Landlord contact:** If you need to reach me, please call my cell phone 000-0000. I will do my best to respond to your concerns or schedule repairs promptly. Email: abcd@alaska.net.

6. **Rent due date and late fees:** Rent is due on the first of each month and is considered late after the third. Please mail your rent check a few days before the due date so it arrives on time (preaddressed, stamped envelopes are provided for this purpose). On the fourth day, you will be charged a late fee of $25, plus $5 for each additional day it's late (as stated in the lease).

Welcome to your new home.

Sincerely,

[Landlord's Name]

## Creating Tenant Files

Create a hard-copy file for each new tenant's rental application, lease, checklist, and related documents. As soon as you get home from the signing, place your signed lease, and any cosigner agreements or other documents in this file.

As a part-time landlord, you can keep your filing system fairly simple for tenant records. It is actually easy to handle the paperwork if you file it right away (knock on wood, I have never lost a lease). The paperwork should not be that overwhelming. I have had eight different rental units over the past decade, and I still haven't filled up one file cabinet drawer. I retain all past leases and tenant information.

It's important to keep your tenant files organized and easily accessible. That way you can quickly pull up the tenant's vehicle information off their lease or rental application if you see a strange car; you can look at the lease move-out and move-in dates for determining your rental income for taxes; you can pull up the leases quickly for a lender or buyer; and even simply check when the leases expires.

Some landlords will want to sign and record their tenant documents electronically by scanning them. Use the level of technology that works best for you. I get applications by email and keep them online, but I still do the lease and the condition checklist on paper in person—because physically walking through the unit with a hard-copy checklist works better for me—plus, I can give tenants a paper copy right away.

## What's Next?

Ideally, you've prepared the unit and the tenant for a long, trouble-free tenancy and selected a good tenant who is on board with your processes and procedures. Your obligations from this point on are primarily routine maintenance and individual service calls (covered in Chapters 3, 4, and 5). You will also have to handle ongoing tenant communications and resolve issues with tenants. I'll discuss that next, in Chapter 9. ●

# Effective Landlord Communications

One overarching theme in this book, and especially in this chapter, is the importance of effective communications with your tenants. From the initial settling-in process to arranging a trouble-free move out (covered in Chapter 10), what you say and how you say it are key to gearing tenant expectations and behaviors. Positive communications can build your relationship with tenants and make it work over the long term. Destructive communications erode that relationship and may even lead to your losing good tenants. In the worst case, this can lead to legal confrontations.

Despite your best efforts, your relationship with tenants will likely be tried by a variety of circumstances: late rent, lease breaks, pets, unauthorized roommates, and more. This chapter offers practical tips, strategies, and scripts to help you deal with many of these

Of course, this is not the only chapter relevant to these topics. Chapters 7 and 8 also cover building trust and communicating with tenants before the tenancy starts—for example, with honest advertising, a clear lease and written policies, a helpful move-in letter, and so forth. This chapter continues that theme and is about maintaining the tenancy through its duration. Chapter 10 then explains how to end the tenancy smoothly with trust as a centerpiece for the tenant returning the unit intact and the landlord returning the deposit.

# Best Practices for Landlord Communications

The following general communication guidelines can help you build trust and effectively handle all types of situations with tenants. I provide more specific advice on dealing with common issues such as late rent and pets later in the chapter.

## Establish a Basis for Mutual Trust

Like any relationship, whether it's in the office or with your family, the landlord-tenant relationship can break down when the parties no longer trust each other. One of the ways trust erodes is when people don't communicate well. See "When Trust Breaks Down" below for an example.

---

### When Trust Breaks Down

Tessa has been renting an apartment from Lee for six months. She has never been late with rent or caused any problems. One month, however, Tessa forgets to put her rent check into the mail before she leaves town for a few days at the end of the month. While she is gone, Lee posts a three-day nonpayment of rent notice on Tessa's door, just two days after the rent is due, without first making other attempts to contact Tessa. The next day, Tessa comes home and sees the jarring legal notice. She quickly pays her rent and late fee, but is upset and embarrassed by having had the notice posted on her door for others to see. Tessa is angry and hurt because she has never paid rent late or caused any problems and hoped for more understanding. But Lee explains coldly it is a legal relationship and her responsibility to pay rent on time.

Given Lee's rush to serve her a late-rent notice, Tessa decides to take advantage of her tenant rights a few weeks later when Lee fails to fix her broken oven in a timely manner. Rather than find out the reason for Lee's delay, and put up with the inconvenience of having no oven for a while, Tessa checks her state law and finds she has the right to withhold rent until Lee makes the repair. She follows the state procedures for doing so. Tessa now communicates with Lee through certified mail, and Lee is looking for a good landlord-tenant lawyer.

---

In the Tessa-Lee example, above, trust has broken down. Each side is appealing to legal authority and heightening the tensions because they don't trust one another to fulfill their obligations in the relationship. The communication is often more legal sparring than actual communication, meant to gain leverage or pressure the other side.

If the parties keep this up month after month, it will likely escalate to its logical conclusion: The tenant moves out or they get entangled in a legal case. By this time, both sides will have a laundry list of the other's transgressions. Whatever the outcome, be it a broken lease or lawsuit, the tenancy is not sustainable.

> **RESOURCE**
> **More on the importance of trust.** For an overview of Stephen Covey's view on how trust is vital to business (any business) and how to diagnose a high- or low-trust environment, see *First Things First*, by Stephen Covey (Simon & Schuster), and *The Speed of Trust: The One Thing That Changes Everything*, by Stephen M.R. Covey, the eldest son of Stephen Covey (Free Press).

Despite extensive landlord-tenant laws across the U.S., the tenant still has to rely on the individual landlord, and the landlord on the tenant. The laws and legal system should really be used as a last resort. Regular communications and interactions between landlord and tenant will be much healthier when based on reciprocal trust— for example, that the landlord will make a repair and that the tenant will pay the rent on time.

A key rule of good communication is always do what you say you are going to do as a landlord. Suppose a tenant mentions a shrub needs to be trimmed, so you say you will get to it when you come by next time. When you stop by a few days later, you notice that the shrub is not really overgrown. Trim it anyway. You have said you would, and the larger issue is not the shrub, but the trust. If you leave it undone, it will serve as a daily reminder of something you said you'd do but didn't.

## Think About How You Phrase Your Communications

As a landlord, you will face many situations that offer alternative ways to phrase a communication with a tenant. Let's say, for example, you see that the tenant's backyard is a mess. How can you best address this? You could go with "Your yard looks like a pig pen," which may be the truth. However, it may not build the relationship or even get the area cleaned up. By changing the focus, you can get the same message across and maybe even enlist the tenant in the cleanup, by saying something like the following.

> *Let's think about how we can spruce up your backyard so it will be a fun and useful area for you.*
>
> Or (drawing on a more practical consideration): *It may be easier to mow the yard if we move some of your larger items like the broken bicycles, then the place will look great for you. Let's look at maybe storing these items elsewhere or making a dump run.*

Often, the goal will be to get the same message across, but to do so in a way that builds rapport or preserves the larger relationship. So, to borrow a theme from a popular book series, think about "how" you say it as a landlord.

**RESOURCE**

**Landlord communications.** In a popular book on communications in the workplace and in business, author Jack Griffin outlines words and phrases to use (and to avoid) in a variety of contexts. While the entire book is helpful for landlords, the sections on working with clients, customers, and vendors, and on handling complaints and working with lenders are all directly applicable. Griffin even covers nonverbal communication and a wide variety of communication pitfalls to avoid. For more information, see *How to Say It at Work: Power Words, Phrases, and Communication Secrets For Getting Ahead*, by Jack Griffin (Penguin).

## Avoid the Power Play

At some point, you may be tempted to say something like, "Because I'm the landlord and I say so." Such power plays don't usually work. As a part-time landlord, you rely on your tenants as much as they rely on you. So the power relationship should be a balanced one. Some land-lords may not be able to resist the temptation to overreach, however.

The most common example of the power play might be where the tenant violates a minor rule like parking in the wrong spot or running the vacuum a few minutes after nighttime quiet hours. These violations of policies or rules require a reminder, yes, but they are not major violations. Rather than a simple email reminding the tenant: "The rules help us all live together better if we can follow them," the power-play landlord attaches a note on the tenant's door in large bold print with lots of exclamation points citing the egregiousness of and spelling out the violations. The landlord's note generally threatens the tenancy in some direct or indirect way, as well. While the landlord is technically right about the violation, the tenant is likely to move out as soon as the lease term ends.

Landlords who resort to the power play will run through tenants at every lease or even sooner. No one wants someone else literally lording over their lives, so people will move on quickly, taking their reliable monthly rents checks with them.

Use of power play maneuvers can indicate a larger communication and relationship problem. Landlords who find themselves resorting to this blunt instrument might look more closely at why they aren't tailoring a more careful or balanced communication. See if it is the tenant's behavior, a lack of comfort with the role of landlord, or a feeling that tenants won't listen otherwise. Remember, you can and should set the rules, but using the power play to do so is seldom a wise strategy.

 **TIP**

**Novice landlords often overestimate their power in the landlord-tenant dynamic.** Property rights are a concept (often thought of as a bundle of rights), and the legal fact is that many of the rights related to the property have been granted to the tenant in the lease. So the naive "My property, my rules" approach simply won't work well even from a legal perspective, for the property is legally the tenant's to use and enjoy for the term of the lease. Indeed, the tenant has the right to enjoy the property free from an angry landlord disturbing him or her unnecessarily.

## Don't Rush to Judgment

One tip to help build your relationships with tenants is to shift from making judgments, right or wrong, and assigning blame right away (especially when you experience what may seem, at first glance, like careless tenant behavior). Instead, try an approach that looks at how and if you can retain the tenant through the situation—regardless of the cause.

For example, a tenant who backs into your fence with a car is in the wrong. The tenant knows it. You know it. Most any objective observer knows it. So repeating it to the tenant does little to help. When you get this call or email, stay focused on keeping the relationship intact. If the damage is not too bad and the incident isolated, you may be able to replace a few fence slats for $20 and gain a grateful tenant who will stay longer than ever. Of course, if the tenant is absentminded and keeps damaging property, you may think carefully about renewing the lease. Either way, the issue is not really about fault and assigning blame so much as whether you can keep the tenancy together long term or need to reevaluate it.

I have had tenants ruin ovens when cleaning them, shatter shower doors, and even break windows with odd objects. Even with this litany of dings and cracks, when I step back and look at the cost of repairing one window, replacing a few boards on a fence, or even losing a used oven, keeping the good tenant long term is usually worth it. The lifetime value of a customer, especially one writing a four-figure check like clockwork every month for several years, *far* outweighs the cost or inconvenience of the minor repair.

## Match the Communication Tone With the Situation (Legal or Business)

The landlord-tenant relationship is highly regulated, and every state has developed a series of standard notices for certain purposes and violations. You'll need to become familiar with how to use these legal communications, such as a notice to pay rent or quit, or a notice of a major lease violation, such as illegal activity on the premises. But don't get trapped into thinking that every transgression by the tenant requires a formal legal notice.

If your tenant is very late paying rent or commits a serious lease violation, then yes, you will need to serve the tenant the proper legal notice, following state rules as to the content, timing, and delivery of that notice. Your state may, for example, require landlords to give tenants a certain number of days to pay the rent, or to remedy ("cure") the lease violation, before you file an eviction lawsuit. Some states don't require any notice—that is, the landlord may immediately terminate the tenancy by serving a notice (called an "unconditional quit") making the tenant leave. (See "Who Should Handle Evictions: You or an Attorney?" at the end of this chapter for more on this.)

When and how often you need to resort to using legal notices is part of the art of landlord communications. Keep in mind that you also have a business (not just a legal) relationship with tenants. And from a business perspective, you also will want to use a wide range of communications and reminders to keep the relationship productive and on course. Keeping the tenant relationship within the framework of landlord-tenant law is just the bare minimum goal. Tenant satisfaction, lease renewals, and a long-term prosperous landlord-tenant relationship are the higher business goals.

It's crucial that you tailor your communications to the given situation. For more egregious violations, like rent that's a week or two late or a loud party past midnight, you will need to use the more formal written notice. Serving this notice will be a prerequisite for a potential eviction and will document the violation and start the process. For minor tenant issues, which should be what you typically encounter (with well-screened tenants), try to employ a range of less severe messages, as described throughout this chapter.

Really think about your end goals. Are you reminding a good tenant (one you want to retain) about your policies? Or are you dealing with a problem tenant and starting down the road to documenting repeat lease and policy violations to substantiate an eviction for cause? This can often help determine the type of communication.

> **TIP**
>
> **Good communications can personalize your service.** Unlike a 200-unit apartment complex, the small-time landlord with just a few tenants has the luxury of a crafting more thoughtful (less legalistic) communications, an approach that can help retain tenants. Using a range of communications may actually give you more leverage and options, setting you apart from the competition.

## Start Friendly, Leaving Room to Get Tough

Having worked with tenants through many issues over a decade, one question I have with the "post the legal notice first and ask questions later" philosophy is: Where do you go if you have already drawn your most severe communication card? Granted, you could shock some tenants or scare them into compliance for the short term, but you haven't really built much of a foundation (other than fear) for a long-term landlord-tenant relationship. Worst case, you may come home one day to find that the favor has been returned in the form of a legalistic letter from your tenant explaining that he didn't pay the rent because you have not fixed a major plumbing problem after several requests. Now, you both may be on the way to court.

---

### The Long Line for Legal Help

I know from personal experience where many landlords' quickly drawn-up legal notices end up: the local legal aid office (where I volunteered a couple of summers). On the day the office holds legal clinics on evictions, a long line of disgruntled and frightened tenants will appear with the landlord's notice in their hands. Working with an experienced landlord-tenant lawyer, the tenant soon finds out more about tenant rights, including everything the landlord got wrong (for example, how the wrong notice was used or was served sooner than state rules allow) and how to craft a strategy and response. Often, tenants leave finding a few dozen legal errors their landlord has made regarding their rights as tenants, from the minor to the quite serious, including a host of counterclaims.

Try other options to communicate with your tenants before using a legal notice. Friendly reminders may be more effective for day-to-day issues. See if you can meet your goals with friendly reminders, for example when:

- a dog is barking too much or a tenant did not pick up after a pet
- on trash day, the tenant parked too close to the dumpster and it wasn't emptied
- a tenant leaves a broken bicycle or other large item by your garbage, instead of taking it to the dump
- you get a note from a tenant saying that another tenant was doing laundry after quiet hours, or
- a tenant needs a late rent reminder every once in awhile but then mails the rent check right away.

This may be the sum total of your problems in a year or two with good (well-screened) tenants in a small multiplex. You can simply handle them with friendly reminders and your ongoing tenant communications about maintenance and rules discussed in this chapter. Many months you may have no complaints or issues at all, if you have great tenants.

Of course, if you have more serious tenant problems (the tenant's dog barks incessantly), or even repeat minor offenders (the tenant who needs a reminder to pay rent every month), you can always alter the tenor of your messages. You can use an elevated warning letter (a notch above the friendly reminder) as an intermediate level response. Then, if need be, you could employ the proper legal notice giving the tenant a set time to correct a problem or to move out.

This three-step format has worked well for me: (1) friendly reminders, (2) more serious warning letters, and finally (3) serving legal notices. However, I seldom if ever need to resort to number three, and rarely use number two with well-screened tenants. The smartest part about starting with a friendly reminder is that you can always increase the intensity and severity of a future communications (and I have found this especially impactful).

## Fewer Communications Have More Impact

You don't need to barrage your tenants with messages all the time. Indeed, this could distract from when you really do have an important message. Rather, your philosophy ought to be to *get good people and leave them alone.* But there will be a variety of ways in which you will need to communicate with them during the tenancy about common issues that arise.

## Avoid Polarizing Topics

The U.S. is an increasingly pro and con, or red and blue society, and some issues can be polarizing. As a landlord who accepts checks from all parties and ideologies, be vigilant to avoid politics and sensitive topics in any in-person or online discussions with tenants. Fraught topics might include presidential elections, religion, gun rights, military actions, and even sports (*especially* in areas with two competing teams, be they high school or professional).

You don't want to label or put yourself on one side. Tenants may not like to listen to or communicate with—much less write out a check to—someone on the other side of an issue they see as important. My advice: Don't take the bait if a conversation with a tenant steers in a polarizing direction. You may feel pressure to agree or nod your head when someone starts off on an issue, but avoid it. Change the subject—talk about the weather, the flowers coming up, the snow coming down, or your upcoming maintenance plan.

## Control Your Response Patterns

Whether it is a salmon head stuck in the garbage disposal or an unauthorized occupant, tenants will do things that make you scratch your head. And your first reaction may not be the best one to share in these cases. Losing your cool could cause you to lose any tenants who see or even hear about the outburst.

For example, I rent out a condo in a development that allows only cats. This rule was strictly enforced. One day, a newer tenant showed up with a dog, even after having been fully briefed on the association's rules. Of course, I got several calls about a dog tied to the tenant's porch. My first reaction was to be upset by how blatant the violation was, and I questioned whether I'd made an error in tenant selection. It was a black and white rule: No dogs (even visiting ones) were allowed. And here the tenant was tying up her dog right in front of the condo complex for everyone to see all day long! I worried I might have a sociopath tenant with a dishonest streak. Of course, I thought about reading the tenant the riot act. Luckily, I asked the tenant about the dog first. My tone was more to find facts, "*So, I got multiple reports about a possible dog around your condo unit tied to your porch. I just wanted to check if the dog was yours or if you knew anything about it...*" I found out that a dog was indeed there—but it was a lost dog, which my tenant had found in a nearby busy street. Worried it would get hit by a car, she took the dog home (but not inside the unit), and found the owner that day with the phone number on the dog's tag. The condo board understood, no fine was given, and I kept the tenant. Even the dog found its owner. It was a happy ending that easily could have been a bad one if I'd gone with my first reaction.

Everyone has different sensitivities, pet peeves, and issues that irritate them. Try to learn about your landlord triggers—the things tenants do or say that could set you off or cause an emotional (typically angry) response. For me personally, some of my triggers occur when a tenant:

- does not respond right away to a request about maintenance
- has a car that leaks excessive oil on the driveway, and
- always seems to have an idea for an expensive, impractical improvement to the rental property.

Knowing your own triggers is half the battle. The other is coming up with a more tempered response (see my guidance and scripts in this chapter). If you are dealing with a behavior that crosses a line for you, pause. Unless it is an emergency, you probably do not need to call or confront the tenant while you're upset. Nor do you want to be passive and let the situation go unchecked. Wait a day or so and craft a message. You don't need superhuman self-control to be a landlord, just some moderate self-awareness and a few communication strategies.

## Stay on Script

Another way to avoid communication problems is to stick with your message and follow a script or theme. While it is possible you may spontaneously come out with just the right message when you happen to see the tenant, you're more likely to phrase the message in the best way if you develop it ahead of time (with the help of the suggestions in this book).

If in doubt about whether your message might offend or alienate a tenant, try it out on a spouse, partner, or friend first. After smoothing out the rough spots, prepare and have the script ready for when you may meet or receive a call from the tenant.

For example, if you leave a message for a tenant saying that you want to ask about the boxes and trash bags outside the apartment door, outline your planned script on a sticky note on your cell phone or in your pocket. Then when the tenant calls, you can convey the message smoothly. Try to anticipate any questions and have your answers already in your script.

What if you are caught by a surprise request—for example, by a tenant who sees you mowing the lawn or runs into you at the grocery store and mentions an issue at the unit? The tenant may not even realize all the thought that goes in to your response to a request and assumes you can spontaneously give an answer about buying a new appliance, adding a roommate, or getting another cat. None of these are issues you want to address off the cuff.

Eager to get back to your shopping or mowing, you may be tempted to just agree to the request. A refusal, for example, may prompt lots of questions from the tenant, clarifications by you, or just awkward silence. But you may have just committed to a new refrigerator or the tenant adopting a third feral cat. Worse yet, there may be no turning back once you agree. Tenants are amazingly fast actors once you agree to something they want. A tenant will have a cat picked out, a refrigerator already in mind, or be moving in a friend by the time you've driven home. You'll find yourself regretting the answer or backpedaling (and losing credibility).

Just tell the tenant: *"I'll look into it and get back to you as soon as I can. Thanks for letting me know."* Or use the classic lawyer answer *"It depends."* This is really not dodging the issue; your answer may depend, for example, on the age and condition of the current refrigerator; the qualifications of the potential new roommate and size of the rental unit; and the behavior of the cat and compatibility with current pets. So, have a catch phrase to give you more time to think about the request before getting back to the tenant with a firm answer.

## Put It in Writing

While the oral tradition is great in some contexts, you will need to write to be an effective landlord. It helps you preserve and clarify your messages and instructions. Whether it is a tactful email to decline a tenant's request for a third large dog or a careful way to let the tenant know his or her late-night laundry schedule will need to change, landlords need some command of the language.

Writing helps in at least three ways. First, the tenant can keep the message, and refer to it over time. Second, you can refer to it and remember your position on the issue so as to stay consistent. Third, it is important to keep a paper (or electronic) trail in case a tenant later complains you didn't handle a repair in a timely matter or never warned about excessive clutter. Keep copies of all written communications in the tenant file created when you signed the lease, as mentioned in Chapter 8 (print out any email or text correspondence).

One advantage of electronic communications such as email is that you can just copy and repurpose messages for similar situations, be they pet problems, noise, or clutter reminders. Use the topic heading to search your email box or put the message in a document file for later use.

If you were never a stellar writer in school, don't worry. No one will be grading your notes and messages. The following writing tips will help you be effective even if you aren't going to write a novel.

**Try short sentences.** It worked for Hemingway; it can work for landlords. Longer, complex sentences can be harder to read and often get novice writers in trouble with run-ons, chaotic clauses, and other errors. Instead of telling tenants not to wash their cars near the building due to water streaking its windows, causing puddles by the steps, and spraying other tenants' belongings, simply try *"Do not wash cars near the building. Thanks."*

**Simplify your message** Nuance can be tricky. Instead of trying to convey subtleties of animal waste and personal responsibility, just say, *"Please pick up after your pet. It makes the place more pleasant for all. Thanks for your help."*

**Talking still helps.** A landlord can (and should) talk to tenants and reinforce any written reminders and policies. Often, you can soften any hard edges and prevent misunderstandings when you talk to tenants directly. This may be especially true if you can't convey nuances in your writing or have sent a direct message. For example, if you get a noise complaint, but can't discover the exact origin, you might justifiably email a terse reminder about no noise after 10 p.m. to everyone in the multiplex. But you'd do well to follow up with in-person conversations later, such as: *"This noise reminder may not be directed at you. I sent it to everyone because we did not know which unit was making the noise. Don't fret: It just works better to send a reminder to all the units."*

# Handling Common Tenant Communications

You don't need a daily newsletter to communicate and keep your tenants informed, but consider developing a handful of periodic communications for regular issues. Many other messages, you'll want to craft on an as-needed basis. Here are some of the common communications I use.

## Starting Tenants Off With Enough Information

Remember, if you do a good job informing new tenants of all your policies and procedures (from late rent to pets to new roommates) before they move in, you can set tenants on information autopilot for much, if not all, of their tenancy. Make sure your onboarding process is information-rich, as described in Chapter 8. You'll avoid having to send constant reminders later if you cover everything up front.

## Updates, Ongoing Maintenance Information, and Schedule Changes

The most frequent reminders you'll want to send tenants will probably be about maintenance—the painting project out front or a new hot water heater installation. Also keep tenants in the loop on new trash pickup schedules, snow removal routines, and the like. Do so by phone, email, or text—whatever works best. If you tell a tenant something important in person (such as when a plumbing repair will be made in the unit), it's usually a good idea to follow up in writing (especially if your state requires written notice of entry to make repairs).

It's also a good idea to provide brief tenant introductions when someone new moves into a multiplex. Get permission first, and then just give the first name(s), unit, and any pet info. I send out a welcome email to all residents in my fourplex, so they at least know the first names of the people living nearby.

Here are some special maintenance and repair situations when good communication is especially important.

### Utility Shutoffs

The inevitable water or power shutoff can be a crucial thing to communicate—it directly affects the tenant's daily activities or convenience. A utility shutoff usually accompanies a repair or replacement of something like a broken water pipe. Don't roll the dice and hope the tenants aren't at home when the work will happen. (The few times I've done that, I've heard from a tenant who was in the shower covered in soap or unable to flush the toilet.)

Give tenants as much advance notice as possible of a water or power shutoff, with a quick email, text, or phone call, or a post a note on the tenant's door. Provide a rough time for the utility shutoff, and add a cushion on both sides. If you have an emergency water leak and need to turn off the water, notify tenants immediately of the situation and that you are working on it.

## Inclement Weather and Emergencies

Whether you face extreme cold, extreme heat, mudslides, floods, earthquakes, wildfires, lava, or local emergencies, be sure to pass on the proper precautions for tenants in your area (cover these precautions in your onboarding process; see Chapter 8). Tenants may not be as attuned to how the issues can impact residents as the property owner.

Often, I just send tenants the same information my municipality gives the public for extreme cold (the main issue in my area) about keeping the heat at a certain level, letting water drip, and opening cabinets under sinks. Let tenants know what steps you are taking related to the common areas and outside of the building and any steps they may take in the tenant's units or precautions outside the unit.

## Your Repair Schedule

You can't make a repair inside a unit if you can't get clear and comfortable access to the area. Let the tenant know well in advance about the repair, and (unless it's an emergency), provide the minimum amount of notice required by your state (typically 24 hours), ideally in writing. The crucial information is the time, day, and scope of the repair. If you have a good idea how long a repair will take, you can estimate a window. See Chapter 5 for more on working with tenants during repairs, and Chapter 6, which covers service contractors and the landlord's role in managing them.

My newer tenants typically like to be there for the repair (which is great), but by year two or three, the tenant tends to just trust me to be there and watch the contractor the entire time. I do give tenants the option to be at home when repairs are made, and I let them know everything about the time and process.

Here are some more tips on what to include in repair messages:

**A request to clear the affected area.** Make sure the tenant has moved any furniture, food, or personal items that may be in the way or that could get damaged in the repair process.

**Timing of tenants responsibilities.** For a common refrigerator replacement, for instance, ask the tenant to start unloading the old refrigerator about a half-hour before the delivery is scheduled to arrive. That way, the tenant's food is on the counter for just the short time it takes the old refrigerator to be hauled away, and the new one wheeled into the unit. The tenant can then begin reloading the new refrigerator right away.

**What to do about pets.** Arrange for pet care or barriers when repairs are being made in the unit. You may open the door with the plumber for an easy leak repair, but if the tenant's cat darts out the door, you can spend all day (and then some) trying to lure the cat back inside. Make sure the tenant has any pets kenneled or placed in one bedroom (with the door closed), particularly if the tenant cannot be there for the repair. Dogs should be in the backyard or kenneled when possible. Many service contractors will walk away if a large unrestrained dog is barking at the window when it is time to go inside. Worse yet, you may still get billed for the minimum service call and the contractor may not be eager to come back.

## Correspondence Related to Tenant Requests or Concerns

Responsiveness is a way small-time landlords can outcompete larger ones, so try to respond to most tenant communications within a day or two, or even on the same day. Use of email, texts, and cell phones may allow you to respond in an even shorter time. Even if you don't give a final answer immediately, let the tenant know you got the request and will begin looking into it. Thank the tenant for bringing the issue to your attention.

> ! CAUTION
> **Respond to urgent repair requests right away, such as a broken front door lock or a major heating problem.** Otherwise, tenant satisfaction and trust could erode, and they could even withhold rent or pursue other legal options.

## Behavior-Based Reminders

Some common behavior issues for otherwise good tenants may be related to day-to-day living, such as making sure tenants park in the correct spots (and not the neighbor's); that they not vacuum before 8 a.m. or after 10 p.m., and that they clean up after their dog (every time). Often you can get newer tenants on course with early reminders. By keeping your messages friendly and direct whenever possible, your longer-term tenants will soon have the routine and policies down pat. They will see that you really do enforce and follow up on the rules you mentioned at the lease signing. You can provide additional reminders if needed, but you are probably on course (with good tenants) for the duration of the lease and perhaps even a renewal or two.

## Annual Maintenance/Safety Letter

You can develop an annual checklist for tenants to report safety and maintenance problems, inside or outside the building, such as a window that is not opening properly or problems with hot water not lasting long. (See the sample Safety and Maintenance Update form in Chapter 5 for a sample checklist.) Getting this feedback can help improve tenant satisfaction and also help you catch minor building issues early before they become major ones, like a hot water heater on its last leg or a broken bath fan (that prevents mold by pushing moisture out of the unit).

## Move-Out Information

This is one of your last but most important communications to tenants. Your move-out letter with information on check-out, wear and tear, and other topics that will help tenants through the process can be provided in one move-out packet (as explained in Chapter 10).

## Thoughtful Communications: Say Thank You

Eventually, your tenants will save your bacon in some large or small way. They might catch a leak early or simply right the garbage cans a dog turned over. Some will grab a shovel in a record snowfall before you can get there. Tenants will also keep watch for bad actors in the area, rogue cars, and wayward rodents. I have even had tenants assist other tenants who were having medical emergencies.

My number one positive reinforcement is a thank you note and a gift card (usually $10–$25) from a local store. A gift card from a popular nearby restaurant works, as well. This is not compensation for a job or task but a show of appreciation for being a helpful tenant and stepping up voluntarily. I also use these thank you gifts for contractors who go the extra mile or even when a tenant refers me a great new tenant (saving me from having to search).

# Communicating About Delays in Rent Payment

Cash is the life's blood of your rental operation. So you need to make sure rent gets in every month on time. Developing a good communication strategy to address common late-rent issues will help with cash management and enable you to keep your good credit and make timely mortgage payments.

Getting rents on time will ordinarily be easy with good tenants (and if you've used the screening methods described in Chapter 7, you should have good tenants). You just go to the mailbox and open the rent envelope. With marginal tenants, it may take more work, and even good tenants can forget sometimes. Having a multiple-point program, as described below, can help you get the rent in on time and address the various issues you may face in a late-rent scenario.

This section is especially geared for good tenants (ones you want to otherwise retain) who may occasionally be a day or two late or have the occasional cash flow crunch. For habitually late rent or tenants unable to pay the rent, use your state's notice to pay rent or quit forms and procedures. This section also assumes that you have clearly laid out your rental policies and procedures, as discussed in Chapter 8.

> **TIP**
>
> **Schedule and simplify your own mortgage and other payments when possible.** If you have several rentals, each one may also have a mortgage (or two), insurance, utilities, trash, condo association dues, taxes, and more. Instead of writing a dozen checks every month, try and schedule an auto payment plan so these bills will be pulled a day or two *after* your rental due dates. For example, I've been able to schedule mortgages and other bills so they're pulled from my account between the fourth and the seventh of the month. This helps ensure most rents are received before or by the time these major bills are pulled from the same account I deposit rents into. When all goes smoothly, the rental units literally pay for themselves.

> **TIP**
>
> **Arrange to pick up rent if needed.** If a tenant calls the day rent is due and has the rent ready (and lives close by or on your commute), consider just stopping by to get it, to avoid any potential late rent issue.

## Tenant Who Is Rarely Late With Rent

Even the best tenant may forget to drop a check in the mail every once in a while. Perhaps the tenant is out of town or is preoccupied with a work or personal matter. This is not the time to cite your lease provision on late fees chapter and verse. This situation is usually easy: Send a gentle reminder, and you'll probably see the rent right away. An email or text with the subject or theme: *"Just checking whether you mailed the rent yet"* usually does the trick. You remind the tenant and never speak of it again.

If that gentle nudge doesn't work, try letting the tenant know more about the economic reality of the situation.

---

*Hi (tenant name), I was wondering if you could help me out. I may have mentioned that I don't have your place on Elm paid for, so I have a mortgage payment, as well as insurance, trash, water/sewer, and taxes for your unit pulled from my account every month. But if I don't have the rents in by the (insert your late-fee cutoff date, the third or the fifth for example), I have to cover the costs out of my own pocket or pay late fees. So I was hoping we could figure out a way to make sure I get your rent in by that time every month. Thanks again.*

---

With such a script, you are letting the tenant see that payment for the property doesn't come from a magical, inexhaustible fund or a corporate deep pocket, but from a real person.

## Tenant Who Is Short on Cash

In this scenario, the tenant has a job and is solvent but often lacks money management skills. Unexpected expenses may come up or the timing of the tenant's paycheck and rent do not match up, so the tenant runs a few days late from time to time.

Something also may have happened since the tenant first applied for the unit, such as a change of job (and pay) or reduction in hours. More elevated communications may be required here. You could try asking the tenant for help in getting the rents in on time (using the previous script above) and may have to keep the reminders coming. Your late fee may also provide some incentive.

If it is becoming too much effort to collect the rent, then you probably do not want to renew the tenant's lease. Maybe you will even aim at a mutual agreement to end the tenancy early, if the unit is no longer affordable. In the worst case, you may have to tell the tenant you will need to post a legal notice for nonpayment of rent.

## Absent-Minded Tenant

A third type of tenant has ample resources to pay the rent but lacks the personal management skills to remember that the first of the month is coming, and the rent will be due. This is an odd situation. The tenant has the funds and knows the process, yet can't seem to follow it. Consider a tickler email if you don't get the rent the day it's due. Over the long term, this tenant can be a reliable source of late fees! Alternatively, some tenants with the means have paid me multiple months in advance—sometimes three to six months.

 **TIP**

**Time your on-site maintenance toward the end of the month.** This helps some tenants remember the landlord's existence and thus the rental due date. I've been out trimming weeds or trees and had several tenants come out as if on cue and hand me checks.

## Tenant Who Pays Partial Rent Each Month

If you have a good long-term tenant who can pay three-quarters of the rent now and the other quarter in a week after getting paid, it may be acceptable to work out this agreement, at least on a one-time basis. How you handle this situation may depend on whether you want to retain the tenant or not. But if the tenant can't come through with the remainder, be prepared to serve your nonpayment of rent notice.

If you are prepared and interested in evicting a tenant who pays rent either partially or late, see a lawyer. Do this before accepting a partial payment, full payment without the late fees, or before making any type of agreement (or anything that can be construed as an agreement).

## Tenant With No Money

By far the hardest case in the late rent category is the person who might like to pay the rent, but simply does not have the money or means to do so in full. You can't get blood from a stone, so your clever communications and toolbox of landlord tricks aren't that useful. A tenant unable to pay the rent may indicate a failure in your tenant selection process, but not necessarily. The tenant may simply be experiencing a temporary job loss, a major family issue, or unmanageable medical bills. You will likely have to find a way to end the tenancy; a suggested method for winding down the tenancy follows.

## Appealing to a Nonpaying Tenant's Self Interest to Wind Down the Tenancy

It's time to face facts, not fantasy, when a tenant clearly can't pay the rent. Make sure you tell the tenant simply and clearly that *you cannot house a tenant who cannot make the rent payments*. You may think the tenant has little incentive to voluntarily move out and leave the place in good condition, but you still have some leverage with which to encourage the tenant to leave voluntarily, and soon.

**Your shared interest in avoiding the eviction.** When communicating with the tenant, also explain that *you don't want to have to evict, which will go on the tenant's legal or credit record*. Logical tenants know they will likely seek housing again, and an eviction could hinder their efforts.

**Any remaining security deposit.** A tenant who is just a week or two behind may be able to move out quickly and, if nothing is damaged in the rental, get part of the deposit back. You might even offer the whole deposit if the tenant presents a clean unit, fully vacated, and signs a mutual lease cancellation at the walk-through. Or, even if you could legally deduct for the rent owed or for minor damages, it may be worth overlooking this, just to get the tenant out.

**Your permanent place on the person's rental record.** While you don't have to give a glowing reference, you could offer that, if the tenant lists you as a reference, you will mention the dates the tenant lived at your rental, that there was no damage, and that the tenant paid the rent on time up until the month you mutually ended the lease. Or maybe you can agree to just verify the dates and leave it at that. At any rate, a tenant who hopes to rent again may still have some interest in not alienating you.

Even the hard case—a tenant with no money and no clear place to go—will often take the deal you are offering, especially if it includes a full deposit. Your script is pretty simple in this case.

> *Here's the best I can do. If you are ready for a checkout by (insert date), I can do the paperwork to end the lease, do a walkthrough, and (if the place looks good), I will have a check for you (for amount of full or partial deposit depending on your strategy), and a short letter that says you lived here and did not wreck the place. There will be no legal action or negative credit history.*

Often, this is a stressful and uncertain time for the tenant, so you are going to have to carefully craft the way forward and try to sell the tenant on the benefits of your arrangement. It is more than fair, but you have to get the tenant to answer the door and listen. Tenants may even get some money in their pocket with your option (especially important if they are broke).

Of course, if the tenant has absolutely no place to go or won't talk with you, it may take an eviction to get the tenant out. But most people have a relative or friend or temporary place to live while they work out their financial situation, so your negotiated move-out terms should work most of the time.

> **CAUTION**
>
> **You can't be the tenant's housing safety net.** But you can suggest the best way forward and help tenants find a safe landing place as soon as possible–which is far preferable to having a tenant face mounting past-due rent, late fees, and legal action while living in your unit. You may hear some sad stories, but it's an occupational hazard, and you can't be swayed by emotion.

# More Strategies for Serious Late-Rent Situations

If you are careful when you select tenants, serious late-rent situations may be rare in your landlord career. But you still need to be prepared for them. The serious late-rent situation is one where the rent has not arrived after a week or two and the tenant hasn't called or contacted you (or responded to your gentle inquiry). You will approach this situation calmly but from a slightly different angle based on the more serious potential consequences. This guidance applies to the harder cases (not a one-time or one day late rent example).

With very late rent, I become more of a presence in the tenant's life. I just can't let it go or the situation just gets worse. After the initial subtle messages, starting with an email or text reminder, I call the tenant by phone, and may even stop by to talk about the situation.

Some of the normal rules about building relationships and trust with tenants become less applicable when you don't get paid and haven't been given a good reason for it. The tenant hasn't held up his or her end of the bargain. You need to get firm to prevent your tenant from facing homelessness. If the tenant hasn't grasped this possibility, your tone and seriousness should begin to convey this message.

Here are some guidelines for the serious late-rent scenario. These tips may help preserve the tenancy if there is any chance it can be saved.

## Find Out the Rest of the Story

Ask the tenant questions. Was the rent mailed? If so, when, where, and did the tenant use the SASE or not? If the rent hasn't been mailed, find out when rent may be coming or when you can stop by and get it. You can usually tell if a tenant is being forthright or making something up. I write all the tenant's answers down. That helps me check on whether the story changes later.

You may find that a tenant has not paid the rent because of some other event: a medical bill, car repair, job loss, or anything from a death to an impromptu wedding. The reasons may be compelling;

but you must also let the tenant know that he or she will be hearing more from you until the rent comes in (or you wind up the tenancy).

> *I hate to bother you, but I just can't let tenants get behind on rent. It doesn't help them or me. It just gets too hard for a tenant to come up with two months' rent plus late fees. So we want to keep you on pace so you can stay in the unit.*

CAUTION

**Check your state rules.** While in many states, you could post or serve the tenant with a legal notice to pay rent or quit when the tenant is even one day late with rent, you'll probably want to use that step as a last resort. In addition, some states have grace periods mandating that landlords wait a set time before serving notices. In either situation, good communications prior to resorting to a legal notice can help preserve the tenancy and your options.

## Follow Up

After you have heard the tenant's side and gotten some assurance the rent is forthcoming, then make sure you follow up regularly and let the tenant know when you receive the rent (if the tenant said it was mailed). Keep track of whether the tenant's scheduled (late) payment comes in on time. Make sure the tenant knows "rent comes first." If you can keep the dialogue going, you will also be able to gauge prospects for the tenant getting back on track with rent and his or her overall financial situation.

TIP

**If you suspect the "in the mail" excuse is a ruse, ask the tenant to stop payment on the check and offer to take a new check.** Tell the tenant you will destroy the old check once the new one arrives. Or better yet, set a time to pick up the new check in person.

## Consider Stopping by to Check on the Tenant

It does seem a bit stereotypical—the landlord knocking at the door for rent. But nothing says, "This is serious" like a personal visit. Also, you can adjust the focus of your visit to make it less uncomfortable. Try and make the theme something akin to checking if the tenant is alive and well—not just a rent check grab. For example, try *"I came by to check on you and see if everything is going okay or something might be wrong."*

I especially recommend this approach if you have not heard back on any emails, text messages, or phone calls. It may help you discover the reason for no response or rent from the tenant. You should be able to tell if the tenant is still living in the rental unit. If the tenant comes to the door, you can find out more about the situation.

Something could truly be wrong: A tenant could have been in a car wreck, or had a heart attack, stroke, or other medical situation requiring hospitalization. There could even be a potential domestic violence or alcohol or drug addiction situation.

## Use a Tough-Love Approach

You may have to reverse your own psychology to be effective in the serious late-rent situation. A normal person's first humanitarian response to someone in financial trouble may be to try and house the person as long as possible. However, by letting a nonpaying tenant stay, and get further behind on payments, you may only be helping the person dig a financial hole that's impossible to get out of, even subjecting the tenant to legal peril. An eviction on someone's legal record can make it impossible to find future rentals, thus leading to long-term homelessness. Your well-intentioned inaction will likely just delay the next step a tenant needs to take, perhaps moving into transitional housing or living with friends or relatives for a while.

You must get the tenant out as quickly and as painlessly as possible so the person does not fall deeper in debt and face legal action, and so that you do not risk your credit and business.

## Do the Math: How Much Does the Tenant Owe?

Keep a running tally, down to the penny, of how much the late-paying tenant owes you. Then make sure the tenant knows this figure, as well. The farther behind the tenant gets, the higher your fees are likely to be, making it tougher to pay on time next month. By communicating this clearly, you may avert this downward spiral.

For example, a tenant just 14 days late on rent may owe $1,000 past-due rent plus another $50 (with a reasonable late fee capped at 5% of rent). So the tenant would need that amount, plus would have only two weeks to come up with another $1,000 for next month's rent. A tenant three weeks late would have to pay $1,050 and then only have a week to come up with another $1,000 for the next month's rent. The odds of someone who can't come up with $1,000 in 30 days being able to pay over $2,000 in one or two weeks is slim. The odds of a tenant a month or two behind on rent catching up are extremely unlikely.

## Warn the Tenant of a Likely Eviction

The steps above may take a few days to run through; or you may exhaust them all very quickly. If you've tried them all and it still looks like a lost cause, you may be heading toward an eviction lawsuit. Of course, you will have studied your state's process and required notice. Be ready to serve the notice and start the process very soon.

But first, there's one last step I have used a couple of times, which has saved a tenancy or two. It is not really a legal step, but refers to the legal notice to pay rent or quit.

> *I will be serving this notice by posting it to your door and also mailing it certified mail. I have to. Of course, I am very sorry I have to do this. Without paying tenants, I'll go out of business. And this is a legal requirement to start the eviction process in our state. I will have to do this if I don't see the rent check by a given date or we can't work out some move-out agreement.*

With this final warning, the tenant may see the seriousness of the situation and obtain a cash advance, call in debts, or borrow money from relatives (who may be happy to keep the person from moving in with them). Or, the tenant may finally see the light and agree to cancel the lease (as covered above) and move out in an orderly fashion. It is a final, last-ditch effort to work with the tenants and your most serious communication.

# Communicating About Unauthorized Occupants

In this genre of tenant mischief, someone not on the lease, such as a new boyfriend or girlfriend, has come to live in or occupy the unit. This section discusses why unauthorized occupants can be problematic; how to discover them; how to get them on the lease (or out of the unit); and three common scenarios, with strategies and scripts to use in each.

I've seen three main categories of unauthorized occupants:

- the romantically involved couple who is, for all practical purposes, living together
- the economically motivated tenant (perhaps a budding landlord) who wants to make a few dollars renting (subletting) the extra bedroom or space, and
- a tenant who's helping out a relative, friend, or someone else who needs a place to stay.

Every situation involving unauthorized tenants presents a slightly different fact pattern, but the basic issues and script will be similar and are covered here.

## Why Unauthorized Occupants Present Real Problems

Unauthorized occupants can cause a variety or problems for landlords, from the minor to the major, in that they may do the following:

**Violate the lease.** Not knowing who lives in your rental makes it impossible to manage the people living there. It undermines the landlord-tenant relationship, and can erode trust. And you aren't able to screen the unauthorized occupant for safety or fitness as a tenant.

**Give rise to awkward situations.** There's nothing worse than coming into a unit for an emergency leak and meeting someone you have never seen before, but who clearly lives there. I once discovered I housed the clerk with whom I'd interacted with regularly at the local video store.

**Create logistical issues.** How do you properly give notice to (or evict) someone whose name you don't even know? If the person won't leave, you may have to research how your state allows people bringing suit to list "Does" (as in John and Jane Doe), or seek legal advice.

**Lead to additional unknown guests.** Friends of the unauthorized occupant may start stopping by asking for the person or hanging out in front of the unit. You could even get multiple unauthorized occupants moving in if you don't act quickly.

**Could be unaccounted for in emergencies.** While I have never faced this particular situation, if a serious health or building emergency arose, it could be chaos if you can't even tell authorities who the person in the unit is or whether all residents are present and accounted for.

Read on to learn how to avoid these problems.

## Discovering Unauthorized Occupants

Novice landlords may wonder: What sort of negligent landlord has unauthorized people living in the rental unit, anyway? Actually, it happens quite easily. If the unauthorized occupant lives quietly without problems, neither you nor other tenants are likely to notice. And these additional occupants aren't people living in dark corners in shanties. Rather, they can be professionals with graduate degrees. Their upright appearance may be the very reason that no one pays any attention as they walk in and out of the rental property. Some may work odd shifts or not spend much time at the unit (or may hurry in and out). As a small-time landlord, you probably won't have 24-hour surveillance, much less a front desk where people sign in and out. You may only stop by for periodic inspections or maintenance.

Unless you're there at the exact moment someone is going in or out, it could take some time or an interior maintenance check before you discover the situation. And if you are a good, lawful landlord, you don't peek in or surprise tenants without lawful notice, and you respect their privacy. This makes it even easier for unauthorized occupants to avoid detection. But there are telltale signs. Keep an eye on the vehicles in the lot, driveway, or visitor spots. A new car parked there every day for a few weeks is a giveaway. Other modes of transport are worth watching, too: I once found a live-in boyfriend simply by noticing a new bicycle locked out front for a few weeks.

> Hi (tenant name), I noticed that a little green car is always parked at your place, and I often see a new fellow there when I am working on the yard. So I was just curious if you might be interested in getting him on the lease (I have an application attached), or if he has another permanent address and you are just spending time together. That's fine, too, and you can let him know about any building rules or policies when he visits. Thanks.

Also look out for a tenant who is adamant about not letting you or any repair people in for routine maintenance. Other tenants may also ask about or clue you in to a new resident (actually, they do so quite often). A tenant who acts like he or she is hiding something probably is.

**TIP**

**Get information on your tenants' vehicles ahead of time.** Because most Americans own cars, the clearest sign of an unauthorized occupant can be easy: the unauthorized car. So I recommend *strongly* that you collect information (make, model, color, and license plate number) for all tenant vehicles as part of your rental application and lease. Include a requirement that you be given updates on vehicles within your rules and regulations.

## The Unauthorized Occupant Script

After discovering unauthorized occupants—in my case, people who've been living in rental unit in excess of 14 days (the guest limit in my lease)—I find it's best to act quickly. My script is one I'm pretty passionate about. Tenants tend to quickly agree with the reasoning:

> *My goal is to be an effective, diligent landlord, but I can only do this if I know who the tenants are. If I do not know who my tenants are, how can I manage them? How can I contact them? How can I tell them about maintenance or repairs that are ongoing? Or how do I inform tenants of risks or simple wet paint? How can tenants contact me? How can I respond? How can I even ensure other tenants in a multiplex that I have chosen safe, respectful neighbors? I won't even be able to respond to noise if I don't know all the people in the place. In short, not knowing who lives in the unit undermines everything about my management and communication philosophy.*

Either the message or my tone gets through and my tenants have always been interested in following my next simple step, either:

- the unauthorized occupant fills out a rental application; and, if it checks out, I will prepare a new lease for everyone to sign, or
- the unauthorized person moves on.

> **TIP**
>
> **Try to get the person's name as soon as possible.** Until you have a chance to do a full tenant screening, it's worth trying to find out whether you have an ideal tenant or a hardened criminal in your unit. Put on your detective jacket and search public records and online or other sources. Your tenant may think he or she knows the person, but often hasn't done the sort of vetting a professional landlord would.

## Screen All New Tenants

Use the same screening procedures for unauthorized occupants seeking to be tenants that you use with new applicants (the subject of Chapter 7). You may already have a tenant or tenant(s) who can cover the rent, so the individual income may be less critical if the group income is sufficient. In some cases, like with couples, it really is going to be difficult to keep them apart, so you may be better off at least having information on the new partner and letting them both stay. If the unauthorized occupant has lived in the unit for a few months trouble-free, the key screening criteria may be for safety (no felonies, for example) and any serious behavior problems at past rentals (destroying a unit or major disturbances).

I've had unauthorized tenant situations work out just fine—the new person passes the screening and I get two good, rent-paying tenants on a one-year lease when before, I had just one tenant and an unauthorized resident with a month left on the lease. I don't want to encourage the practice, but it can be a manageable. In fact, the twosome may be better able to withstand a rent increase, as they are splitting costs. Yes, there's a bit of extra wear and tear, but it's often negligible. Turning unauthorized occupants into legitimate tenants can be a way through an otherwise problematic situation.

At the other end of the spectrum, you may find that the unauthorized occupant balks at the application. This is a red flag, suggesting that the person either has skeletons in the rental, credit, or criminal closet or is not interested in a long-term lease with your tenant for personal or financial reasons. It's particularly likely to happen with the "charity case" occupant, who's there specifically because he or she can't make rent payments elsewhere and does not want to start now. Of course, I can't make someone undergo the screening; but I can say firmly that the unauthorized tenant cannot continue to live there without doing so.

 **TIP**

**What if an unauthorized occupant doesn't check out?** If someone looks problematic in your screening, it's time to tell the main tenant the person does not meet your criteria and needs to be out of the unit as soon as possible. That may work—or it may not. If your main tenant can't seem to get the person out, either give that tenant a 30-day notice, if you are on a month-to-month rental agreement (name both the tenant and unauthorized resident in the notice), or begin communicating that you don't plan to renew the lease if it's within a few months of ending. Start planning the checkout dates and try for an orderly move out. In the worst case, you may have to evict the tenant and the unauthorized occupant. However, your tenant's deposit is on the hook, so the tenant could be helpful in urging the unauthorized person out of the unit in time. Also, you can use an accelerated notice in many states for an unauthorized occupant. Consider this if you think there is a risk to people or property based on the background of the unauthorized occupant or their current behavior.

## Avoid Discrimination Complaints When Dealing With Unauthorized Occupants

If the tenant has remarried, is cohabitating, or has minor dependents (under age 18) who now appear to live in the unit (but are not on the lease), be very careful to avoid familial status discrimination. Demonstrate your reasonable behavior by simply stating that you would like to get some information about the other residents and add their names to the lease. You need current information on everyone in the unit for safety and management reasons. If the tenants still balk, consider getting legal advice or doing more research before proceeding.

## Terminate the Old Lease and Prepare a New One

The mechanics of how to add a tenant when you have an existing tenant and lease can be confusing, but it can be simplified. The best method I have found is to simply end the tenant's current lease and let the new cotenants embark on a new one together. This works for an unauthorized resident you want to make a legitimate tenant or new roommate you have approved. Simply use a short termination form, the Landlord-Tenant Agreement to Terminate Lease shown below, to terminate the current landlord arrangement right before signing the new lease.

## Sample Landlord-Tenant Agreement to Terminate Lease

**Landlord-Tenant Agreement to Terminate Lease**

__Robert Chin_____ [Landlord]

and __Carl Mosk_____ [Tenant]

agree that the lease they entered into on __November 1, 20xx___ , for premises at

__56 Alpine Terrace, Hamilton, Tennessee_____ ,

will terminate on _January 5, 20xx_____ .

| | |
|---|---|
| _Robert Chin_____ | _December 28, 20xx_____ |
| Landlord/Manager | Date |
| _Carl Mosk_____ | _December 28, 20xx_____ |
| Tenant | Date |

**Source:** *Every Landlord's Legal Guide*, by Marcia Stewart, Ralph Warner and Janet Portman (Nolo). Copyright Nolo 2014

Adding this form at the outset of the signing is the cleanest route to adding a new tenant (or subtracting one). You terminate the current tenant's lease by mutual agreement and then start a new one with both the tenants. Review all the same information, lease terms, and policies, and make the lease signing exactly as you would any other signing (covered in Chapter 8).

Regarding the security deposit: You can either have the current tenant return the deposit, and then have both new tenants repay it if each wants to pay half. Or credit the deposit to the new lease and let the tenants work out any details and note how it will be returned in the lease. The latter seems to work smoothly.

## Take Steps to Evict Tenants for Unauthorized Occupants

While I have never had a tenant be uncooperative about unauthorized occupants, it would be a serious lease violation and there is an accelerated and serious notice procedure for this purpose in many states, meaning tenants would have to "cure" the problem very quickly. Or in some cases, violations can allow a landlord to post an "unconditional quit" notice, meaning the tenant cannot cure the problem and the landlord can terminate the lease immediately. You might try some negotiation, but if the tenant was adamant about keeping an unauthorized tenant, you may have such an undermining of trust and enough risk that you would want to look at termination. Research your state's proper notice for a lease violation and consult with a landlord-tenant attorney if you have questions about the process.

---

### Playing the Bad Guy When Family and Friends Overstay

Your tenant may have a distant cousin or old college friend who drops in and doesn't show any signs of leaving. The guest time frame in the lease (I recommend a maximum of 14 consecutive days) comes and goes. It may be that your otherwise good tenant actually wants this person out of the apartment, but can't muster up the courage to say so.

Here is where you can offer to play the heavy. Let your tenant (in fact, encourage your tenant to) use you and your policies as an excuse. Try this script: *"Hi Tenant, I noticed your brother-in-law has been with you almost two months and the lease allows guests for only two weeks. So please let your brother-in-law know your landlord needs him to be on the lease or moving on as soon as possible (and feel free to tell him it is me and my policy and not you prompting this). Let him know we may have to serve you a legal notice or even terminate your lease if he does not comply."*

Tenants with guests overstaying their welcome may be secretly glad to hear of the policy enforcement. And for unauthorized occupants, who have been living for free, the idea of being legally obligated on a lease is generally not attractive, and they move on.

---

# Responding to Requests to Add a Roommate

Landlords will inevitably face a roommate request from a tenant. It could be the vacant second bedroom, a student wanting to share an efficiency apartment with a friend, or someone who plans to leave town for the summer and wants someone to pay the rent in the meantime. Like the unauthorized-tenant situation, it could be economics, friendship, or love that prompts the request. Be thankful that the tenant asked you first! Nevertheless, there are a number of important points to consider before you reply, as detailed below.

The steps I describe may take some time, but that serves a double function: It helps make sure that the roommate idea is not a whim. If the two people are still intent on the idea after a few weeks, and after investing more time and thought into the arrangement, there is a stronger chance it could work out.

## Be Selective But Keep Context in Mind

All the same screening rules and guidelines in Chapter 7 apply—get a completed application, check references, and do a full screening of the potential new roommate. Make sure the prospective tenant is completely aware of your lease terms and policies and rules. Your signing and onboarding should also mirror the process and procedures in Chapter 8.

Be reasonable, especially if you already have a tenant who can pay the rent. If you turn down a string of applicants, you may find one living there anyway. The main thing to screen for will be risks (you want a clean criminal background and a rental history free of evictions, rule violations, or property damage). If the current tenant is stretched or has any trouble making the rent, a new roommate who meets your criteria may be a blessing in disguise (allowing tenants to split their costs).

CAUTION
**Your tenants may assume they can do the screening for you.** Your tenant can forward the person he or she feels is an ideal roommate, but don't take this selection as much more than a personal reference. The tenant may have no clue about the potential roommate's rental, criminal, or financial history. I had a tenant forward two consecutive roommate requests from people who'd been recently evicted. I told the tenant, "*A person who*

*did not pay the rent before is not likely to pay it now, so you would likely have to cover the full amount. In that case, you may as well have the place to yourself! (It's less stressful than living with someone who owes you money.) Better keep looking for a more suitable fit."* That tenant eventually found another roommate whom I approved, and it has worked out well.

## Establish Equal Rights Between Cotenants

A current tenant tends to think of the unit as his or her own place, with the new tenant having less priority or seniority. Terminating the current tenant's lease and preparing a new one (as described above) helps put the tenants on an equal footing. It's important to emphasize they will be equal tenants, jointly responsible for the rent, and both with equal and full tenant rights and responsibilities.

## Ensure Compatibility Between Cotenants

Make sure your tenant and the potential roommate have sat down and talked about their house rules and expectations. I require them to confirm that they have discussed all aspects of living together and that there are no outstanding issues. Be sure they discuss pets, sleeping/quiet hours, rent payment, utilities, food, guest procedures, and more. Otherwise, the tenancy may not last, and their disagreements may be brought to you later.

> **TIP**
>
> **Make sure any pets are compatible, too.** I've suggested that roommates with pets make sure their animals interact before they decide to share my unit. Otherwise, if their dogs or cats are fighting and chasing each other from the start, it is hard to imagine how the tenants will make it through the lease together.

You might even suggest that the prospective roommate take a compatibility "test drive" and stay for a couple of weeks. This is most appropriate in the classic scenario of an old friend coming to town, whom your tenant might feel sure would be an ideal roommate. My lease allows visitors for up to two weeks. Every time I've suggested this, the tenant was glad we didn't go forward with a lease right away—and the old friend was gone in a couple of weeks.

## Don't Be Afraid to Deny an Applicant Who Looks Like a Bad Fit

Many times, I've seen otherwise logical tenants ready to gladly jump into roommate purgatory with someone whom they didn't realize had a string of evictions or a criminal past. It's up to you to say no. Otherwise, the tenant (in my experience) will come to you in a month or so complaining that you need to do something about the troublesome roommate that you, the landlord, approved, forgetting whose idea it was in the first place. The tenant may be upset when their roommate choice is denied, but this creates far less misery than having someone not pay the rent or cause problems. The tenant will find another roommate.

# Communicating With Tenants Who Break the Lease

People vary in their respect for a signed lease. You'll find tenants who regard the lease as holy writ and won't break it even under hardship. Others may announce they're leaving halfway through, as if the lease didn't exist. Either way, a lease-breaking tenant presents one of the most difficult communication situations for a landlord.

Before you rant, rave, and launch into tirades about social decay and moral responsibility, remember that it's not personal. The tenant may have simply found another job in another state or be moving in with a loved one—you might behave the same way, and your lecture will either fall on deaf ears or hinder the smooth ending of the tenancy. Besides, do you really want to hang on to a tenant who doesn't want to be there? You're not running a jail. Your energies would probably be better spent getting a new tenant.

## Complying With Your Legal Obligations in a Lease Break

The theory behind a lease is fairly simple. It protects the expectations of the landlord and tenant and provides some certainty. In practice, however, tenants do occasionally break leases.

In a lease-break situation, landlords in most states must limit (or mitigate) their damages (such as lost rent) by making efforts to find a new tenant. This means you can't just coast and let the unit sit vacant and still collect back-rent on the departing tenant's dime. You have to use your best efforts to rerent the unit, and because you can't collect double rents, your collectible damages are only rents lost on the vacant days until the unit is rerented. Your best approach in a lease-break situation is normally to follow the law and use your best efforts to immediately rerent the unit.

## The Lease-Break Communication Primer

Inexperienced tenants will often be surprised to find there are no "lease police" who will arrest them for leaving, no fire and brimstone sermons coming their way. In many cases, they may not even be on the hook for much more than part of the security deposit if the unit is rerented quickly.

When a tenant asks about leaving early, see whether he or she is willing to share what's prompting it. It could be a death in the family, job loss or transfer, marriage, divorce or break up, or a move in order to care for elderly parent. Some issues, such as domestic violence, can be valid (legal) reasons for tenants to get out of the lease without liability. A few states even allow tenants in long-term leases to get out of them for health or employment reasons, so check your state rules closely before you consider what rights you might invoke under your lease.

> **TIP**
>
> **National defense trumps your lease!** The Service Members Civil Relief Act (SCRA) is important for landlords to understand, especially if you own rentals near a military base. Briefly, this law allows a tenant to break a lease under any of three circumstances: (1) the tenant enters active duty military for the first time, (2) the tenant is in the military and receives a permanent change of station orders (PCS), or (3) the tenant is in the military and deployed for over 90 days. In these situations, a tenant can provide written notice to the landlord and lawfully terminate the lease without penalty.

If you are getting more than one lease break every couple of years, make sure your screening process is helping you select good long-term applicants with a record of honoring their leases. Also try to make sure that it's not the rental unit or living conditions driving the tenant away early (like a bad neighbor, noise, or dated building). How you handle the lease break may vary by each unique situation, as in those described below.

## The Lease That's Broken Before It Starts

Here, the tenant is eager to move into your rental, but something happens at the last minute to prevent it—perhaps a job falls through or the tenant has trouble getting out of the previous lease. False-start lease break situations are often employment- or housing-related. To forestall such false starts, you should verify employment with the new employer and call the person's current landlord to verify that arrangements have been made to end the existing lease. Someone who can't easily get out of a lease and get the deposit back or have to pay damages on the current rental may not move.

At any rate, if a tenant has not yet moved in, and you don't have to re-prep the place, consider cancelling the lease and returning the money. Chalk it up to experience. Then keep showing the place.

## The Poor-Fit Lease Break

Whether it's location, rent amount, size of the unit, or some other factor, some tenants find your rental is just not the place for them.

Ideally, you will have screened out this type of tenant or ascertained the fit in screening, but no process is perfect. Again, if someone doesn't want to continue renting your place, you probably don't want that person either, so you will want to explain how the lease-break process works in your state (see below) and look at a time to check the person out.

## Sudden-Event Lease Breaks

Any number of circumstances; a death in the family, job loss or transfer, or divorce may cause people to need to get out of a rental lease. For humanitarian reasons, you may simply want to cancel the lease and call it a day, then use the standard move-out procedure in Chapter 10 (provide a move-out packet, set a date to terminate the lease. and schedule a walkthrough inspection). You often can work out a reasonable move-out scenario for most tenants.

## A Couple That No Longer Wishes to Live Together

One of the most common lease-breaking scenarios is when couples separate. You do not want to get in the middle of a breakup or divorce. But let the couple know that, whatever they agree to, you can work with them. Often one person will stay and another will leave, so you can terminate the prior lease with both and start a new one with the remaining tenant (the only required rescreening might be focusing on the remaining tenant's employment and ability to pay the rent). Some discussion on handling personal conflicts and even domestic violence is located later in this chapter, in the conflict management section.

> **TIP**
>
> **Let the departing tenant know if you have vacancies at other properties.** If you have a couple separating and both are strong tenants, mention any potential vacancies you may have (if any). You may solve two problems at once—finding the departing tenant housing and finding yourself a reliable tenant.

## What to Tell Tenants About Logistics and Legalities of Breaking the Lease

Now let's focus on that moment when you get an email, text, or voicemail saying that your tenant needs to leave or move out early, before the lease ends. Consider a response along these lines:

*Sorry to see you go. It happens. In fact, every state has rules that cover this type of situation. This is how our state generally handles the situation (explain in detail how the tenant is on the hook for the rent until you re-rent the unit). The way this process has worked well in the past is that we agree on a date for a walk through, check out, and hand over of the keys. Let me know an exact date. You are paid up through the month and I have your $1,000 deposit. The sooner we can move you out the better, because people will be looking for places toward the end of the month. And if you have the unit in rental condition (like you found it), I can run the ad for the place and start showing it right away. In fact, I will start going over and inspecting everything the day you check out. Then I will stay in touch about the unit, my progress rerenting it, and other details. I can tell you about my showing numbers, any potential tenants, and I will let you know the day I sign a lease with a new tenant. Then I will put your deposit (with any itemization or offset) in the mail that day. Our state allows (insert days) for this. If the unit is still vacant past the required deposit return date, we can touch base.*

Be very clear about how your ability to rerent the unit quickly hinges on the tenant being moved out on time and the unit being in ideal condition. If the tenant leaves you a damaged, dirty unit, it will take more time to turn it around. Any delays in moving or even waiting until the early part of the month can impact the vacancy time, as can the time of year and overall rental market. Let the tenant know the daily rate the vacancy will cost for every day you can't get the place rented, an amount that could (depending on the terms of your lease) be deducted from the security deposit.

> ⚪ **TIP**
>
> **Manage tenant expectations.** Tenants are always curious how long it will take to rerent the unit—that is, when their liability will end and thus whether they will get some or all of their deposit back. I give my best estimate, with a caveat that it really depends on the rental market, the season, and even the economy. But I'm also careful to avoid the impression that I'm promising anything.

Notice also that my script above alludes to the benefits of moving out well before the end of the month. That's when many potential new tenants look for units. They have either given notice on their previous rental or are paid up through the month. If you can get the lease-breaking tenants out by midmonth, you may be able to catch the upcoming rush— avoiding any vacancy.

Here's how you might further explain this:

> *If you are moving out on the fifteenth, for example, I can begin prepping and showing the place on the twentieth or earlier, and ideally rent it by the end of the month. If that works out, then you may even be able to get your full deposit, if the unit is clean and undamaged. The amount of rent is $33.33 per day for your unit. I will deduct the amount from the deposit if it takes longer than that, on a per-day basis. Again, your rent is paid through the 30th, so if we get a new tenant after that, for example, to sign a new lease on the 5th, I will deduct $166.65 (5 days x $33.33 per day) from the deposit and send the remainder with a deposit itemization form within two weeks. Let's work together on this to get me a new tenant as soon as possible and get you all or part of your deposit back.*

I had one long-term tenant who broke a lease in order to leave and care for an ill parent. But she cleaned her unit exceptionally well and had the carpet professionally cleaned, so I put an ad on Craigslist and showed it that night. The first person who saw the unit wanted it and had a great application. We signed the next day, less than 24 hours after the previous tenant left. It's rare to get a unit so well-cleaned and in such good repair, but it can happen. By letting the tenant know she could help speed up the process by returning a very clean, undamaged unit, we both came out feeling good about the result, and she received all of her deposit back.

---

### Required Deposit Return Dates and Rerenting After a Lease Break

What if the vacancy after the lease break exceeds the required days for returning the deposit in your state? That is, you know you need to return the deposit, but you are in a dilemma because you do not know how much to return, as you are still trying to rerent the unit?

**Check your state law.** There may be some tension between the legal requirement and reality, especially if you're in a state with a short deadline (such as 14 days) for returning the deposit. It's probably less of an issue for the states with a longer (30- or 45-day) deadline for returning the deposit, as this is a more reasonable time in which to rerent.

**Do your best.** If you can continue to be in touch with the tenant and explain that you're making reasonable efforts to rerent the unit, with a regular account of your progress, you are probably doing more than many other landlords. This may keep the person from suing you. In the worst case, by the time the person does get upset enough to sue, he or she will have gotten the remainder (if any) of the deposit back, including your meticulous itemization of days vacant and any other deductions, and will realize how lucky he or she is to get anything back at all.

---

## Using Standard Move-Out Procedures— Even for Lease-Breaks

Whether you are willing to cancel a tenant's lease or planning to hold the person to it (seeking vacancy costs from the deposit, for example), try to keep the tenant from feeling like a thief who must sneak out in the night leaving keys on the kitchen counter. You will have far fewer troubles if you can remain cordial, communicating and scheduling the move-out together, in an orderly way. I recommend using all the same move-out procedures discussed in Chapter 10. Set a firm move-out date, carefully go over the unit, get all the keys and a forwarding address, and make sure the tenant doesn't fill the dumpster or leave furniture behind.

While you are not condoning the behavior, you are getting the tenant out of your hair without undue grief. The last thing you want is a house full of abandoned property or any uncertainty about whether the tenant has actually left. In those situations, you could have to research your state's rules on abandoned property and even an eviction process if the tenant didn't clearly move out.

## Documenting Diligent Rerent Efforts

Once your lease-breaking tenant is gone, your works begins. Most states will require your best efforts to rerent the unit as soon as reasonably possible. If you try and let a unit sit vacant and collect against a tenant, you may face a legal challenge in any state. So you need to turn the unit around to prepare it for new renters (See Chapter 4) and run an ad to start screening tenants (as covered in Chapter 7).

Keep in mind the upside of rerenting: you are now free of a tenant who broke the lease and did not want to be there. Plus, you can freely look for a better long-term renter. And check the market, you may even be able to raise the rent.

To avoid any possible claims that you were not diligent in your efforts to rerent the unit (mitigate damages), a few simple guidelines can help.

**Prepare to meet your legal burden of proving reasonable rerent efforts.** That means gathering or creating any documentary evidence of your turnaround activities. Ideally, you will rent the unit right away and be able to return the tenant most or all of the deposit. But keep in the back of your mind that it could be an extended vacancy and a dispute could arise about whether or not you made best efforts to rerent the unit. Document your turnaround and other efforts in greater detail than you might in a normal vacancy. I'll specify the most important documents in the sections that immediately follow.

**Move fast.** As soon as the tenant has moved out, begin preparing the unit for the next tenant. Keep notes on the date, time, and what you did. (They will be part of the documentary proof mentioned above.) It may pay to burn the midnight oil a bit. That way you won't have a unit empty on the tenant's dime and no work done.

**Post the ad sooner than you ordinarily might.** While you never want to show a unit that is not prepared, think about getting the ad up as early as possible, so as to begin scheduling showings. Print it out for your records. If you have prepped and advertised the unit within a short time, this will be a strong indication of your reasonable efforts to rerent the unit.

**Prepare an itemization of your costs—and play it safe.** Whether the vacancy runs a few days or a few weeks, consider listing only the daily lost-rent charges in your itemization (no other related charges, such as for supplies, advertising, or normal turnaround). While you will spend time showing and perhaps cleaning the unit—and doing so earlier than you'd planned—these could be construed as normal business efforts for any vacancy, which would have come up in a matter of months regardless. When it comes to charging for repairs, consider leaving out your own time and charging only for parts or actual contractor bills if there was damage or repair related to the tenancy. That way, you'll avoid the tenant challenging how long you took to do certain work or whether a repair was necessary.

# Communicating With Tenants About Other Common Issues

The examples in this section are everyday scenarios most landlords will face. While some could be emotional triggers, this section has some positive scripts a self-aware landlord could develop and use to avoid responding angrily.

## Tenant Clutter

Americans face a clutter epidemic, and sooner or later one of your tenant's belongings will start to overflow out of the unit. It may be a broken down barbecue out back or cardboard boxes on the porch. I've seen entire bedrooms become floor to ceiling storage.

All people, not just hoarders, have emotional attachments to items, which makes clutter a potentially touchy topic. Subject to health and safety issues, I consider the inside of the unit and its orderliness to be largely the tenant's business. But that has its limits, for example if I can't access a leaking window or check for mold because of boxes piled high. And when clutter finds its way outside the unit, it may not only make maintenance like painting or mowing more difficult, but affect curb appeal. While the first instinct may be to cite a lease a provision, insurance issue, or just messiness, this might alienate an otherwise good tenant. Think about how to phrase a more positive message to tenants here.

> Hi (tenant's name), I'm doing some spring cleaning and painting on and around your area (cite the exact area—porch, deck, or wherever) and will be spraying some cleaner, hosing it off, and clearing the area in a few days. This is to prepare for repainting/staining it on the next dry, clear day. But I don't want to get any of your items wet or get paint on them. So perhaps we could find a place for these items. Thanks.

The idea is to enlist the tenant in the process, state your reason, and mention the welfare of the person's items. After you're done, the tenant may even see how good the area looks and find another place for the items.

> **TIP**
>
> **Dealing with condo clutter.** If your condo or homeowners' association rules and policies restrict what's left out on the porch, deck, or other areas outside the unit, this gives you an excellent way to raise the concern with the tenant. Unlike with your lease provision, you're pointing to someone else as the "bad guy." Cite the rules and let the tenant know you just want to make sure both of you stay within the letter of the condo rules.

Another theme that may be less subtle but has a strong rationale is that you are getting a nearby unit ready for showing.

*Hi (tenant's name). You may have noticed I'm getting the unit (above, below, next door to) yours ready to show to prospective tenants. And I want to make sure we get the best possible new neighbor for you. So that we can make a good impression, I'm gathering up all the loose items out front that an applicant may see right away. I think the better the place looks, the better tenant we may get. So check around out front. I did notice some boxes and if we could find another place for those, it could help us get a really good neighbor for you.*

## Use "We" Not Just "I" to Focus on Shared Landlord-Tenant Interests

In both your written and oral communications with tenants, try to shift to the pronoun "we" instead of "you" or "I." If every notice or reminder is saying "you did X" or "why did you do Y?" it can put the tenant on the defensive. It has an accusing tone that can put a tenant into an adversarial position. The "we" pronoun is actually apt because the tenant and landlord are really in the relationship together. While you have some different interests, you have a large shared interest in making the place as livable and pleasant as possible. Try to focus on your shared interest in the quality of life in the unit.

## Leaking Car Oil

With cars leaking fluids, both you and the tenant have a shared interest in a solution. Some tenants may not know their engine will seize up without oil or how it gets damaged if it's low on oil. (And an expensive repair to rebuild the engine will make it harder to pay the rent.) Landlords can use this shared interest to tailor the message.

> *There seems to be some oil in your parking spot. We ought to check this out soon and get it fixed so your vehicle is not damaged. And we want to make sure nothing leaks into the gutters or storm water system. Minimizing the oil in the driveway means everyone has a nice place to park, too. I put some oil mats by your door that you can place under the car and then throw away (or take to hazardous waste if very contaminated). This will help until you get your car looked at and the leak repaired. Thanks.*

Cars that leak small amounts of fluid are usually not a big problem, but some will leave noticeable amounts. With designated parking spots, it is easy to spot the offenders. You can use a driveway cleaner or oil absorbent pads for minor issues. Some people prefer using cat litter. Large amounts of oil are an environmental and property hazard, so use your messaging to get it corrected.

## Tenant Not Responding Promptly to Your Calls and Emails

Waiting for the tenant to call back? Don't be offended, but you are not necessarily the top priority in a tenant's life. Employment, family, and social obligations typically come first. But you may be able to get higher on the priority list if you (1) make it easy and (2) show how it is in the tenant's interest to respond.

> *The plumber is coming on Monday at 9 a.m. next week for one hour. Let me know if this will not work or you need to be there. Please put your pets in a place where they'll be safe and won't get underfoot.*

I also find that hard-to-reach tenants become more approachable when you let them know how difficult it is to get good service contractors and how much they cost. Most tenants do not know that landlords can pay $50 to $100 an hour or more for a plumber or other contractor, or that it may be hard to even get the best people to come at all.

## The Impractical Request

Some tenants aren't realistic about the costs and work involved in some improvements or additions to the property. Suppose a tenant recommends covering the parking area, an improvement you know will cost $10,000 and not really bring much more in rents. Instead of looking at the tenant funny or telling them "no way," mention your larger rationale and the potential consequences.

> *We try and keep rents low, so if we did that kind of major improvements, we'd probably have to raise the rents by $ (insert amount to recover the costs). I am not sure we could rent the units for that amount and was hoping to not raise your rent.*

When the issue of a major rent raise is involved, you probably won't hear much more about this request from the tenant.

# Communicating About Tenants' Pets

So far, this chapter has covered the communications strategies related to tenants and the myriad of situations landlords face when housing them. But in many cases—if you've gone with my preference, and allowed approved pets on your properties—the majority of your residents (on a numeric basis) may not even be people, but furry, finned, or feathered friends! For example, if you have one tenant in each side of your duplex with two small dogs each, you house two people and four dogs.

Having carefully screened both the pets and their owners as described in Chapter 8, I don't anticipate too many problems. However, issues can arise with dog or cat behavior, waste around the property, or wear and tear on the property itself. Here are some ideas for avoiding pet problems:

**Watch the waste.** Dog waste can draw more ire than almost any pet issue (right up there with barking dogs and cat urine). You may have even heard of disputes among neighbors that have gotten legal and involved DNA evidence to track the waste back to the perpetrator. I tell my tenants at condos or in areas with strict dog waste rules to advertise their plastic bags (often orange or black). In other words, while walking the dog, hold the bags or tie them to the leash so that anyone looking out the window into the common yard or paths (and someone always is), will see them. Don't be subtle about being a responsible owner—advertise it.

**Prepare for some barking.** Often small dogs are the noisiest culprits, but all sizes enjoy an occasional bark. Your key is to find the trigger—the doorbell is often it. If your tenant gets lots of visitors, you may want to unhook the doorbell or ask the tenant to have people call the cell when they're out front. Other common barking triggers are outdoor sources of excitement: the suspicious squirrel or dastardly mail carrier. Heavy curtains or barriers that block the visual path can help, as does leaving a television or radio on low so the dog doesn't pick up noises as easily.

**Make sure owners understand their exercise responsibilities.** Your ideal dog owner, especially for a large active breed, is a jogger or walker, or at least someone willing to hire one. A dog is fairly dormant in a small unit, and anxious pets can be problem pets—tearing up doorframes, chewing up carpets, disturbing neighbors, and so on. So we are often screening not just the pet but the owner's ability to understand pet behavior and properly attend to their pets' exercise needs.

**Keep tenants apprised of condo policies.** For condo renters, let them know about rules, updates, meeting topics, and any pet-related issues. The association may send you the information about its goings-on, so you can share these with your tenant. That way they can see the issues that are on their neighbors' minds and stay clear of controversy.

**Cats up, dogs down.** Whether it is a condo or multistory fourplex, I prefer large dogs to be housed on ground floors and cats or smaller dogs upstairs. Large dogs upstairs can create an issue jumping, playing, and running, thus bothering the downstairs tenant.

> TIP
> **If you replace carpet in an upstairs unit, get the thickest pad possible.** Also, put thick area rugs on hard floor surfaces like kitchens, entries, and hallways.

Here's one general script I use for various pet issues:

> Hi (Tenant's name). We are in the minority allowing pets in all our rentals. We do this because we think pet owners can and do make great tenants, but we have to make sure having pets does not impact other tenants negatively. Try and work on some strategies for helping us with the (insert problem behavior, be it barking, dog waste, digging, etc.) so we can continue to live together with our pets harmoniously. Thanks.

And, of course, the time may come when a tenant wants to add a new pet to the family. Whether you allow adopted or additional pets is also a matter to be dealt with case by case, and with close scrutiny. Consider factors such as how many pets the tenants already have and their likely compatibility with additional ones. Also, probe into how well socialized the proposed pet is. Be on the lookout for behavioral issues. If the pet hasn't been chosen yet, that gives you an opportunity to weigh in, using the same screening criteria as always. Humane Society or shelter staff, for example, want a good fit and will be honest with landlords about a prospective pet's behavior and fitness for a particular environment.

# Handling Conflicts Large and Small

You may encounter various conflicts of all sizes as a landlord. Here we define conflict broadly as any situation where someone has an issue with someone else or some aspect of your rental property, for example:

- A tenant has an issue with the behavior or actions of another tenant, neighbor, roommate, or even you (the landlord). Noise complaints are common issues tenants have with one another.
- A tenant has a problem with some aspect of the property or the policies related to living at the property. It could be a problem with the maintenance needs, property condition, or a community or lease rule. Common examples could be issues with heating or cooling in the unit, parking-spot assignments, or secondhand smoke.

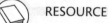 RESOURCE

In *Developing Management Skills,* David A. Whetton and Kim S. Cameron (Prentice Hall) survey the conflict management literature. They encapsulate sound conflict-diagnosis and management approaches from current and past research, which I've drawn on and adapted to the landlording context in this chapter.

Since we can't provide an individual approach to every type of issue you will face, it is useful to have a general strategy or approach. Here is a process I have used with success in the landlord-tenant context, melding both practical insights and the general theories on handling human conflict.

## Start With Some Fact Finding

When you get a report or complaint about a conflict, listen (to all sides) and find out more. You may hear one compelling argument and tale of egregious behavior, but there are always two sides to every story. Your first statement will be: *"Thanks for letting me know. I will look into this and get back with you on it."* Right away, this neutralizes the situation somewhat and prevents the tenant from trying self-help (such as retaliating against a loud neighbor) or from feeling powerless. And you also don't want to jump to any conclusions or make any promises about outcomes until you hear more. No need to be Sherlock Holmes. Just make a call or two and ask other tenants about the issue or stop by and look into it yourself, if it concerns the property's physical state.

I had a tenant, for example, (Joe) who complained that another tenant (Fran) was striking the fence between their property in a loud and frightening way. Upon first reaction, this sounded like problematic and inexplicable behavior. Rather than write Fran a letter or warning, however, I asked her about it. Turns out, she was trying to get Joe's loud dog to stop attacking the fence area. So the facts were more complicated (as they often are). I gave each a friendly reminder, one about the dog and the other about the fence. They went on to live next door to one another in peace for a couple of years.

The run-of-the-mill noise complaint usually calls for some fact finding. A tenant may complain to you about noise the tenant thinks is coming from another unit, but discerning the exact source can be problematic, especially in a multiplex or a condominium complex. You will need to rule out noise from nearby properties or from the building itself (like loud sump pumps, loose pipes, or off-kilter washing machines). Walking around the perimeter of a building may help you zero in on the source. If you are reasonably sure the noise comes from a unit that you own, write that tenant a reminder (just as you would for clutter or leaking oil).

## Recognize That Conflicts Can Lead to Positive Change

Understanding the type of conflict you are facing is important to your resolution strategy. It may help to view some types of conflicts as positive, indicating that people are invested and still care enough to voice their views and press for change. Far worse than getting complaints about noise, trash, or damage at the building would be if residents didn't complain because they'd given up all hope, and feel there's no recourse. A downward spiral could develop, with the good tenants spending their energy looking for a new place to live.

Let's say you're faced with one problem tenant (say, one playing extremely loud music at all hours). You might, at some level, wish the problem would go away without your intercession. But a tenant like that can literally run off all the good tenants in a multiplex. Good tenants do not want to live like that. If they're too afraid or apathetic to complain, you may not learn about the situation until they've all moved on, leaving you with vacancies that are hard to fill. Facing the noise conflict early and reforming or terminating the problem tenant would have been the better resolution for all concerned.

Some tenant complaints might even help you improve your operation, whether the issue is noise, an unruly pet, a dark area of the parking lot, or too few recycling options. Even the best landlord can't know everything that happens on a property, so tenants act as eyes and ears. Keeping open communication will help them share their observations—positive and negative.

## Diagnosing and Dealing With Two Types of Conflicts

Rather than try to avoid or deny any conflict, accept that you will face some conflicts in landlording. This means you will need a strategy to handle it. A key first step is to diagnose whether you face an issue-based or a personal conflict, as your approach will vary depending on which it is. The following parking conflict example illustrates the difference between the two basic types of conflict you will face.

**Sample issue conflict.** A tenant emails you to let you know the parking configuration at your triplex is making it hard to maneuver her car in and out, especially when guests are visiting other units. She has been blocked in or had trouble getting out at times. You may be able to solve such a conflict through your own actions, perhaps with a new parking plan or better communication to other tenants. Issue conflicts can lead to improvements and often can be resolved.

**Sample personal conflict.** In contrast to the above issue conflict, a tenant emails you to let you know that tenant X has deliberately blocked her car in again after several angry confrontations on the subject, and that she strongly dislikes tenant X. Most landlords probably don't have the background to work people through personal conflicts, nor should they have to attempt to play counselor. You have a few angles you can try and ways you can help, but your options may be limited. Your only viable solution may be not renewing one or both of the tenants' leases if they can't work through the conflict.

Start by letting the tenants know your position on their conflict. I ordinarily tell the parties they will need to find a way to work through the issue, or else we will need to look closely at whether they want to stay in their leases or whether I would want to renew their lease(s). I remind both parties that they are in leases for a set term (mentioning the end dates and the required notice), and that I am glad to enforce the policies and lease, but if their conflict is too stressful or disturbing, I would recommend looking at canceling leases or seriously consider not renewing them.

Sometimes the seriousness of the conflict sets in when tenants consider the prospect of finding new housing (especially with your just-below-market rates, good service, and generous pets policy). In a tight housing market, tenants may at least come to an armed truce and avoid one another, agreeing to live together peaceably. I have even seen them reconcile.

With serious cotenant personal conflict, particularly where you suspect some psychological or physical violence or abuse, the best course of action is likely to refer one or both tenants to resources in your area. Get safely away and call the police if you witness actual violence or abuse.

 RESOURCE

**Landlords must know their legal rights and responsibilities around tenant domestic violence.** Over half the states have statutes covering how domestic violence intersects with landlord-tenant law. These typically control how a landlord must handle a domestic violence situation, and the rights of tenants who are victims of domestic violence, such as to break a lease and move out early.

One positive aspect of the transient nature of tenants is that you may be just a 30-day notice away from a resolution. In cases where I can't do anything to help an aggrieved tenant, I have given them the option to cancel the lease and move. Even with longer-term leases, you may find it best not to renew one or more people involved in a personal conflict.

# Formal Conflict Resolution for the Landlord

There may be times when your best efforts to resolve tenant complaints and conflicts nevertheless fail. An unreasonable tenant could flout your rules or seriously damage your property. And, of course, as discussed in Chapter 11, you could be sued (for a slip and fall, for example) or need a lawyer.

Before getting lawyers involved, consider exploring these dispute resolution options.

**Negotiation.** This may be an extension of your conflict-resolution communications, in which you try and reach a compromise with the tenant through meeting and discussing the issue and a possible resolution.

**Mediation.** A neutral third party can help soften the rigidity between the parties and help both sides see their way to a jointly agreed-upon resolution. Mediators can also suggest solutions the parties have not considered.

**Arbitration.** Here, a third party will actually decide on a resolution for the parties, similar to the way a judge would. While more formal than negotiation or mediation, arbitration offers a way to avoid going to court. Yet the decision or award can be enforceable in court.

**Small claims court.** Many people handle their own cases for smaller claims (usually under $10,000, depending on the limit in your state). Security deposit disputes often end up in small claims court (typically the tenant suing the landlord for failure to return the deposit). Although it is a court with a judge, the procedural rules in small claims court are often relaxed and geared for self-represented laypeople.

**RESOURCE**

**For useful articles on mediation, arbitration, and small claims court,** including state rules and dollar limits on small claims court lawsuits, see the Small Claims Court & Lawsuits section of www.nolo.com.

# Who Should Handle Evictions: You, or an Attorney?

The thesis of this book is best practices to avoid a legal situation, like a termination and eviction. If you do reach the point of no return, however, you must make some important management decisions. In particular, you may need to choose between outsourcing the eviction to an attorney or handling it yourself. Think about the following questions and factors (and see Chapter 11 for more advice on finding and working with lawyers):

- Do you have a landlord-tenant lawyer you use often?
- If you do not have a lawyer, can you afford one?
- Is there a landlord-tenant lawyer available to take your case nearby with expertise in your jurisdiction?
- Do you have a good knowledge of the termination and eviction processes and forms in your state?
- Do you have some legal background and writing skills?
- Have you been through the eviction process before as a landlord, representing yourself?
- Will the tenant have a legal aid or private lawyer? Or will he or she even show up in court?
- Do you have the time, disposition, and skills to do the job effectively?
- Might the tenant have a defense to your termination, such as that the eviction is a form of retaliation for the tenant having

filed a housing complaint, or is an act of discrimination? Will the tenant have any other defenses?

As you ask yourself these questions, the answer should begin to present itself. For example, if you don't have a lawyer and are unable to find one in your area (or one you can afford), then you probably are going to be representing yourself. If you have done an eviction before, you probably know the ropes. However, if the entire process is new and seems very technical (and it often is), and you can't make any sense out of the terms and steps, consider finding a lawyer who has experience in the area. The same goes if the tenant has mentioned claiming retaliation or discrimination.

RESOURCE

**The legal process for terminating a tenancy and evicting is beyond the scope of this book.** However, all landlords should know a bit about it. See the Nolo resources mentioned at the start of the book. Also, check your state's attorney general's office, the state bar association, and your state court's self-help centers for more information on the eviction process in your state. Some apartment associations in more populous states may also offer information and forms used in the process.

## What's Next?

We have covered communications and conflict strategy through the entire tenancy, but even when your tenant gives you notice that he or she will be moving, your communications duties don't end. They actually increase for a short time during the move-out period. You will need to share your move-out procedures and tips to guide the tenant through the transition smoothly, as described in Chapter 10, next.

# Moving Tenants Out

Most property management books provide ample coverage on how to get new tenants—advertising, screening, prospecting, and moving them in—perhaps because it is human nature to focus on the future tenant and not the outgoing, past one. After all, the new tenant is the source of the future revenue stream, while the departing one, you may never see again.

But moving tenants out smoothly can be as important as moving them in. Not everyone is aware of the issues you can face in a move-out. First and foremost, the interests of the tenants have shifted. Your rental unit is no longer the tenants' present and future home; so while tenants may have covered the carpets and carefully avoided damaging walls moving in, they may not behave with the same care on the way out. The unit is now just a storage place for the tenants' belongings until they get everything moved. Your walls and any floor protection may just be in the way.

All you really have with which to motivate a tenant to get out on time and without damage are your communications, assistance, and the deposit offset.

## How a Tenancy Ends

Many tenancies run their natural course—the lease expires and the tenant is ready to move on to other things, or a month-to-month tenant gives the required notice and then departs. In other cases, either you or the tenant will end the tenancy early.

States vary as to the amount and type of notice landlords and tenants must provide in order to end a tenancy. Most states require 30 days' notice to end a month-to-month rental agreement. A lease lasts for a fixed term, such as one year; neither you nor the tenant may end the lease early, with some exceptions, including a violation of the lease terms by either party. (That said, tenants break leases occasionally, so I include a whole section on the topic in Chapter 9.)

States also have specific laws and procedures regarding the return of security deposits. You will likely have between 14 and 30 days after the tenant leaves to return the deposit, along with an itemization of any deductions that you took before returning the remainder—such as to fix damage (outside of ordinary "wear and tear") or to make up for rent that the tenant failed to pay.

# Four Major Move-Out Pitfalls to Avoid

If you've had good communications with your tenants during their stay, your move-outs will be few and far between (as many tenants may renew their leases) and those that occur will go smoothly. Nevertheless, even a part-time landlord using one-year leases will need strategies to handle some of the major move-out pitfalls listed here (and in the section below on security deposits). A good move-out letter, also described below, will help minimize some of these problems.

## Extra Wear and Tear

Landlords may get more wear and tear on the move-out than the move-in. Tenants who are leaving may be less concerned about their past rental. They will be moving tons of property out of your unit—often with the help of people who were never your tenants. You don't want to rely on the kindness of strangers to make sure it goes well.

Dings and dents are likely. The floors also take a beating from very heavy traffic. A moving crew coming in and out dozens of times on a wet day can ruin the carpet. Doors left open long-term will swing in the wind; insects may even move in en masse.

Sometimes just being on site can make a difference. You'd be there if professional delivery people were moving in objects, for example, so you may want to check in from time to time, especially with amateurs running the move-out show.

## Property Left Behind

You may have even driven by other rentals and seen the mattress mayhem of debris littering the curb at move-out time. There is a very real risk of unwanted items, large and small, being left behind in the move out. If that happens, you may need to dispose of all these items or, worse, use your state's abandoned property rules, which may require you to provide the tenant a legal notice describing the personal property and what will happen if it is unclaimed within a specified period of time. Some states even require landlords to inventory, store, and sell tenants' property at a public sale.

## Noise and Disturbances

Moving can be controlled chaos. There are hundreds of trips back and forth between the unit and the moving vehicle. Add in noise, foot traffic, extra vehicles (trailers and trucks backing in), and strangers helping out, and it can be a minor circus. A lot can go wrong: from someone backing a moving van into your fence to general noise complaints or building damage. Late-night packing and people going up and down the steps all day can disturb other tenants or neighbors.

## Overflowing Trash Receptacles

A top issue I have worked on correcting is the tenant's overuse of the garbage can or dumpster when moving out. You have to be diligent to avoid an overflow—the scheduled pickup may still be a week away. You also need to be concerned about proper disposal of household hazardous waste, such as half-used cans of paint or lighter fluid. My strategies for a greener move out (see below) have helped out with both these issues immensely.

# Preparing a Move-Out Letter

To avoid pitfalls such as abandoned property or damage, give tenants move-out guidelines. Also try to get them started on the process early, rather than enabling a rush at the last minute. Good tenants will let you know well in advance of when they will be moving. Others may not give as much notice, or even clear dates or deadlines.

But whenever a tenant gives you notice, send a move-out letter covering your check-out, walkthrough, and inspection procedures. I suggest you set a tentative date for the inspections and walkthrough as soon as possible after the tenant gives you notice of leaving. Be sure your tenant knows to expect an inspection for damage *after* the move out, as well. Some states require a pre-move-out inspection or that the tenant be present at the inspection; you will need to find out and follow any such laws in your state.

Your move-out letter should explain the types of deductions from the deposit you may legally make, such as for damage (include specific examples of wear and tear versus damage); when and how you will send any refund that is due; and what you expect in terms of cleaning (for example, that the unit be as clean as when the tenancy began). The more detailed the move-out letter, the better. Some landlords provide tenants a checklist as to their specific requirements—such as to clean the refrigerator inside and out. You can also remind tenants of quiet of hours and to be watchful about damage or debris.

Almost all tenants have more stuff than they can or will move, so make sure your move-out letter clearly lets the tenants know that disposing of items means getting everything out of the rental and premises. This includes not putting items out front, in the back, or on the side of the unit. Your letter should include specific tips (see "Green Tips for Moving Out With Minimal Waste," below) to help the tenant dispose of various types of items.

Finally, be sure your move-out letter alerts tenants to return all keys and provide their forwarding address (where you will send the refunded portion of their deposit).

Start early and often in reminding the tenant about the major issues and themes in the move-out process. Check in a few times during the course of the move-out month to see how things are going (or not going). This is important for several reasons. It will let you know when you can really expect the tenants out. Only then can you begin the turnaround and search for a new tenant. Also, it lets you make sure the tenants don't get into such a rush that they damage the unit or leave items behind, sitting out front, or piled on the trash receptacles.

If other tenants will be affected by the move (for example, if you own a duplex), make sure they know about the move-out, the process, and what to expect (or to forgive).

# Reviewing Your Security Deposit Return Rules

It's worth double-checking that your guidelines on deposits (and return of deposits) mesh with your state's deadlines, procedures, and rules for returning deposits. States' laws vary, but the key points that follow can help landlords avoid conflicts over the deposit at the end of the tenancy in every state.

## Be Lenient Regarding Minor Wear and Tear

Life happens, and the tenant shouldn't—by common sense, and often by law—be held responsible for every little scuff. If spills on the carpet or scratches on the door keep you up at night, you might consider using the time to learn about how to touch up scratches and remove stains at the next turnaround. Most minor damage can be repaired fairly easily. Getting the unit back in reasonable condition and turning it around for the next tenant is the best use of your time.

## Explain How Tenants Can Help You Return the Maximum Deposit Amount

Probably 90% of the time, I fully return deposits, within two weeks (my state's deadline for returning the deposit). I let my tenants know I am on their side, and that they can help me by returning the unit like they found it. Ideally, you will have done a move-in inspection (using a checklist like the one shown in Chapter 8), so you have a record of the rental's condition at the start of the tenancy, for comparative purposes.

Be sure to tell tenants that your preference is to give back their deposit—always referring to it as their money—and let tenants know how they can help you do that. You want long-term tenants to be careful, but not paranoid. If tenants know they have a real chance of getting their money back, you also stand a better chance of getting your unit back in good condition. You can even give a form reference letter to great tenants who leave the unit in ideal condition (a parting item I find tenants appreciate).

## Don't Be Pennywise and Pound Foolish

Yes, you can collect a few hundred dollars off a deposit here and there. But it could cost far more than that in the end to defend against a tenant's claim that you wrongfully held or deducted from the deposit. Any landlord could find the dings and dents, no doubt.

But remember that your tenant will probably be asking for return of the full deposit if the unit is basically intact. Tenants often need every penny of the deposit in order to move into their next unit, and can be quite vociferous in their requests. Indeed, you could burn up a few hours (worth a few hundred dollars to most people) just explaining the damages to the tenants and showing them photographs of before and after the tenancy.

When it comes to money, tenants can be quite savvy about the deposit rules (which are widely available online). Even tenants who are not legal experts can represent themselves effectively in small claims court (again, information on rules and procedures is readily available). Tenants often have another advantage, in that many landlords fail to follow their state's deposit rules to the letter—often by forgetting about any state requirement for handling interest, failing to properly segregate the accounts, or just being a few days late returning the money.

So, if a dispute ends up in small claims court, you may have to walk in already admitting you did not follow the deposit law (by which time you will likely wish you had just given the money back in full). Further, you could end up paying thousands of dollars in penalties and legal fees (yours and maybe even your tenant's), so it seldom makes sense, from a risk-management perspective, to keep the deposit unless absolutely warranted.

As a volunteer legal aid lawyer, I once worked full time for several weeks just to secure part of a security deposit for a low-income tenant. I think it may have been $600 or less. The landlord had a private lawyer and no doubt racked up thousands of dollars in legal expenses. We had numerous meetings and court filings, and probably spent over a hundred of hours in total. It made no sense from an economic perspective.

## Be Precise in Itemizing Deductions

If you are going to hold part of a deposit—as is perfectly warranted and within your rights, when a tenant has damaged a unit or done something else to trigger a deduction under your lease (for example, by leaving with unpaid rent)—just remember to be exacting in accounting for the amount. Your offset or reduction may need to hold up in court, so you can't just approximate the repair costs or give ballpark figures.

This advice applies even if it was the tenant who pointed to something broken and volunteered part of the deposit. (I've had tenants do just that.) Such a tenant may still balk at being apparently taken advantage of if you overcharge for the repair.

If you hold back part of a deposit, you are on perilous legal ground. Your own rough estimates on the repair cost or value (if you did the work yourself) won't necessarily hold up. If you have work done by outside contractors, you will need the exact bill for the replacement or repairs. Even better would be having multiple estimates.

If you do the labor yourself (for example, to replace a doorknob), it may be cleaner to just charge for the parts you purchase, unless you can demonstrate that you used a set, reasonable labor rate. The few times I've kept a small part of a deposit, I used exact parts-replacement costs. I don't have a labor fee—so it would be harder to set, prove, or assess that.

Take a photo of the damage, the repair you made, and the receipt for the parts or materials. Send all of these to the tenant, attached to the offset form (itemizing your deductions from the deposit), along with a check for the remainder of the deposit. If you use a contractor, put in any contractor bill.

The more reasonable your fee and meticulous your documentation, the less likely the tenant will be to challenge your deduction. Tenants also put some value on their time and will estimate their chances in court before filing a small claims lawsuit.

**TIP**

**Using the deposit for prorated rent after someone broke a lease?** Be sure to document your efforts to refill the unit, document the days the rental has been empty and your advertising and marketing efforts, and make sure the tenant knows exactly how this process will work. See Chapter 9 for further guidance on dealing with tenants who break a lease.

# Green Tips for Moving Out With Minimal Waste

If you are new to landlording and fairly thrifty or environmentally conscious, it will surprise and shock you when you see what some tenants throw away. It did me. You may find most of your tenants' useful, half-used, and even new items overflowing your trash cans.

It may be that the tenants are getting on a plane, can't afford to pay movers or store the items, or are just in a frenzy to downsize their belongings. It was probably late at night, under the stress of a moving deadline, and the car or moving van was full. The end result is always the same: A dumpster or garbage can full of useful items that look as good as any in the thrift store or better. You can fish out things to donate, if you have time. But make a note to yourself for the next tenant to redouble your efforts to get the person started on the process early, with your guidance.

Before the move-out day has arrived, you can help tenants (and help the environment) by explaining how they can create less waste when moving (and can thereby let your remaining tenants continue to use the dumpster). You can't really forbid tenants from taking everything to the landfill or mandate that they give their useful items to those in need. But you can guide tenants in the right direction.

The following tips have helped me (and my tenants) get through move-outs with only minor damage and not much, if anything, left behind. The dumpster gets some attention, but is not packed full. I do still see the occasional disaster move-out in other nearby rentals. So, I hope for the sake of our overflowing landfills that more landlords will take some steps to help tenants conduct the transition out of their units in environmentally friendly ways.

**Start early.** If you show up the last week before a tenant will be moving and offer some bright ideas, it's too late. I start a month out, at a minimum. As soon as I get a tenant's notice that he or she is leaving, I start educating the tenant. Someone who has not lived in the community long might not know about the resources that are available. I give tenants a handout that covers all the options for disposing of unwanted items.

**Know your state law on abandoned property.** The key is that you do not want any property left at your unit—or in legal terms, "abandoned." It can slow down your turnaround process by requiring you to follow strict notice and even storage and disposal procedures. It's always easier to have an empty unit; a mantra to share with the tenant from the beginning of your contacts concerning the move. Emphasize all the numerous ways tenants can find people who may want their unwanted items. Otherwise, the items could be your headache later.

**Help tenants help others.** Give them the locations, hours, directions, and tips for donating used items to the local Salvation Army, Goodwill, or other charity thrift stores. You might put consignment stores on the list, too, for tenants whose goods might actually be worth money.

**Check with other tenants.** Help the moving tenant by coordinating a group email to see if others in a multiplex want any items. A number of neighbors will often be happy to take useful items in good condition like bookshelves, chairs, and small appliances (keeping these out of the dumpster and out of the unit you are turning around).

**Harness online and social media contacts.** People are more connected than ever. And your tenants can harness the power of these connections to sell all their unwanted items or give them away. Let the tenants know of any social media or online sites for free items in your area (such as Freecycle, Facebook, Craiglist). It's better to let a stream of people come by and haul away the items than have them left behind for you to track or dispose of.

**Don't forget local food banks.** Suggest that tenants take unopened nonperishable food to the local food bank.

**If viable, allow a garage, yard, or moving sale (with proper instructions).** If you have a single-family home or multiplex with a yard and space for people and cars, a moving sale may work. Recommend this only if you have the space and the tenant has the organization and time to pull it off. Be sure to tell the tenant that just piling things out in front and hoping for the best is not a yard sale.

---

### You Can Leave the Household Cleaners, Thank You

The one minor exception to my "leave nothing behind" rule is that I prefer tenants to leave any household cleaning items, such as cleanser and window cleaner, in a box under the sink. This is very minor and would not be considered abandoned property. You can even confirm in an email that the tenant will be leaving cleaning supplies for you. The reason is twofold. One, I got tired of seeing half-used bottles of glass, bathroom, and oven cleaner in my dumpster when I was using this stuff all the time. Two, it really made no sense to have tenants put this useful cleaner into the landfill (where it could pollute the earth) when, as a landlord I would likely be using it on their unit within the next day, or on other units in the future. It's a win-win.

---

**Instruct on disposal of household hazardous waste.** Do *not* allow a tenant to leave behind any fuels, corrosive chemicals, lighter fluid, paint thinner or half-filled cans of paint, or auto fluids. Instruct the tenant in detail about your local household hazardous waste procedure. Most municipalities have drop-off times and locations. Be sure you get this info early to the tenant, otherwise you will find all sorts of chemicals in your unit and spend your afternoon in line dropping these off.

**Allow or coordinate a curb alert.** While not ideal, a free sign on items near a well-traveled street can make them disappear like magic. First, assess whether this is appropriate or allowed in your neighborhood. Use good judgment. Also, make sure the items are not trash.

> **CAUTION**
>
> **Strict condo associations may forbid leaving items on the curb.** If I put a sign on a free item at a tightly controlled condo complex, I would probably get a letter from the board and be slapped with a fine. Check the norms and rules and make sure the tenant knows them, as well.

**Give recycling instructions.** I started doing this when I saw how much of the material filling my dumpster was recyclable. Make sure the tenant knows how to recycle cardboard, paper, glass, metals, and plastics. (You should have done this at the start of the tenancy, too, but a reminder never hurts.) If tenants fill up any on-site bins, let them know where the local recycling station is located.

**Direct tenants away from the path of least resistance (your dumpster or trash receptacles).** Let tenants know the dumpster is absolutely not the place for their unwanted items—only for trash. In the move-out process, I have seen tenants develop a new relationship with a dumpster, spending hours stuffing, filling, and piling things inside. They will visit it ten times a day and resort to all sorts of odd behavior to increase its capacity. And when the dumpster fills, tenants will stack large items next to it that will never fit inside, as if the items may magically find a way into the dumpster sometime. If this happens, your other tenants have no place for their trash and the trash truck may not even service an overloaded dumpster or haul off the items piled next to it.

> **CAUTION**
>
> **Filling or overloading a dumpster at a condo association is especially problematic.** It may be the trash container for 50 people for the rest of the week. A full dumpster could draw complaints from angry residents and even result in a fine for you. Be especially clear about the proper use of the dumpster at the condo or at your own multiplex.

# The Landlord Cycle: Preparing for the Next Move In

As you move out one tenant, you should already be thinking about moving in the next one. Survey the unit once again and make your to-do list for minor repairs, cleaning, and any painting (see Chapters 3 and 4). After you turn the unit around and do any maintenance (discussed in Chapters 5 and 6), begin to craft (or reuse) your rental ad and start showing the unit and screening tenants once again (following my advice in Chapter 7), and ideally select an ideal tenant who signs a lease (see Chapter 8). Then communicate with your new tenants through the tenancy (Chapter 9) up until it ends and you help them move out (this chapter). Then do it all over again!

---

### Nolo Resources on Moving Out Tenants

*Every Landlord's Legal Guide*, by Marcia Stewart, Ralph Warner and Janet Portman (Nolo), provides detailed advice and forms for returning security deposits and handling other move-out issues, such as abandoned property.

For dozens of free articles on the subject, including state-by-state rules on deposits, notice required to end a tenancy, and small claims court (in the event that a security deposit dispute ends up in court), see the Landlords section of Nolo.com.

---

# What's Next?

Much of our work with tenants, from screening applicants to move out (covered in Chapters 6–10), has been primarily do-it-yourself, and the core job of the part-time landlord. But there are areas where calling on help can add value to your operation. Just as blue-collar service contractors can help with tricky building issues (our Chapter 6 topic), Chapter 11 discusses how white-collar professionals can help with complex tax, legal, or insurance issues in your rental operation. ●

# Understanding and Using Professional Services

Part-time landlords can handle many everyday issues on their own. But they may also find it more efficient to use a professional for help with legal issues, tax preparation, insurance coverage, real estate transactions, and other tasks. We already looked at how landlords facing a thorny building problem might use a contractor (our Chapter 6 topic), and this chapter follows the same theme, but with professional services.

Intangible areas like law or tax may not result in a puddle on the floor when you have an issue, but there can be serious consequences if they are not handled properly. Professional advice or assistance, especially when it comes to law and taxes, can add value to your business by preventing liability and creating certainty.

## Lawyers and Legal Help for the Small-Time Landlord

Because the landlord-tenant relationship is a legal arrangement with statutes and cases outlining the parameters of the parties' obligations, lawyers are often the first professionals a small-time landlord may think about using. But it doesn't make sense to call a lawyer every time a rent check is a few days late or you suspect your tenant has moved in a person who's not on the lease. In most situations, knowing and complying with your legal obligations and using good communication and negotiation strategies (discussed in Chapter 9) are your best bets.

The key is to identify what's a run-of-the-mill matter versus a potentially expensive legal liability (like a serious tenant injury on your rental property). Also watch for issues that can get out of hand quickly (like a fair housing complaint) and end up in an expensive court battle. Such matters may require a lawyer's help—though you may not need to hand off all the work to the lawyer. For example, if evicting a tenant, you might handle the termination notice yourself (or run it by a lawyer), at least up until filing the actual complaint in court.

## Legal Matters You Can Usually Handle Yourself

Even a novice landlord should be able to handle the legal tasks listed here, after some study of your state's landlord-tenant laws and obtaining the appropriate forms and documents (Nolo resources, including the free online Legal Encyclopedia and Legal Research center on Nolo.com, can be especially helpful—see the introductory chapter for details):

- post a rental ad that does not discriminate against any protected class of persons
- present prospective tenants with a valid rental application
- screen and select tenants using neutral business criteria and avoid discrimination during the term of the tenancy
- prepare and sign a lease or rental agreement, covering key terms such as rent, late fees, security deposit, occupant limits, and pets
- make all required landlord disclosures
- meet property habitability requirements, comply with state and local housing codes, and handle tenant repair complaints
- handle all nonlegal tenant reminders, updates, and communications
- understand and enter routine agreements with service contractors
- add a cotenant or roommate to an existing or new lease
- follow state notice rules before you enter rental property
- terminate a month-to-month rental notice with appropriate notice (30 days in most states)
- check out tenants and return the deposit with any itemized deductions
- mutually terminate a lease with a tenant
- use and apply your state's abandoned property statutes
- navigate an early lease break efficiently
- negotiate or enter mediation for a minor claim
- prepare for or defend yourself in a small claims lawsuit (typically involving security deposits), and
- do some legal research on your own, such as finding out local housing codes or noise ordinances.

Assuming you carefully follow state rules and procedures and use the proper forms, you should be able, with a little experience, to handle more sophisticated matters like these:

- serve the proper termination notices required in your state (such as a pay rent or quit, cure or quit, or unconditional quit notice for a given scenario), or
- file a complaint and summons in an uncontested eviction lawsuit.

## Common Scenarios When You Might Need a Lawyer

Here are some issues that may be best handled (in part or in full) by a lawyer, either because the risks of doing it wrong are high, or because an experienced attorney can do the job much more efficiently than you.

### Substantive Change to the Lease

Assuming you start with a legally accurate lease (discussed in Chapter 8), you'll want to consult a lawyer if you have questions about a particular term, especially anything involving:

- deadlines, such as when you will return the security deposit
- late fees
- notice requirements, such as for landlord entry to the rental property or to end the tenancy
- liquidated damages, requiring a tenant to pay a set amount of money (damages) for losses if the tenant breaks the lease and leaves early
- any attempt to absolve yourself from your legal responsibilities, such as to provide habitable housing
- any attempt to remove a tenant's right, such as to file a fair housing complaint, or
- anything that changes the meaning of your lease or that may run afoul of the law.

## Contested or Complex Eviction

You'll probably want to hire a lawyer the first time you have to evict a tenant (hopefully, that will seldom, if ever, happen) or for any contested or complicated eviction. A lawyer will be invaluable in handling any tenant counterclaims or defenses that arise (for example, based on habitability, discrimination, or retaliation). Going it alone will put you at a great disadvantage, especially if the tenant has a lawyer.

It also makes good sense to hire a lawyer if you are evicting a tenant who:

- has a mental illness or other disability
- has a criminal background
- is filing bankruptcy
- is renting property that is rent controlled, or
- is renting under the Section 8 program (you might try working first with a Section 8 housing authority representative, who may convince the tenant to move without resorting to an eviction, which could impact the tenant's ability to qualify for future Section 8 housing).

---

### Legal Issues When You Inherit Nightmare Tenants

If you are selective in screening your tenants, the most troublesome ones you will ever face in your landlording career are probably any you inherit (by acquiring a rental property with tenants already in place). You may get a great deal on a rental property specifically because the unruly tenants (or even squatters) have run the prior landlord off. When their leases are up (if they even have one) or if these tenants don't pay the rent or follow rules, you'll want to give them the proper notice and try to negotiate and reason with them about a smooth departure. If that does not work, consider using a lawyer for the eviction process. It will be a one-time expense (a tax-deductible one, at that) and can add a lot of value simply by getting the property vacated.

If you make major errors in how you prepare and serve eviction papers, you will have to do the process over again. Worse, if you try to force a tenant out illegally, you could find yourself paying hefty damages for a wrongful eviction.

> **CAUTION**
> **Be careful about spending legal resources (and your money) to go after a tenant for damages or back rent.** Whether it's a tenant you inherited or one you chose yourself, be careful pursuing a tenant for funds he or she does not have. The tenant may be judgment-proof (having no money to pay back rent if ordered to do so by a court).

## Personal Injury or Property Damage Claim

If a tenant or another person is seriously injured on your property, notify your insurer and seek legal advice right away, regardless of whether the person has yet filed a claim. In addition to the general liability coverage provided by your insurance company for personal injury or property damage costs, your insurer has the duty to defend you in a lawsuit—that is, to hire a lawyer and pay the legal fees and costs to represent you in the claim. This is a very important provision, because in some situations, the total legal fees and costs may exceed the damage amount for the actual claim or injury.

If there is any doubt about coverage or your insurance firm is not cooperating, it may be helpful to get a legal opinion on coverage and the insurer's duty to defend in your state.

See the "Insurance" section below for more details.

## Contractor Dispute

Disputes with a contractor that involve a significant dollar amount may require a lawyer's help. It is likely the contract you signed has a mediation and arbitration clause. These are alternative forms of dispute resolution done outside a court and not always with a lawyer's help. You may nevertheless want to hire a construction lawyer if the arbitration involves a large dollar value. Many states have specific laws about construction defect claims, which the lawyer can help you interpret. For smaller claims, however, negotiation and mediation are something an average landlord can do. Indeed, many of the communication strategies and tips in Chapter 9 are designed for this process.

### Real Estate Purchase and Sale Transaction and Title Issue

Legal advice can add value in a real estate transaction, such as if you are:

- preparing an offer or purchase contract when buying property (or getting out of a contract), especially for a nonstandard type of purchase, such as taking over an existing mortgage or buying a foreclosure at auction with multiple mortgages or liens
- selling and owner-financing a rental property, including verifying that you have a valid, properly recorded first mortgage or deed of trust
- dealing with a contractor who has placed a mechanic's lien on your property or made any filing that clouds your title (legal ownership), or
- handling any complex real estate issue or dispute related to an easement, zoning rule, boundary line, or land use.

## Finding a Lawyer

Once you determine you need a lawyer, your next step is to find one with the relevant expertise and experience, and who comes highly recommended.

### Expertise and Experience Your Lawyer Should Have

You want an attorney who specializes in the key issues you are currently facing. If you have a pressing eviction question, you don't want a great criminal lawyer or even a generalist, but rather a landlord-tenant expert. If the issue involves a personal injury on your property or a construction defect, you'll want a lawyer with expertise in these areas. Better yet is someone who has worked through the legal issue—be it an eviction, a discrimination complaint, or other matter—many times before. Lawyers bill by the hour, so a lawyer who has *been there* and *done that* will generally be less expensive and more efficient. If your lawyer has to spend hours researching a new topic, it will be on your dime. However, a lawyer who just handled three similar eviction cases last month may only need to change the names and dates on the documents, file them, and keep in touch with you—a far less time-intensive scenario.

If you are in a large metropolitan area, some lawyers will specialize in particular landlord-tenant issues, such as discrimination complaints or evictions. If you are in a small town, your best bet may be a good civil or business lawyer who has done some landlord-tenant work (maybe even as a property owner!), or a former legal aid lawyer (a major part of legal aid work involves landlord-tenant and fair housing law).

You can usually find out which areas a lawyer lists as main practice areas or specializations on the lawyer's website, in the firm's promotional materials, or in online lawyer databases such as those listed below. Some lawyers may list that they are certified by a board, commission, or other entity. This ordinarily indicates some experience or having passed an exam and pursued continuing education in a particular area. Entities that certify lawyers can be found by searching "sources of certification" at the American Bar Association (ABA) website, www.americanbar.org.

## Getting Names of Well-Respected Attorneys

Ask business contacts, fellow landlords, property managers, bankers, real estate and insurance brokers, and well-connected friends for leads on lawyers they have used or who they know to be effective. Keep track of who gave you which names—a good way to break the ice with a prospective lawyer is to say, "[*Name*] told me about you and I was hoping to meet with you about an issue I have."

One tip you may find that could work to find the best lawyer in town is to follow the smart money. That is, identify the largest and most reputable businesses or organizations that house people in your area (the ones engaging the most in landlord-tenant matters). It could be a large property management firm, a family company that owns several large apartment complexes, or even the local public housing agency. Then find out the lawyer it uses for landlord and tenant legal services. Such an entity could have afforded anyone in town, so this candidate likely has the expertise and experience you need.

To get this information, check your state or local court system's online database. A simple search for the organization as a party name should turn up the name of its counsel (or lawyer) of record. But you may be small potatoes for the same lawyer or firm the largest apartment complexes use. As an effective part-time landlord, you won't generate a high frequency of legal work (like most clients of large firms), so you might have even better luck with the lawyers who work for smaller independent apartment owners or the best small property management company in your area. Many of these are solo practitioners who may have actually left one of the large firms for more control and autonomy, so these lawyers can bring the same skill to your case—and they may have more time (and lower overhead) for a small client like you.

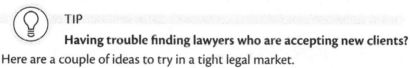

TIP

**Having trouble finding lawyers who are accepting new clients?** Here are a couple of ideas to try in a tight legal market.

- **Check out associates.** If the lawyer you want is a partner in a firm and can't take your case, see if an associate in the same firm may be able to handle it. You may even get a lower hourly rate, and the associate can still call on the senior partner's experience. Partners usually are the senior people in a firm and command the highest hourly rates, whereas associates are more junior and can even have lower hourly rates.

- **Think regional.** You don't necessarily need a lawyer in your city, though it can be helpful. A lawyer in a nearby city, county, or borough may be a fine choice to handle the case. This lawyer will still know all the relevant state law and likely even be familiar with the local courts.

## Searching for Lawyers Online

Thanks to the Internet, you have many resources for finding legal services. Here are just a few places to start your search:

- **Nolo's Lawyer Directory.** Nolo has an easy-to-use online directory of lawyers, organized by location and area of expertise, such as landlord-tenant. You can find the directory and its comprehensive profiles at www.nolo.com/lawyers.
- **Lawyers.com.** At Lawyers.com, you'll find a user-friendly search tool that allows you to tailor results by area of law and geography. You can also search for attorneys by name. Attorney profiles prominently display contact information, list topics of expertise, and show ratings—by both clients and other legal professionals.
- **Martindale.com.** This site offers an advanced search option that allows you to sort not only by practice area and location, but also by criteria like law school. Whether you look for lawyers by name or expertise, you'll find listings with detailed background information, peer and client ratings, and even profile visibility.

## Researching Prospective Lawyers' Experience

After you've got a list of names of recommended lawyers, it's time to learn more about them. Probe the lawyer's online information (including biography or resume) or ask in person about his or her years of experience in a given area. Also, ask whether the lawyer has handled cases independently or in tandem with other lawyers. Depending on your legal needs, a lawyer's trial experience may be important.

After you've narrowed down your list of prospects through such research, schedule appointments with the lawyers whose credentials most impressed you (such as authorship of articles or presentations at Continuing Legal Education (CLE) sessions), or who seem most suited to your needs.

Many lawyers and firms allow a free initial consultation, which can be an ideal time to ask about the lawyer's case volume and years representing landlords or experience with your particular legal task.

## Confirming What the Lawyer Will Do
## for You and Billing Practices

Once you find a lawyer you like, one of the first steps will be to settle on the scope of the representation (that is, exactly what the lawyer will do). This can run the gamut from being your go-to person for leases and other tenant communications to handling a one-time eviction. It depends in part on how much you want to do yourself, and how willing the lawyer is to help you represent yourself, if that is your goal.

Another important topic to discuss up front is the lawyer's billing practices. Some may ask for an advance payment (a retainer) up front, and then will bill you hourly after that runs out. Of course, you'll want to know the attorney's hourly rate (this will vary a lot depending on the location and type of lawyer), and get some estimate of how many hours the work you are requesting will take. For a discrete task, like reviewing your lease or insurance coverage, a few lawyers will work on a flat-fee basis.

While many of the same rules for hiring contractors (discussed in Chapter 6) apply to hiring legal professionals, a few differences apply. A major one is that the attorney-client relationship is closely regulated and subject to many professional obligations and duties to the client, including duties of:

- confidentiality—the lawyer can't disclose what you talk about or reveal anything adverse to you
- loyalty—the lawyer has to work on your behalf and can't jump ship and switch to the other side, and
- competency—lawyers are held to a professional standard of skill.

Lawyers also can't commingle, lose, or take your money improperly, but must hold it safely segregated in trust and draw from it only to pay legal fees.

Check your state bar association website (find yours on the American Bar Association website, at www.americanbar.org) for information about rules and regulations governing attorneys in your state.

CAUTION
**Attorney ethical and professional conduct rules are very serious.** Lawyers can face discipline and even disbarment for breaking the rules of conduct. The attorney is one of the few professionals you'll deal with who has an ethical and legal duty to put your interests ahead of his or her own—called a fiduciary relationship. Many contractors or service providers, white and blue collar, may talk about putting you first, but lawyers have a real duty to do so and can lose their license if they don't.

# Accountants and Tax Help for the Small-Time Landlord

Probably the most important consideration for new or ongoing landlords is determining their role in the tax process. Many may choose to use an accountant. Others may choose to try it alone. Either way, landlords should understand the tax process and some basic concepts. Whether you have one accessory apartment or seven duplexes, you have to account for the income and expenses from your rental activity every year. This process culminates in filing your taxes each year but in any case, your filing obligation will require year-round record keeping (covered more in Chapter 12).

Your tax preparation may be a situation where it is more effective for you to delegate, but because every landlord has a different background and situation, I will try and lay out some guidelines to help you make this decision. In fact, you need to know quite a bit about taxes to make an informed decision about whether you can do them yourself.

## How to Decide Tax Matters You Can Handle Yourself

It is possible to effectively handle your taxes as a landlord—but only if you have some tax background and experience. The questions below may help you understand whether you are able to tackle your rental property taxes.

**Do you prepare your own personal income taxes?** If not, you probably don't want to try to do your rental taxes. It will be even more complicated.

**When completing your personal or family taxes, did you use Form 1040 and itemize (using Schedule A), handle capital gains (using Schedule D), or take other deductions and credits that required extra worksheets or forms?** If you have done only a simple 1040-EZ and not tackled itemized deductions, the rental property taxes may be too extensive for you to comfortably take on.

**Have you taken formal accounting, finance, income tax, or tax law courses? Or through self-study, do you understand concepts like depreciation, deductions, and the difference between repairs and improvements?** If not, you will need some background work to handle your rental property taxes effectively, so it may be wise to hand the process off until you learn more.

**In examining the Schedule E form (discussed in Chapter 12) and your income and expense records, can you understand where every expense fits, and grasp the language and concepts involved?** Take a few minutes to read the publications for tax topics (like depreciation) and forms (like the Schedule E) provided by the IRS for free on its website. If the terms and concepts still seem foreign, consider handing off your taxes until you learn more.

In short, if you have already been doing some tax puzzles and know the language and process of federal income taxation, taking on your rental taxes would simply be an extension of this activity. However, if taxes are new or still a bit unfamiliar to you, get help.

## Pros of Doing Your Own Taxes

While the paperwork and legal concepts can be complicated, there are some benefits of doing your own taxes. A few are listed below.

**You will save money on the accountant's fee.** Of course, this fee is also tax deductible.

**Doing your own taxes may be the only viable choice if you live in an area with few qualified accountants.** If there aren't any available qualified accountants in your area, then it may not only save money to do it yourself, it may be the only feasible choice.

**Doing your taxes serves as a financial performance review.** Seeing all your yearly income and expenses (literally every bill and receipt) can help you understand your business in depth. You will be examining every expense category and all the revenues for each rental, so you'll get a great view of your overall performance. Of course, you can also look at the Schedule E your accountant does, but it may not get you into the finances in the same depth as doing it yourself.

## Tax Resources for the Small-Time Landlord

You are not alone in trying to understand the taxes related to your rental properties. Ten of thousands of small landlords are puzzling over their tax situation every year, and many resources have been developed to walk you through the process.

The IRS website (www.irs.gov) even has some user-friendly features. When you pull up a tax form that you need, the site will also show all the associated publications, worksheets, and tax guidance available. Whether you are doing your own taxes or just want to understand them to help your accountant, try some of these resources.

- IRS *Tips on Rental Real Estate Income, Deductions, and Recordkeeping* IRS website: www.irs.gov/Businesses/Small-Businesses-&-Self-Employed/Tips-on-Rental-Real-Estate-Income-Deductions-and-Recordkeeping
- IRS Publication 527, *Residential Rental Property*
- IRS Publication 946, *How to Depreciate Property*
- Nolo free articles on landlord tax deductions at www.nolo.com/legal-encyclopedia/tax-deductions-landlords
- *Every Landlord's Tax Deduction Guide*, by Stephen Fishman (Nolo), a book designed just for landlord tax issues, and
- *J.K. Lasser's Your Income Tax* (John Wiley & Sons), published annually. While primarily for individual income tax, *Lasser's* has updated sections on rentals and related transactions like tax-free exchanges, property sales, deductions, and depreciation, as well as personal tax issues each year.

**You make the decisions and control the level of risk.** Studies have shown that the same business or family's taxes taken to different CPAs can yield different results. Why? The CPAs differing attention to detail, choice between options (like taking bonus depreciation in one year or over time), and approach (aggressive or conservative) on a particular deduction in a gray or questionable area all make a difference. If you do your taxes, you can control these variables.

**You will learn more about the tax code.** An understanding of the complexity of tax rules can also help you conform your business behavior in a way that takes advantage of certain deductions. You may also learn to time an expense so as to offset gains or take advantage of accelerated depreciation or new changes in the tax code. Careful planning of capital expenses and other purchases can help minimize tax liability.

**They are your taxes.** No one will have the same incentive to work to round up a lost receipt or explore a possible deduction as you. Your accountant will have many other clients and can't devote the entire tax season to you. There may be a $50 deduction that you can take advantage of after some research through IRS publications and worksheets, but it may not make economic or practical sense for a paid accountant to pursue it.

**The learning curve will flatten out.** If you jump in and start, you will pave the way for doing your own taxes for years to come. The process can even be streamlined in future tax years. Using prior tax returns as guides, you may be able to simply adjust the numbers for the current year and plug them in. Of course, if you do a new type of transaction (like owner finance a unit), or buy new rentals, some of the complexity comes back.

## Common Scenarios When You Might Need an Accountant

If any of these tax conundrums are present, consider using a tax professional:

**Entity complexity.** Most small landlords will own their rentals alone or with a spouse and can add a fairly simple Schedule E to their personal taxes (Form 1040). But if you own rentals through a partnership or corporation, or have some fractional ownership in a venture, the added organizational complexity can increase your tax complexity and hiring a professional may be advisable.

**Complicated tax credits or deductions.** No two landlords will be exactly alike in their personal and rental situation, and tax laws frequently change in both minor and major ways. You'll want to seek professional advice if you face a novel situation or an unknown area. Depreciating personal property, for example, can be tricky. Even some of the personal tax credits can be complicated.

**You get stuck.** My cautionary reminder to avoid getting stuck does not just apply to a plumbing problem that delays turning around a rental unit. You can also easily get stuck on a tax form, concept, or worksheet. And remember there is a deadline (April 15—although you can request an extension). Your taxes are an interlocking series of line-by-line calculations, each one sequentially working off the next, so if you get stuck on some complex deduction on one line, you literally are stuck and can't move through the form and complete your taxes. There is some risk of late or improper taxes, and a major tax error could take extraordinary amount of time to redo.

**Complex and gray areas.** Many of the IRS rules are set up for clean, clear transactions. But real life can be filled with gray areas, so you may have questions that aren't clearly answered in the IRS tax guidance. You may even find areas with judgment calls involved.

Your taxes will also be more complex (and require professional help) if you:

- own many rentals
- are owner-financing properties on an installment basis
- are facing a large project that you are not sure is a repair, which could be written off in one year, or a remodel that improves the building, which should be written off over several years
- are selling a property and adjusting your basis to determine your capital gain (or loss), or
- live in one of the units in a multiplex and later sell the property or are completing a tax-deferred 1031 exchange.

> **TIP**
>
> **Don't forget state taxes.** The majority of states impose their own income taxes, and while many try to mirror and use your federal return (Schedule E and Form 1040), they can have unique aspects and deductions. Consider using a professional if you own rentals in multiple states, out of state, or if your state has some complicated tax rules you need help with. Only seven states currently have no state income tax: Alaska, Florida, Nevada, South Dakota, Texas, Washington, and Wyoming.

## Finding a Good Accountant

By now, you know the drill: As with lawyers, get names of prospective accountants from other professionals in your industry, and plan to meet with more than one of them before making your choice. You'll also need to narrow in on exactly what type of accountant you're looking for.

## Expertise and Credentials Your Accountant Should Have

In choosing an accountant, you may be confused as you survey the variety, which includes providers of accounting, bookkeeping, and tax advice. To ensure a high level of accuracy and competency, think about finding a Certified Public Accountant (CPA). This credential is a reliable gold standard, indicating that the person has a minimum level of education and training needed to offer you expert help. But the CPA designation is just a threshold filter. You should then select from CPAs based on their ability to work with small-time landlords and their experience with your type of tax issues. A good CPA can even help with business planning and strategy built around your tax situation and considerations. Your CPA will know about the newest deductions and ways to categorize transactions for the best results.

The ideal candidate would be someone who does work for other small-time residential landlords. Perhaps even better is an accountant who actually owns a residential rental property (not uncommon). However, if you get a good accountant interested in working with residential landlords, he or she may be able to learn and grow with you.

> **RESOURCE**
> **For more on CPA requirements and their certification.** The American Institute of CPAs (AICPA) website (www.aicpa.org) includes each state's information and links on CPAs (search "CPA Licensure" for details).

What about a tax lawyer? Some even have an L.L.M. (a one-year degree focused on tax law) or a CPA designation, but this may be more firepower than you need. The exception might be if you require complicated sifting through statutes, regulations, court cases, and IRS interpretations. If, however, you are using trusts, have very large transactions and deductions, or are in a serious dispute with the IRS, a tax lawyer may add value. One with a specialty in tax law and past experience working for a taxing authority or law firm specializing in tax could be ideal.

CAUTION

**The ideal candidate to do your taxes is not a mere tax preparer.** The tax preparation franchises in strip malls or temporary kiosks at a big box retailer offer services best suited for simple individual taxes—not the more complicated tax issues landlords face.

## Paying and Working With an Accountant

The accountant's fee structure will no doubt be at the top of your list of questions. If you will want this person to work with you year-round, the rate will probably be hourly. Your tax preparation fees may also be hourly, as it may be hard to determine how complex your tax situation will be from year to year. Perhaps after a long-term working relationship, you might arrange a flat fee with an accountant in a year with no tricky tax issues, but then the hourly rate may be advantageous if the work is routine (see the cost-plus versus fixed-price discussion in Chapter 6 for the merits of each type of payment arrangement).

Working with an accountant year-round can be helpful, because your behavior and transactions during the year will determine your tax liability. If you have questions about things like whether a project at your rental property is a capital improvement or simply an expense, or about whether your home office qualifies for a deduction, it will be too late by tax time to structure your transaction or change your behavior. With advice during the tax year, you can make sure you meet the requirements of some tax deductions from the outset.

Also, ask whether the accountant will be available to help with a potential IRS audit (if it should happen) and whether he or she will offer advice on personal tax questions, planning, and deductions.

You will likely need someone who can help with both your personal and business taxes due to the interrelated nature of Form 1040 and Schedule E.

> **TIP**
>
> **Start your accountant search early!** If you gather your records a couple of weeks before taxes are due, don't expect to find a good CPA who can handle your taxes. The good ones are likely booked solid well in advance. Start several months out to find a good tax accountant; ideally in fall, so you can hand off all your year-end records early in January.

## Insurance Professionals and Coverage for Your Rental Property

As with any home or property, you will need to purchase insurance coverage in case of damage, liability, or certain other losses. Insurance is a unique product, in that you pay regularly for something you hope you will never use. It also represents an ongoing responsibility to check your coverage and pay your premiums. But aside from initiating and reviewing coverage, you should not have to spend an undue amount of time on insurance, especially if you don't have any claims or buy any new properties.

Whether you are new to landlording or looking for a new provider or products, a few guidelines can help you find a professional and products to meet your insurance needs.

**Captive or independent.** Some insurance brokerage firms sell only one company's products (their brokers are "captive," and will not sell you coverage from any other company). Other brokers sell insurance products from multiple companies. You could probably work with either scenario as a small landlord, provided the company issuing the policies is solid and the other criteria are met. Just be aware that an independent broker could shop around and get you the best rates, offer more unbiased advice, and present more choices.

**Personal or commercial.** Some insurance brokers may work only with businesses and some only handle personal lines. But as a landlord, you are somewhat in the middle. So a firm that offers only personal insurance is not ideal, while one with multimillion-dollar major commercial insurance is not a good fit, either. Look for a firm or broker that handles small business and personal insurance.

**Proper policies and coverage.** A company or insurance broker that doesn't have a landlord policy or personal umbrella coverage for a small-time landlord is not for your rental business. (But if you can get your car, house, umbrella, and landlord policies all (or mostly) in one place, it can help in getting discounts and make it easy to adjust coverage with one call.)

Cost is not the only factor to consider. The actual insurance company's products, financial stability, and claims practices are also important. For independent ratings of insurance companies, go to:

- JD Power, which measures customer satisfaction: www.jdpower. com (under "Ratings and Awards, click "Insurance"), and
- A.M. Best Company, which rates insurance companies on financial strength: www.ambest.com (check the "Ratings and Criteria" section).

## Manage Risk Through Best Practices

The best defense is safety. No injury, no claims. So use best practices for maintenance and inspections, do careful tenant screening, and take safety precautions as recommended throughout this book. Using these practices along with a good landlord insurance policy and umbrella insurance (both discussed below) forms my three-point risk management plan for part-time landlords. You can't eliminate all risks, but you can minimize and insure against them.

## Type of Expertise Your Insurance Broker Should Have

Here are key traits to consider when choosing a broker:

- **Experience.** The broker you choose should ideally have many years of insurance industry experience and expertise working with both personal and small business lines.
- **Licensing.** Each state regulates the operations of the insurance industry within its borders, and you should be able to confirm your broker's license. Start with your state's department of insurance, which you can find through the National Association of Insurance Commissioners at www.naic.org (click "States & Jurisdiction Map").
- **Certifications.** You can check whether your insurance professional has some of the recognized insurance certifications such as a Chartered Property Casualty Underwriter (CPCU), Certified Insurance Counselor (CIC), Chartered Life Underwriter (CLU), or Accredited Adviser in Insurance (AAI). These may indicate a minimum level of experience and education and greater understanding of insurance concepts and risk management.

## Landlord's Insurance Policy Tips

Along with the standard advice for buying insurance, there are some unique aspects to keep in mind for landlords seeking the protection that insurance offers.

### Buy a Landlord's Policy

It goes without saying, but there are landlords who may have the wrong coverage. For example, if you rent out your own home after you move away, inertia may keep you buying the same insurance. But if a claim arose and the insurance adjustor discovered it was a non-owner-occupied property (which may be considered a higher risk), it could be very easy for the insurer to deny coverage. Bottom line: Make sure the insurance broker knows what property you are renting and that you get appropriate coverage.

At least half a dozen major insurers offer a landlord's policy or some equivalent product (there are enough landlords out there to create a market!). So be sure you have this category of policy. And pay attention to liability, dwelling replacement, and even features like wrongful eviction coverage. Also, check whether your property manager is covered if you use one. These are all features you may find on your landlord's policy.

### Aim for Full Replacement Cost

While policies and terms vary, get the closest you can to 100% replacement value for your dwelling. This way your insurance will cover the loss. Often, state court rulings will outline how insurance contracts are interpreted in each state. Talk to your broker, attorney, or expert in the area. If you are not able to get guaranteed replacement cost, look at extended dwelling coverage options.

### Stay Safe Under the Umbrella

Small landlords can also use an umbrella insurance policy to help guard against risks. This type of insurance is just what it sounds like—an extra layer of coverage in excess of your underlying insurance. The good news for small landlords is that these policies are available to those who have a few residential properties (four units or less). My insurance company allows up to six residential properties, for example.

Read your fine print and make sure the accurate number of rentals is listed in your renewal application each year. You will also have to set your levels of auto and home liability coverage at required amount ($300,000 liability coverage, for example) and the umbrella policy covers liability in excess of the underlying coverage. You can likely find a one million dollar umbrella policy for a few hundred dollars per year depending on your circumstances. If you have too many properties or do not qualify for a personal umbrella policy, look into a commercial umbrella policy.

## Keep Your Insurance Updated

Unless you adjust it periodically, your insurance coverage may stay the same while rebuilding costs and property values rise. Remember, you will be insuring the building, not the land, so to gauge whether you are properly insured, check the cost of construction per square foot to rebuild a new home in your area. This will help you determine if your coverage would be adequate to rebuild the structure anew. Ask your insurance broker or contractor if you are unsure about rebuilding costs. Also, just as building costs rise, building codes also get updated and modernized, so be sure your policy has a clause or coverage to rebuild the structure to current code.

## Consider Lost Rental Income

A clause covering lost rents in case of a damaged or destroyed building could be very important. Otherwise, you'd have to cover the monthly mortgage (your payment obligation does not stop even if the building is damaged).

## Get Adequate Premises Liability

You absolutely want to check your premises liability. This pays the legal and medical liability for accidents like a slip and fall injury. Also make sure the underlying insurance covers an amount required by your umbrella policy, if you opt for one. For example, your umbrella policy may require $300,000 per occurrence coverage, then would only cover liability in excess of that amount. Premises liability for landlords can also cover invasion of privacy and wrongful eviction. So check your policy.

## Purchase Extra Coverage for Any Condominiums

Your association will have some form of master policy that will cover the structure, likely as it was built. But in addition to the master policy, you may want one for excess coverage if you rent out a condo, because it could cover dues or rental income if the unit is damaged, as well as personal property, additions, or upgrades you have made.

> **TIP**
>
> **Don't forget renters' insurance.** In most states, you can require tenants to buy insurance covering losses to their belongings (such as from theft), injury to other people or property, or damage caused by the tenant's negligence. I have even given tenants contacts for local insurance brokers and articles on renters' insurance to help emphasize its importance.

## When Your Interests Diverge From the Insurer

In the event of a loss, your interest may diverge from your insurer. You'll want your claim paid and the damage repaired, and the insurance adjustor will closely scrutinize costs and coverage. While your insurance company may have the advantages of size, resources, and expertise, you still may be able to negotiate a fair settlement if you can arrive at an agreement about the value of the loss. You'll need to document your dealings with your insurer in a claim scenario as meticulously as you would with a tenant in an eviction case. It can be a high-stakes and high-risk situation. I would use old-fashioned certified mail and letters, especially in a large claim, and build a file. If you had a major fire, you could be in for a very long process and need to produce quite a bit of documentation.

If you think you are being treated unfairly and your negotiations have failed, consider using these tools (you may need an experienced insurance attorney's help):

- **Unfair claims practices.** Most states have uniform rules and standards about such things as times to respond and settle claims, and these can be indicators of whether an insurer company is meeting its duties to policyholders in good faith.
- **Bad faith.** If you think your insurer has been dishonest, is wrongly denying or unreasonable delaying your claim, or is otherwise violating their duties to policyholders, explore a bad faith claim. You'll want to hire an attorney experienced in bad faith claims and insurance law on the plaintiff's side (that is, pursuing insurance firms). The possibility of a bad faith claim that results in hefty punitive damages can be a powerful incentive for insurance firms to settle your claim and act fairly.

## Understanding Insurance Language

Insurance is an area of business and law with its own language, terms, and meanings. Even words like "occurrence" can have a special meaning, so be sure you clearly understand all definitions and their impact.

Surveying the terms and their definitions used in the insurance context is too complex for this book, and meanings can differ by state, as some terms can depend on how your state courts interpret them. The goal here is to help you be aware of the major issues so you can understand your coverage. Your insurer's website may also have more information and definitions, and your broker can be a source of information. Also, check out the extensive glossary on the Insurance Information Institute's website, www.iii.org.

# Other Helpful Professionals

A number of other professionals can add value to your work as a landlord beyond the lawyer, accountant, and insurance broker. Primarily, you will use these around a particular transaction (such as a real estate sale or purchase) but you may also build working relationships for other mutually beneficial networking purposes.

## Bankers and Lenders

Small-time landlords looking to purchase one or more new rental properties are in a middle ground in terms of lending opportunities. You don't really want a multifamily commercial lender (that handles large apartment complexes) and you also aren't an ideal fit for the average home loan officer. Your goal is to find someone who can arrange non-owner-occupied loans for residential properties (one to four units). So it can pay to cultivate a relationship with a mortgage broker or banker who has skill and expertise in putting funding together for this type of loan. If you need some leads, simply ask the listing agents of recently sold multiplexes who set up their loan.

TIP

**Got a tenant who needs a loan broker?** If your tenant asks about purchasing the condo or property you are renting, or just buying a place in general, send the person to your banker or mortgage broker. Your tenant will receive help qualifying for and getting funding to buy your place (if you are interested in selling). Or if the person buys elsewhere, you will build up some good social capital, so that next time you need a loan, your lender may be extra eager to help you.

## Real Estate Professionals

A good real estate professional can help you find the right property with which to start or grow your rental business. When the time is right, this person can also help you market your property and get top dollar.

Part of what you look for in a good real estate professional is market knowledge. You want someone who can stay abreast of pricing trends, spot values, and find properties before they've even been listed. Often, you can find a real estate professional who works with landlords or has some property management background—both are ideal. Such a person will understand, for example, why you'd prefer not to have a house with a pool or a huge (maintenance-intensive) yard.

Look for a real estate professional who comes highly recommended and has met your state's licensing requirements; the National Association of Realtors® offers a variety of additional credentials and certifications (see www.realtor.org).

## Property Managers

Your interests and abilities may change over time (or sooner than you expected), and necessitate stepping back from your rentals a bit. The most commonly thought of professional to help you at this stage would be a property manager. Hiring someone to take on this role would allow you to maintain ownership (and keep collecting checks) while handing off the day-to-day repair, maintenance, tenant screening, and other duties. The property manager will essentially be replacing you.

TIP
**All the same rules on hiring contractors (from Chapter 6) apply to hiring a property manager.** Check insurance, license, references, and research property managers to make sure they can realistically act as independent contractors (not employees).

## Getting Names of Good Property Managers

Even if you think you're years away from hiring a property manager, start asking around and keeping your eyes open for the ones that:
- present the cleanest, best ads, websites, and contact information
- are being hired to handle the top properties regularly in your area
- regularly call you to check on references or send you an online questionnaire, and
- have been established and successful for a significant period of time in your area managing properties.

Once you have a good idea of some possible candidates, check out their backgrounds and credentials.

## Credentials Your Property Manager Should Have

The activities associated with property management are often, but not always subject to state licensing (usually in connection with existing real estate agent/broker laws). In addition, there are several credentials a property manager could have, some of them quite rigorous, such as those from the Institute of Real Estate Management or IREM (www.irem.org). IREM offers designations, such as the CPM (Certified Property Manager) and Accredited Residential Manager (ARM). The National Association of Residential Property Managers, or NARPM (www.narpm.org) also offers designations, such as Residential Management Professional (RMP), Master Property Manager (MPM) for individuals, and Certified Residential Management Company (CRMC) for companies. However, you probably just need someone to manage a couple of duplexes—not a towering office building—so experience in residential property management may be more relevant than these designations.

## Researching Prospective Property Managers

Check out your short list of prospective managers based on the following.

**Experience and references.** See if you can talk to some of the manager's current and past clients. Verify the years of successful management and units under management.

**Greater focus on management versus property sales.** In a less densely populated region, some managers are likely to sell a few listings on top of their property management duties. You want someone who isn't just managing as a sideline when sales are slow, which might lead to the manager neglecting your tenants in order to chase after large sales commissions.

**The terms of the management agreement.** Look at fees and costs, as well as how the manager communicates with you, which decisions you will make, which ones the manager will make, and so on.

**Quality of the manager's forms (leases, applications, and checklists).** After all the work you've done developing policies and paperwork that works for both you and your tenants, you don't want some management company to sweep in with an incomprehensible lease and off-putting tenant application.

**Degree of help with the transition from owner management.** The new manager should be prepared to supply transition information, explaining to the tenants what's going on, whether they need to sign or do anything in the short term, and who to call for what in the future.

> **TIP**
>
> **Try a trial step-away period.** Perhaps you aren't sure if you will like having someone else run your rental (or are even afraid you'll get bored with no walls to paint). You could hire a manager on a test basis for six months or a year. This could combine well with a long vacation or when you're deep in another project (or your day job). If the arrangement works well, you can keep it going for the longer term.

## Networking Without Trying: Cultivating Your Professional Landlord Network

Many formal groups for landlords are organizations of large apartment owners like the National Apartment Association (www.naahq.org). There are some online sites for smaller-level landlords, and your local area may have an organization (perhaps called a real estate investor group) where landlords network and share ideas. If there is one in your area, maybe check it out.

But even if there is not a formal group in your area for landlords to share ideas, you can still network with others in your business—often without even trying. Nearby landlords are ideal resources. Often buildings in the same area may face a common enemy—be it termites, dry rot, or soil subsidence. And there is no reason you can't also ask local landlords for advice about the best snowplow driver, carpenter, or handyman. Also, think about cultivating contacts with your own contractors (like your plumber), vendors (like your specialty paint store expert), and the other professionals listed in this chapter. Be it putting them on your holiday card list or just saying hello from time to time, other landlords can often help you with information about a maintenance issue or even the direction of the local rental market.

# What's Next?

Our survey of professionals focused on how they can help you meet certain goals (like evicting a tenant) or help with periodic tasks, like doing your taxes. Our final chapter turns to a specific ongoing landlord task: tracking your income and expenses in order to prepare your taxes (or help your accountant prepare them). It also marks the culmination of the year's economic activities, a time for reporting income and expenses to the IRS and also some reflection on your financial performance. ●

# Tracking Landlord Income and Expenses for Tax Time

Like all businesses, some of your years in landlording will be smoother than others. You may have busy years—when you buy a new unit, have several turnovers, or do some major repairs. Others years can be quite tranquil, with no major building issues or significant tenant problems. But even in a quiet year, you will always have record keeping and tax work to do.

And taxes are not just a once a year event where you scramble to meet the mid-April deadline. You really need an awareness of taxes to document your income and expenses year round. In addition, if your profits reach a certain threshold, you may need to pay quarterly, estimated taxes in order to avoid a penalty. (Many part-time landlords can avoid this, however, by simply having an extra amount withheld from the paycheck at their day job.) Tax deadlines present an ongoing record-keeping responsibility; it is *not optional* for landlords to track their income and deductions (it is required by law).

Luckily, the task of tracking your income and expenses is not that hard for the small-time landlord. The Internal Revenue Service (IRS) has even made the process somewhat easier through the use of Schedule E, a short form that guides rental property owners through their annual income and expenses. While this chapter won't attempt to provide a complete lesson in tax law, it will acquaint you with the basics of how you'll report your income and expenses on Schedule E.

## Where You'll Report Income and Deductions: Schedule E

Put aside your tax phobia for a moment: The simplest way to start is, in fact, to look at the tax form known as "Schedule E." Here, the IRS has boiled down the core of what you will need to report, by means of an attachment (Schedule E, *Supplemental Income and Loss*) to your Form 1040. You'll find a sample below (the 2014 version—it may change year by year), and you can access it on the IRS website, www.irs.gov. Although Schedule E is two pages long, you will probably need only page one unless you own your property under a more complicated organizational form.

Every landlord, whether handing off the taxes or tackling them from start to finish, ought to understand what's on Schedule E. It is the primary mechanism used by the IRS to track and account for the income and expenses of small residential landlords in America.

Even if you know you'll be using the services of an accountant, you can't really keep up with the needed record keeping, nor communicate with your tax professional, without some understanding of what's on Schedule E.

Instead of handing off a huge box of receipts and hoping for the best, you will be able to hand your accountant neat copies of expenses (already totaled up) in each of the relevant categories, matched up to the right rentals. This will keep down your accounting fees—it can take accountants hours to go through those receipts, too. And who knows, after a few years of handing off your tax return preparation, you may begin to study the concepts, analyze your prepared returns, and realize you can complete the process yourself.

### Exceptions: Landlords Who Won't Use Schedule E

The vast majority of small landlords will use the Schedule E. The only exceptions may be landlords who own their property through a partnership or corporation; they would likely use IRS Form 8825, *Rental Real Estate Income and Expenses of a Partnership or an S Corporation*, which is beyond the scope of this book. Even if you have your property in an LLC and you are the only member, then you will still use the Schedule E. Also, spouses who co-own residential rental property will use the Schedule E, as they are not generally considered a partnership in a standard residential rental scenario.

The way that Schedule E works is to have you set forth your income and expenses on a per-property basis, after which it guides you to calculate a total gain or loss from all your rental properties. The end result, be it a gain or loss, will be inserted on a line on your personal Form 1040. It's a fairly simple concept in theory, but can get more complicated in practice, as we will discover.

## Sample Schedule E, Supplemental Income and Loss

**SCHEDULE E**
**(Form 1040)**

Department of the Treasury
Internal Revenue Service (99)

**Supplemental Income and Loss**

(From rental real estate, royalties, partnerships, S corporations, estates, trusts, REMICs, etc.)

► Attach to Form 1040, 1040NR, or Form 1041.
► Information about Schedule E and its separate instructions is at *www.irs.gov/schedulee.*

OMB No. 1545-0074

2014

Attachment
Sequence No. **13**

Name(s) shown on return

Your social security number

**Part I**   **Income or Loss From Rental Real Estate and Royalties**   **Note.** If you are in the business of renting personal property, use **Schedule C** or **C-EZ** (see instructions). If you are an individual, report farm rental income or loss from **Form 4835** on page 2, line 40.

**A** Did you make any payments in 2014 that would require you to file Form(s) 1099? (see instructions)    ☐ Yes   ☐ No

**B** If "Yes," did you or will you file required Forms 1099?    ☐ Yes   ☐ No

| 1a | Physical address of each property (street, city, state, ZIP code) | | | | |
|----|----|----|----|----|----|
| **A** | | | | | |
| **B** | | | | | |
| **C** | | | | | |

| 1b | Type of Property (from list below) | 2 | For each rental real estate property listed above, report the number of fair rental and personal use days. Check the **QJV** box only if you meet the requirements to file as a qualified joint venture. See instructions. | | Fair Rental Days | Personal Use Days | QJV |
|----|----|----|----|----|----|----|----|
| **A** | | | | **A** | | | ☐ |
| **B** | | | | **B** | | | ☐ |
| **C** | | | | **C** | | | ☐ |

**Type of Property:**

1 Single Family Residence    3 Vacation/Short-Term Rental   5 Land      7 Self-Rental
2 Multi-Family Residence    4 Commercial            6 Royalties    8 Other (describe)

| **Income:** | Properties: | | **A** | | **B** | **C** |
|----|----|----|----|----|----|----|
| 3 | Rents received . . . . . . . . . . . . . . | **3** | | | | |
| 4 | Royalties received . . . . . . . . . . . . | **4** | | | | |
| **Expenses:** | | | | | | |
| 5 | Advertising . . . . . . . . . . . | **5** | | | | |
| 6 | Auto and travel (see instructions) . . . . . . | **6** | | | | |
| 7 | Cleaning and maintenance . . . . . . . | **7** | | | | |
| 8 | Commissions. . . . . . . . . . . . | **8** | | | | |
| 9 | Insurance . . . . . . . . . . . . | **9** | | | | |
| 10 | Legal and other professional fees . . . . . . | **10** | | | | |
| 11 | Management fees . . . . . . . . . . | **11** | | | | |
| 12 | Mortgage interest paid to banks, etc. (see instructions) | **12** | | | | |
| 13 | Other interest. . . . . . . . . . . | **13** | | | | |
| 14 | Repairs. . . . . . . . . . . . . | **14** | | | | |
| 15 | Supplies . . . . . . . . . . . . | **15** | | | | |
| 16 | Taxes . . . . . . . . . . . . . | **16** | | | | |
| 17 | Utilities . . . . . . . . . . . . . | **17** | | | | |
| 18 | Depreciation expense or depletion . . . . . . | **18** | | | | |
| 19 | Other (list) ► _____ | **19** | | | | |
| 20 | Total expenses. Add lines 5 through 19 . . . . . | **20** | | | | |
| 21 | Subtract line 20 from line 3 (rents) and/or 4 (royalties). If result is a (loss), see instructions to find out if you must file **Form 6198** . . . . . . . . . . . . | **21** | | | | |
| 22 | Deductible rental real estate loss after limitation, if any, on **Form 8582** (see instructions) . . . . . . | **22** | ( | )( | )( | ) |
| 23a | Total of all amounts reported on line 3 for all rental properties . . . . | **23a** | | | | |
| b | Total of all amounts reported on line 4 for all royalty properties . . . . | **23b** | | | | |
| c | Total of all amounts reported on line 12 for all properties . . . . . . | **23c** | | | | |
| d | Total of all amounts reported on line 18 for all properties . . . . . . | **23d** | | | | |
| e | Total of all amounts reported on line 20 for all properties . . . . . . | **23e** | | | | |
| 24 | **Income.** Add positive amounts shown on line 21. **Do not** include any losses . . . . . . . . | **24** | | | | |
| 25 | **Losses.** Add royalty losses from line 21 and rental real estate losses from line 22. Enter total losses here | **25** | ( | ) | | |
| 26 | **Total rental real estate and royalty income or (loss).** Combine lines 24 and 25. Enter the result here. If Parts II, III, IV, and line 40 on page 2 do not apply to you, also enter this amount on Form 1040, line 17, or Form 1040NR, line 18. Otherwise, include this amount in the total on line 41 on page 2 . . . . | **26** | | | | |

For Paperwork Reduction Act Notice, see the separate instructions.      Cat. No. 11344L      Schedule E (Form 1040) 2014

## Looking at Schedule E

The first part of the Schedule E is fairly simple: You list your name and the address of each property. You won't have to worry about the fair rental days for each property, unless you used the property for personal use during the year (if you did, see the IRS *Instructions for Schedule E* for guidance).

If you have more than three rentals (each Schedule E currently allows you to enter only three properties), simply use a second Schedule E (or a third if you have more than six properties), but then list the total income or loss from all the properties only once, on lines 23 through 26 of the first Schedule E.

## Rents Received: Just Add It Up

When you own just a few rentals, it's fairly easy to calculate the rents you received in a year. If your units were full all year (and rents were kept steady), you multiply the monthly rent for each property by 12 months. If you had a vacancy or the rents went up during the year, simply adjust the calculations accordingly. Use your leases and move-out documents to remind you of the exact lease start or end dates.

## Expenses Paid: Hang on to Those Receipts and Records

Many expenses on the Schedule E are relatively simple to understand, record, and calculate. Several are more complicated and require some higher-level understanding of tax concepts and even the minutiae of IRS regulations. So, if you encounter any complex questions, consider using a tax professional (as described in Chapter 11).

The Schedule E lists many of the major expenses small landlords will face. Your task will be to match the listed expenses with the right property and find the best category for each expense. If you can't find a match, don't give up: The list is not comprehensive, and if you have a legitimate business expense outside these categories, you can still write it off (most likely using the "Other" category).

What's a legitimate business expense? It's not a personal expense, for starters—any time you mix business and personal activities or expenditures, you'll need to keep track of which is which. It's also defined as an expense that's "ordinary and necessary" (a term that comes from Section 162(a) of the Tax Code):

- **By "ordinary," the IRS generally means a common expense for your trade or business area.** A landlord could ordinarily deduct the cost of cleaning supplies, for example, but probably not baking supplies (unless baking cookies for the staggered open house showings!).
- **"Necessary" means what is useful, helpful, and needed in the business or trade.** A landlord could deduct the cost of renting a truck to haul away junk from a rental property that was left by tenants, for instance. But if the landlord rents an exotic, luxury sports car to drive to and from the rental for fun, the IRS is probably not going to view it as necessary.

 **TIP**
**Some expenses will need to be allocated across several units.** This needn't be scientifically exact; simply spread the cost across the units as accurately as possible. For example, if you have a cell phone you used for fielding rental calls at five units and your phone service costs $1,000 per year, you could allocate $200 per unit, likely as an "other" or "utilities" expense.

Now let's look at the Schedule E expenses one by one.

**Advertising.** This can include classified ads, signs, and other forms of marketing. While advertising was once a staple landlord expense and a source of deductions, it has largely given way to low-cost and even free online services like Craigslist. Don't be alarmed if you have no advertising expenses to report at all.

**Auto and travel.** The details of writing off auto and travel expenses can be complex. Your main expense in this category is likely to be use of your vehicle. In theory, you can write off the cost of traveling to and from your rentals. You'll likely make many trips each year, in order to work on your properties, show units to prospective tenants, and check on tenant or building issues.

But you have to make a choice between two options for writing off vehicle expenses. The first option is to track the actual number of miles you traveled in order to manage your rental properties, and write off a standard, IRS-provided rate (56 cents per mile in 2014). The second option is to track your actual auto expenses (gas, repairs, tires, insurance), and deduct those. However, there's a catch if you use actual expenses. You cannot write off *all* your car expenses for the year unless you used the vehicle only for rental-related work, which is unlikely for the small-time landlord. You are limited to the percentage of the car's use that was dedicated to business. For example, if you use your car 60% for business (and 40% personal) and you spend $5,000 per year total on your car, your deduction is $3,000 ($5,000 x .60) or just the ratio of business use of the car. That means you'd have to carefully track the purpose of every car trip. See "Put Your Mileage Records on Cruise Control," below, for more on this.

RESOURCE

**More information on deducting vehicle expenses.** See IRS Topic 510, *Business Use of a Car,* available at www.irs.gov. It covers some key requirements for deducting your vehicle expenses under either the mileage or the actual expense option, and provides links to other relevant IRS publications (like Publication 463, *Travel, Entertainment, Gift and Car Expenses*).

If you use a car for your business, you can also write off the value of the vehicle over time, otherwise known as "depreciation" (Schedule E includes a special item for depreciation, described below). Your depreciation deduction will, of course, be limited to the percentage of your vehicle usage that's for business purposes. For a full (albeit long and complex) discussion of vehicle depreciation, see IRS Publication 946, *How to Depreciate Property.* This 100+ pages of definitions, examples, and tables may soon have you calling an accountant. Keep in mind that you do not have to take the depreciation deduction on your auto. But it can be a substantial deduction, especially if your vehicle is new (or fairly new) when put into service, and you use it substantially for business.

## Put Your Mileage Records on Cruise Control

You could spend hours tracking your auto use, only to claim a relatively modest tax deduction, especially if you make many short trips. The most obvious way to record your vehicle use is to use a mileage log and track every business trip, but this is tedious, and may not be sustainable for everyone. You could forget some trips, lose your record book, not want to take off your gloves in the cold to write, lose your pen, and so on. Keep in mind, if you were ever audited, the IRS would want to know the mileage, date, place, and purpose of your business trips.

Some landlords decide to forgo the mileage tracking and try actual auto expenses—which may be easier to track and yield a higher deduction, in the end. Another possibility for tracking mileage is to harness technology for the task. Good news: There's an app for that! Try *MileIQ* (*see* www.trymileiq.com) to track mileage in an IRS-compliant way.

Or if you are low-tech, find out the exact distance from your home to the rental and back. If you're like most small landlords, your business driving is primarily back and forth to the rental (shoveling snow, showing rentals, and so forth). Then just log each visit on a calendar and jot down the purpose of the trip (then you'd have the date and purpose, plus you'd know the mileage and location already). You need only calculate the total visits at year-end and multiply by the number of miles. Of course, you'd have to add in occasional hardware store trips.

Whatever method you use, the key is to start tracking your mileage right away, because you're not going to remember every trip to your rental after the fact, especially weeks, months, or even a year later. And the IRS will look for contemporaneous, not after the fact, calculations.

**Cleaning and maintenance.** This expense represents the staple of landlord duties, and is also fairly easy to understand and track, especially if you save all your receipts. Maintenance is how you keep your building up and running All the supplies, and contractors' service fees that you spent to keep your gutters clean, trees trimmed, snow removed, paint in good condition, and so forth, can be entered here. General maintenance expenses that may not fit another place can go here.

The key is to allocate cleaning and maintenance expenses to the right property. Jot an address on any receipt, so that you know where it goes at tax time. If you are sprucing it up, cleaning it, oiling it, painting it, tightening it, or replacing a worn out part (the routine of the DIY landlord) the associated cost is probably a maintenance expense. Almost all the cost of materials and items used in the turnaround process (see Chapter 4) will be categorized as cleaning and maintenance. The only exceptions would be if you replace something major—like an appliance or flooring—which may have to be written off over time (depreciated). You will accumulate more receipts in the turnarounds than any other common landlord routine.

A related expense category, Repairs, is discussed below.

---

### Sorry, a Landlord's Work Hours Aren't Deductible

If this possibility occurred to you, nice try, but you can't deduct your own labor. Of course, you might want to track your hours for your own planning purposes, so that you'll know how much time you're spending on each unit. The IRS, however, won't be interested in this information.

---

CAUTION

**Try to use incorporated contractors whenever possible.** Otherwise, you'll need to prepare a tax form known as a 1099-MISC on any payments to an individual over $600 in a year (and you will need the contractor's taxpayer identification number), and note this on the top of Schedule E. For example, if Carl's Carpentry, a sole proprietor, does a week-long repair on your deck that costs $1,000, you would need to do a 1099-MISC.

**Insurance.** Your insurer won't forget to send you the annual bill and statement, so record keeping will, in this case, be easy.

**Legal and other professional fees.** All the amounts you spend on legal, accounting, and other professional services for your rental property business are deductible. But watch out for transactions that mix personal and business matters. For example, your accountant will do both your rental and personal taxes of necessity, because they merge in the same form (your IRS Form 1040). Similarly, you might ask a lawyer a question about your personal and business affairs in one visit. In such cases of mixed transactions, you'll need to ask the professional to differentiate the fee or hours. This way, you can deduct those professional fees related to your rentals on your Schedule E.

**Management fees.** A property manager's fee will be a deductible expense you can write off here. Also, all or part of the management fee for a condo or homeowners' association could go here, provided it was designated as a management fee. If your condo or homeowners' association uses the monthly dues for a variety of purposes, the "Other" expense category may be the best place to claim it as a deduction. Any special assessments for capital projects, however (like a new roof or parking lot), should be written off (depreciated) over the useful life of the improvement.

**Mortgage interest paid to banks, etc.** This category is another large deduction for landlords. Each of your financial lending institutions will report interest to you annually, using IRS Form 1098, *Mortgage Interest Statement.* (Don't forget to add these up if you have two mortgages on a property—it's not uncommon.) There are more details to be dealt with, for example if you want to deduct the points you paid on a loan (you have to do it over the life of the loan), or if you refinance and get cash out of your rental. IRS Publication 936, *Home Mortgage Interest Deduction,* covers this topic.

**Other interest.** Interest paid on a business credit card (for a business expense) may be deductible. Many landlords keep a separate card for business purchases, to simplify accounting and tax matters. Of course, the efficient landlord will save money by paying the card off monthly, but if you have racked up some interest on your business purchases, track and deduct the interest. If you paid interest on a construction loan for a rental property or a car loan for your business vehicle, research further into how to possibly deduct these expenses.

## How Do You Write Off Your Condo Dues?

Monthly condominium dues are a major expense for many landlords. Yet, highlighting how the tax code and reality diverge, you may find your monthly dues go to pay a mosaic of expenses such as insurance, maintenance, repairs, cleaning, a management fee for on-site or contract property management, and even toward a capital account. IRS Publication 527 (*Residential Rental Property*), Chapter 4 "Special Situations," offers a bit of guidance:

*You can deduct as rental expenses…any dues or assessments paid for maintenance of the common elements. You cannot deduct special assessments you pay to a condominium management corporation for improvements. However, you may be able to recover your share of the cost of any improvement by taking depreciation…*

This makes some sense: You can write off repairs and upkeep in the current year, but need to write off improvements over time, depreciating them. Luckily, most condominiums will segregate out bills for capital projects, often "special assessments" for a new roof, driveway, or other upgrade. But the IRS guidance does not really tell the average condominium owner where to place monthly condo dues on Schedule E. The dues are legitimate business expenses, but cover the whole range of expenses listed on Schedule E. The "Other" category at the end of the Schedule E expense categories seems to be the best place for it; you can just list "condo dues" on the line. But if you have special assessments, look into expensing these over time.

**Repairs.** If something breaks (a window, closet door, handrail, faucet) and you repair or replace it, then the Repairs category is ideal. But the categorization isn't always so easy. For example, if a carpenter fixes a broken railing on the back deck of your duplex for $300, that's a repair. The same goes if the carpenter finds rot in the deck and needs to replace a few boards. If the entire deck is rotten and needs to be replaced, however, this is not just a repair, but an "improvement" (in fact, it's a listed example of an "improvement" in IRS Publication 527, Chapter 1 Table 1.1, *Examples of Improvements*). You would need to write off the costs of the deck slowly, over the useful life of the deck. To help with the complexity and confusion, see IRS T.D. 9636 *Guidance Regarding Deduction and Capitalization of Expenditures Related to Tangible Property*.

A complete discussion of repairs versus improvements is beyond the scope of this book. However, the IRS has created some "safe harbors" to help small-time landlords through the storm. These new safe harbors allow, as a practical matter, most small-time landlords to expense (meaning write off in one year) many typical repairs, subject to some limitations. See "IRS Safe Harbors for Landlords," below, for more on this.

**Supplies.** Stocking up at your local big box store can be a good idea, especially when things are on sale or to consolidate buying in one trip. But keep your receipts, because all the items purchased for your rental are deductible business expenses—especially if you don't know when or where you might use the gallon of glass cleaner or primer, lightbulbs, caulk, painter's tape, disposable gloves, screws, and nails. I generally put items in the Supplies category that I didn't buy specifically for one maintenance or repair job. If you have multiple properties, you can allocate supplies pro rata across your rentals. Also, don't forget office supplies, like stamps and envelopes for tenants' SASEs, and paper with which you printed leases and checklists. Small improvements (under $200) can also be listed as supplies, meaning you do not have to capitalize small improvements (even if you miss the safe harbor).

**Taxes.** The Schedule E is for calculating your federal tax obligations. Here, however, you can deduct your state and local property tax payments. You should be able to find this amount from your taxing authority or by checking your tax bill. There are tax credits related to energy efficiency, accessibility, or other categories that may be relevant.

**Utilities.** Landlords can write off all the utility expenses incurred on their rentals. Common bills to track include water, trash, electric, and gas. Of course, whether you can deduct these will depend on whether you actually paid them, as opposed to having passed the costs on to your tenants. If you had vacancies, however, track the period between tenants, and be sure to deduct the corresponding utility costs that you yourself paid.

## IRS Safe Harbors for Landlords

The IRS actually calls the regulation (IRS Reg. § 1.263(a)-3h), passed in 2014, the Safe Harbor for Small Taxpayers (SHST). And it is really for small-time landlords (not owners of major apartment complexes), because the requirements are that (1) the building basis (or what you paid for it, not including the land) is below $1 million, and (2), you expense no more than $10,000 per year or 2% of the building basis (or amount you paid for it, minus the land value). This should cover the buildings of small-time landlords in all but the most expensive areas of the U.S., and the $10,000 or 2% limit probably covers many routine repairs and updates. Major renovations or repairs above that amount can be depreciated over time. The IRS also offers a safe harbor for routine maintenance and a *de minimis* exception (meaning minimal or minor) primarily for expenses under $500.

**Depreciation.** This category can be a challenge for the average landlord. The concept of depreciation—writing off property slowly, over its useful life, rather than not all at once in one year—is not hard to grasp. But different property must be written off over different time frames, and the tracking can be tricky. IRS Form 4562 (*Depreciation and Amortization*) is the form used for reporting depreciation, but you can include the final number in the Depreciation category of Schedule E.

One important aspect of depreciation to keep in mind is that your largest and most consistent depreciation deduction will be on your rental building (but not the land, which you cannot depreciate). You'll need to figure out the basis or initial cost of the building, then write this amount off over 27.5 years, by dividing the building cost by 27.5 and claiming that amount every year under the depreciation category. That means your largest depreciation deduction is fairly simple to calculate. Depreciation can, however, get more complex when tracking personal property, improvements, or a vehicle, or adjusting your basis in the property (based on depreciation) when you sell. These topics are beyond the scope of this chapter, so consult your accountant or the references listed in this chapter for more details.

**Other.** Not every expense fits in the listed categories. Schedule E acknowledges this with a catch-all, "Other" category. Some items that you might list here include expenses that span several categories (like condo association dues) or costs that just don't quite fit in any other category, such as cell phone charges or landlord training materials (like this book). You can also briefly list the expenses you are listing here, in the space provided.

> **RESOURCE**
> **Detailed instructions for completing Schedule E and related IRS publications are available on the IRS website at www.irs.gov.** Also, check out *Every Landlord's Tax Deduction Guide*, by Stephen Fishman (Nolo), which takes you step-by-step through the process of completing Schedule E. For more information on doing your taxes, see "Tax Resources for the Small-Time Landlord" in Chapter 11.

## The Grand Finale: Inserting the Total into Your Form 1040

All of your work (or your accountant's) adding up the year's expenses and deducting them from your rental income will boil down to a single number on your personal Form 1040. It may seem a very small gain for all your efforts, or even a loss.

If the numbers don't look quite right to you—or even if they do— double- and triple-check them. If just one number in your calculations is off in any category or column on the Schedule E, it will throw off your Schedule E total, which will in turn mess up your Form 1040 amounts. Also canvass for any more expenses or income you may have left out before entering your rental total on your 1040.

# Don't Sweat a Tax Loss (Especially in Your Early Years)

It's not uncommon for a small-time landlord to show a tax loss, especially in the first few years. Don't panic. It doesn't mean you are a failure. Many small businesses show losses in the early years. It might not even be a "real" loss.

## If You Are Making Big Money, Be Sure Your Withholdings Keep Pace

If you have significant taxable income from your rentals (good for you!), make sure your tax withholdings are keeping pace. The easiest way for the part-time landlord to do this (and indeed what the IRS Form 1040 ES *Estimated Tax for Individuals* directs), is to ask your employer to increase your withholdings. This is actually a simple issue (that can seem complex). In our pay-as-you-go tax system, the IRS wants its money sooner not later (at year end)—so you can easily give them any taxes due on your rental activity throughout the year through withholdings at your day job. Form W-4 (*Employee's Withholding Allowance Certificate*) includes a special line for you to enter the additional amount you want your employer to withhold. But see a tax professional if you have questions. Search the IRS website (www.irs.gov) under "estimated taxes," for instructions and forms for figuring and paying any estimated tax.

Remember, owning residential real estate is a long game. One year's statement does not reflect the overall financial position of your rental business. Without having claimed large deductions, like depreciation for your buildings or personal property, you might have broken even or even shown a gain. Plus, your rental property value may have increased over the year (something not reflected on your taxes).

If you are an active landlord (and ran the property yourself), your tax loss may be used to offset your income from your day job and lower your overall tax liability. However, there are limits and restrictions on losses. As a hands-on or involved landlord who participates in the management of the property (not just an investor), you can deduct up to $25,000 in losses against your income, provided your modified adjusted gross income (MAGI) is under $100,000. The $25,000 deduction phases out at income levels between $100,000 and $150,000. There are other important rules to deducting losses; see the *IRS Passive Activity Loss Audit Technique Guide*, available at www.irs.gov.

# Keeping Records of Your Income and Expenses

There are various strategies and methods for effective record keeping. The key is to have a system that will help you both understand how your business is doing and report to the IRS without using excessive amounts of your time over the course of the year. The landlord with just a few rentals can use a simple system with file folders, and do everything at a kitchen table. Just make sure to choose a system that can expand with your business.

## What Records to Keep

Although you won't have to actually submit all your receipts with your tax return, you may need to show them to an IRS agent if some day you get audited. Without any record, you really can't legally or practically make a deduction, or have a clear financial picture of your business. To the extent possible, therefore, you'll want to keep your receipts and other forms of substantiation. The IRS lists a wide range of supporting documents that can be used to document and substantiate your business income and your expenses, in IRS Publication 583, *Starting a Business and Keeping Records*.

You may be able to let your bank and credit card company do some of your record keeping for you, for free. If you use a separate bank account to deposit all your rents, you will instantly have a record of all rental deposits. Probably one of the best friends of the small landlord is the auto-pay function for reoccurring payments:

You can have your mortgages, insurance, trash, water, and electric charges pulled automatically from your account.

And if you use a separate credit card for business expenses, your monthly statements become a form of documentation for every expense—though they might not show the details of what you spent the money on. The IRS accepts electronic records, bank statements, and credit card receipts for substantiation. But you'll also want to log all your rents in a journal or ledger and save all the actual receipts; noting on the actual receipt the type of expense and the property address it's attributed to (such as "123 Elm St."). Still, if you lose a receipt but made the purchase on the credit card, the statement will work as a record, particularly if you note the property and any details of the purchase on it.

If you're more tech oriented, you might scan your receipts into a digital file and go paperless. There are many ways to make paper records into electronic files. The IRS will also accept this form of substantiation of your expenses. Check with the IRS or your tax professional if you have questions about the adequacy of any records.

## How to Keep Your Records

The complexity of your filing system may mirror the complexity of your rental operation. For example, if you own one rental property, then you could simply create a manila file labeled "Business Expenses 2016." Any time you get a bill or make a purchase, put the receipt or record in the file. Then categorize your receipts and records at tax time, and prepare your taxes (or give everything to your accountant).

The business file could sit right next to your "Personal Tax" file, in the same drawer or file cabinet. Keeping all tax-related materials in the same place might even serve as a reminder that you'll constantly need to allocate business receipts to the business file and personal receipts to the personal file. This is easy, cheap, and very simple. It has worked for me.

The key is to be able to get the sum total of all your "ordinary and necessary " business expenses for your rentals each year without playing hide and seek around your car, house, or even online for lost records. Missing one large receipt or figure can stop the progress of doing your taxes completely (until you track it down) or mean you miss a deduction.

---

### Which Is Which? Prevent Multiple Property Confusion With Good Records

Tracking which expenses apply to which property is important if you have multiple properties. The Schedule E is organized by property (not units, so a duplex is one property), and you need to connect expenses with each property where they occur. If you have one property, this is easy—all the business expenses apply to that property. But if you have three, six, or nine properties and you buy a gallon of paint during the year, you may not remember which property it was used on nine months later when you do your taxes (or give them to your accountant). Don't end the year with a thick file of receipts wondering which expenses apply to which rentals. Keep track of them as you make purchases. If you just have one rental (be it a condo or fourplex) it will be fairly easy to just put all your business expenses in one "business expense file," but if you have two or three, have a file for each property and even write down on the receipt the address for each item as soon as possible. Of course, some products will be used on multiple rentals (like a box of nails or bottle of cleaner), so do your best to allocate the expense across rentals where it is used.

---

If you have a larger property portfolio, you could create separate files for each property. Inside each of those files, you could create separate categories that mirror the Schedule E expense categories. If you have several multiplexes, you are going to be producing more and more paperwork, which will be harder to sort at tax time if you haven't organized them well throughout the year.

You might wish to take advantage of technology, perhaps by using *Excel* to record every receipt, or expense program like *QuickBooks*, or *Quicken's Rental Property Manager,* which integrates your personnal and rental property finances. Commercial property management software programs are also available (like *Yardi, Buildium, Appfolio Property Manager, Propertyware*, and others), which help track and account for expenses and rents (but are geared more toward landlords with many properties or apartment complexes).

Once your system is set up, the important thing will be to develop a habit of using it. Drop your receipts in the same place every time, all the time. They should go into your wallet or purse at the store or rental. As soon as you walk through your front door, drop receipts in the proper file. If you don't do this, you'll be endlessly frustrated trying to "gather all the bills" at tax time.

> **TIP**
>
> **Couples should sync up their filing habits.** If you are co-landlording with a spouse or partner, and both are paying bills or making purchases, beware of situations where a receipt can go astray because you're not implementing the same filing habits. If it doesn't go in the file, it likely won't get deducted.

---

### How Long Should You Keep Your Receipts?

You don't need to keep your receipts and records forever—but don't throw them out when you're done with your taxes, either. The IRS lists some "Periods of Limitations," and notes that business owners should keep the relevant record till this period runs out. (You can still be audited years later!) Seven years is a safe time frame for most tax situations. You may want to save your records for even longer, for your own, nontax reasons. For example, you may want to remember when you replaced a faucet or door a decade later. Also, keep in mind that if you sell your rentals in 20 years or so, you will need to account for depreciation or capital improvements. Also, note there is no time limit on the IRS screening you for a fraudulent return or taking action because you failed to file a return.

## What's Next?

Being a part-time landlord isn't for everyone, but it can be manageable for almost anyone with the right attitude and knowledge. It can even be a fulfilling way to play a useful role in society (in addition to your day job). It may even make you some money over the long term. Everyone needs a place to live, and affordable, well-managed housing is often in short supply in many areas. By providing such housing, the part-time residential landlord can make a difference in the everyday lives of others. Even though this is the last chapter, keep reading, and learning all you can about landlording topics (many are cited throughout this book), including the valuable lessons your tenants and properties will teach you. I hope this book helps you in that mission and on your journey as a landlord, whether it is just beginning or coming to a close. ●

# Index

## A

Abandoned property, 357–358, 367

Accessory (in law) apartments, 46–47

Accountants, 380–387
  certification requirements, 385
  CPAs, 385, 387
  finding, 29, 385–386, 387
  for IRS audits, 386
  paying and working with, 381, 386–387, 401
  for tax preparation, 380, 383–384, 385–387, 401, 408
  when to use, 380, 383–384

Adverse action letters, 253

Advertising rental property
  after lease breaks, 340
  antidiscrimination law compliance, 199–200
  crafting advertisements or postings, 203–205
  handling inquiries, 205, 223
  key terms and details, 204–205
  online rental scams, 215
  overview, 203
  sample ad, 205–210
  Schedule E expense reporting, 404
  screening role, 235
  security deposit laws and, 268
  street addresses and photos, 211–212
  when to advertise, 206
  where and how to advertise, 203–204

Air conditioners
  energy efficiency, 280
  maintenance requirements, 135, 148
  permits required to work on, 59

Alcohol abuse
  driving under influence, 243
  landlord visits to assess, 320

Amending leases, 272, 372

American Institute of CPAs (AICPA), 385

*American Renters and Financial Fragility*, 246

American Society of Home Inspectors (ASHI), 63–64

Antidiscrimination laws
  advertisements and, 199–200
  cosigners and, 275
  discriminatory communications, 199–200, 232
  legal advice on, 376
  legal requirements, 199–200
  rental applications and, 217
  renting to drug addicts, 244
  screening prospective tenants and, 234
  Section 8 vouchers and, 241–242
  unauthorized occupants and, 327

Apartment management, 15–16

Appliances
  compactors, 117
  depreciation of, 407
  dishwashers, 115, 117, 119
  energy-efficient, 117, 119
  exhaust fans, 117, 118
  explaining at walkthrough, 279
  freezers, 117
  garbage disposals, 117, 119
  information resources, 115
  life spans, 117

# ⚖ NOLO  *Online Legal Forms*

Nolo offers a large library of legal solutions and forms, created by Nolo's in-house legal staff. These reliable documents can be prepared in minutes.

## Create a Document

- **Incorporation.** Incorporate your business in any state.
- **LLC Formations.** Gain asset protection and pass-through tax status in any state.
- **Wills.** Nolo has helped people make over 2 million wills. Is it time to make or revise yours?
- **Living Trust (avoid probate).** Plan now to save your family the cost, delays, and hassle of probate.
- **Trademark.** Protect the name of your business or product.
- **Provisional Patent.** Preserve your rights under patent law and claim "patent pending" status.

## Download a Legal Form

Nolo.com has hundreds of top quality legal forms available for download—bills of sale, promissory notes, nondisclosure agreements, LLC operating agreements, corporate minutes, commercial lease and sublease, motor vehicle bill of sale, consignment agreements and many more.

## Review Your Documents

Many lawyers in Nolo's consumer-friendly lawyer directory will review Nolo documents for a very reasonable fee. Check their detailed profiles at **Nolo.com/lawyers**.

## On Nolo.com you'll also find:

### Books & Software

Nolo publishes hundreds of great books and software programs for consumers and
business owners. Order a copy, or download an ebook version instantly, at Nolo.com.

### Online Legal Documents

You can quickly and easily make a will or living trust, form an LLC or corporation, apply
for a trademark or provisional patent, or make hundreds of other forms—online.

### Free Legal Information

Thousands of articles answer common questions about everyday legal issues
including wills, bankruptcy, small business formation, divorce, patents,
employment, and much more.

### Plain-English Legal Dictionary

Stumped by jargon? Look it up in America's most up-to-date source for
definitions of legal terms, free at nolo.com.

### Lawyer Directory

Nolo's consumer-friendly lawyer directory provides in-depth profiles of lawyers all
over America. You'll find all the information you need to choose the right lawyer.

PROP1